THE SPIRIT OF
Spinoza

Healing the Mind

Neal Grossman
With a Foreword by Huston Smith

ICRL Press
Princeton, New Jersey

THE SPIRIT OF SPINOZA: Healing the Mind
By Neal Grossman
Copyright © 2003, 2014 by Neal Grossman
ISBN: 978-1-936033-263

This is a revised edition of *Healing the Mind: The Philosophy of Spinoza Adapted for a New Age*, originally published by Susquehanna University Press in 2003.

All rights reserved, including the right to reproduce this book or portions thereof in any form whatsoever. For information address:
ICRL Press
211 N. Harrison St., Suite C
Princeton, NJ 08540-3530

TABLE OF CONTENTS

Foreword by Huston Smith 8
Introduction 13
Who is Spinoza? 19

1. Metaphysics 20

    FIRST PRINCIPLES 21

    THE EXISTENCE OF GOD 23

    A PRACTICAL APPLICATION 29

    THE WHOLENESS OF CREATION 32
        Holism and Atomism 33
        The Demise of Atomism 35
        Holism and Quantum Physics 38

    THE CAUSALITY OF GOD 41
        Divine Necessity 41
        Could It Really Have Been Otherwise? 44
        The Illusion of Free Will 46
        The Importance of Practice 48

    MIND AND BODY 50
        Some Considerations Against Materialism 51
        The Relationship Between Mind and Body 56

    SPACE, TIME, AND ETERNITY 61
        The Expanding Universe and the Limits of the Imagination 61
        The Emanation of the Spatio-Temporal Order
            from Its Eternal Source 62

2. The Mind 67

THE GENERAL NATURE OF SENSE EXPERIENCE 67
- The Myth of a Homunculus 68
- Structural Parallels Between Mind and Body 69
- The "Illusion" of Sense Experience 73
- The Mechanics of Sense Perception 75
- The Dependency of the Visual Appearance of Things
  upon the Optical Properties of the Body 77
- A Wonderful Mystery 80
- Spinoza's Metaphysical Parallelism Applied to the
  Mystery of Perception 83
- Anthropomorphism and the Imagination 85
- The Inadequacy of Imaginative Experience 88

RELATIONSHIPS AMONG MINDS 91
- The Concept of a "Larger" Mind 91
- An Example of Direct Communication Between Minds 93
- Reincarnation 97
- The Mind of the Earth 100

3. Desire and Emotion 103

THE NATURE OF DESIRE AND INTENT 103
- Understanding the Emotions 103
- The Metaphysics of Desire 106
- Determinism and the Illusion of Free Will 112
- Wholistic Embedding and the Metaphysics of Choice 118
- Psychophysical Parallelism, Causation, and Purpose 123
- An Objection to Parallelism, and Spinoza's Reply 126
- Dreaming, A Context that Exhibits the Causal Structure
  of Spinoza's Psychophysical Parallelism 130

THE DEFINITION OF EMOTIONS 132
- Power of Acting 133
- Joy and Sorrow, the Primary Emotions 138
- Love and Hate 142
- Some Additional Consequences 145

SELF-KNOWLEDGE AND THE EMOTIONS 148
    Beliefs and Emotions 148
    The Social Conditioning of Belief... 150
    The Programming of the Mind by Western Society—
        A Major Impediment to Self-knowledge 154
    Social Schizophrenia, the Split Between Feeling and Behavior........ 158
    A Reminder... 160
    Knowing Our Emotions 162

4. Freedom From Bondage 167

EMOTIONS AND THE PROCESS OF IMAGINING 167
    The Nature of Our "Inner Dialogue".. 168
    The Causal Role of the Inner Dialogue in Producing
        Our Emotions... 173
    Summary, and More Examples 179

SECOND ORDER AWARENESS... 180
    While Watching a Movie 181
    Shifting from the "There and Then" to the "Here and Now" 182

RESISTING OUR OWN HAPPINESS 188
    The Metaphysical Impossibility of "Good" and "Bad"................... 188
    Some Harmful Consequences of Believing in "Good and Bad" 190
    Discernment 192
    Resistance, Denial, and Emotional Bondage................................. 194
    The Cause and Structure of Human Bondage 200
    Reason and Rationality 203

PROGRAMMED PATTERNS OF FEELING AND BEHAVIOR.....207
    Identifying Our Patterns...207
    Infections of the Mind, or the Power of Conditioned Patterns 209
    Principles for a Mentally Healthy Culture.................................... 212
    The Irrational and Unhealthy Nature of Contemporary Society..... 213
        1. Competition vs. Cooperation.. 213
        2. Advertising, or the Unhealthy Programming of Desire 216
        3. The Avoidance of Nurturing in Contemporary Society 218
        4. Education: Analysis vs. Appreciation 222
    Summary, and a Step Toward Freedom..225

5. Transcendence 228

SEXUALITY: TRANSCENDENCE OF THE BODY 228
Sexuality and the Metaphysics of Holism... 229
Exploring Our Programmed Sexual Patterns 233
Union with the Earth... 235

BLESSEDNESS: TRANSCENDENCE OF THE MIND................... 237
Imagining the Temporal, Understanding the Eternal..................... 237
A Brief Metaphysical Review... 240
The Essence of the Body.. 244
The Eternality of the Mind.. 246
"Becoming" Eternal, or the Possibility of Direct Experience 249
Spiritual Love.. 251
The Shakespearean Metaphor: "All the World's a Stage"................ 253
Shakespeare's Metaphor and Spinoza's Metaphysics 255
Rational Faith and the Satisfaction of Longing............................... 262
Concluding Words... 264

Glossary... 266
Index.. 269

List of Exercises

EXERCISE 1.	Practicing removal of guilt	31
EXERCISE 2.	Practical response dispelling guilt and blame	49
EXERCISE 3.	Enhancing feeling of awe	87
EXERCISE 4.	Understanding feeling, desire, and behavior	104
EXERCISE 5.	Establishing comfort with desire	110
EXERCISE 6.	Free will and decision making	113
EXERCISE 7a.	Holding a thought	114
EXERCISE 7b.	Choosing thoughts	115
EXERCISE 7c.	Imaginative thinking	115
EXERCISE 8.	Exercising "free choice"	122
EXERCISE 9.	Accepting circumstances	124
EXERCISE 10.	Recognizing decrease in power of action	137
EXERCISE 11.	Developing sensitivity to our own body	145
EXERCISE 12.	Repression of feelings	159
EXERCISE 13.	Ownership of emotions	164
EXERCISE 14.	Awareness of pleasant and unpleasant sensations	169
EXERCISE 15.	Experiencing our inner dialogue	170
EXERCISE 16.	Inner dialogue and the understanding mind	172
EXERCISE 17	Inconsistency of emotional responses	174
EXERCISE 18.	Anatomical awareness of physical responses	177
EXERCISE 19.	Allowing emotions to be controlled by external events	179
EXERCISE 20.	Experiencing first-order awareness	181
EXERCISE 21.	Creation and analysis of a thought log	183
EXERCISE 22.	Judgment	195
EXERCISE 23.	Development of awareness of feelings and behavior	198
EXERCISE 24.	Self-image	199
EXERCISE 25.	Identification of behavior patterns	207
EXERCISE 26.	Awareness of irrational infections of the mind	216
EXERCISE 27.	Observation of feelings when touched	221
EXERCISE 28.	Recollection and analysis of Childhood	227
EXERCISE 29.	Conscious awareness of sexual conditioning	234
EXERCISE 30.	Recollection of emotional and unemotional events	250
EXERCISE 31.	Viewing the world as a stage	254
EXERCISE 32.	Understanding transcendence of spiritual love	260

FOREWORD

Neal Grossman was a student of mine while I was teaching at MIT, which means that I have known him for forty-some years. Only during the latest of these years, however, did he tell me of an experience that dates back to when he was fifteen or sixteen years old, one that I find so prescient of the book in hand that I can think of no more appropriate way to open this foreword than to relate it.

Neal was exploring the streets of Boston one summer afternoon when he found himself passing its public library, and with nothing better to do he entered. Dazed by its seemingly endless corridors of books, he wandered down one of them, and there his eye fell on Plato's dialogues. He had heard of Plato, and to satisfy his curiosity he pulled the book from its shelf, took it to a reading table, and let it fall open. *Mirabile dictu*, what then greeted him was the most famous passage in all of the dialogues, the Allegory of the Cave, which together with Moses' vision of Mount Sinai in flames, is one of the twin foundations of Western civilization. When he came to the end of the allegory with its moral that education is not what most people take it to be, but instead should be "to put true knowledge into souls that do not possess it, as if inserting vision into blind eyes," he found that tears were streaming down his cheeks.

When Grossman reported that episode, I heard it as a harbinger of the book in hand, but to bring out the full force of that book I need to say something about the years that intervened between the afternoon I have recounted and the writing of this book.

Innately intelligent and in search of truth, which our culture assumes can be most assuredly found in science, Grossman entered M.I.T., where his undergraduate major was physics. That institute requires its undergraduates to take 20 percent of their courses in humanities and the social sciences, which led him to my two courses on world religions. There he found echoes of Plato's idea of a domain more ultimate than the physical universe, and he staked out as his life's project to investigate whether the concept of a transcendent reality was compatible with our best scientific understanding of the world. To qualify for it he entered the then-strongest graduate program in history and philosophy of science in the country, at the University of Indiana, and when his doctorate was in hand the University of Illinois at Chicago hired him to teach that subject. Ten years later, having satisfied himself with regard to the basic compatibility of physics and spirituality, he lost interest in the philosophy of science per se and turned to teaching those philosophers whose first ambition was to change people's lives.

This book, originally entitled *Healing the Mind*, is the first printout of that switch in his career and, to put the matter bluntly, it is one of the very few books that makes me regret that I am not still in the classroom where I could teach from it. It has taken its author a decade to get it published, for it falls between two stools. Academic presses wouldn't touch it, even though Spinoza scholars gave it flying colors for its understanding of Spinoza, but because of its New Age mentality and the exercises Grossman includes to open readers to where Spinoza's ideas can enter the lives they are actually living, thus effecting the improvement that Spinoza hoped for. Meanwhile, New Age presses all assumed that Spinoza was too heady for their audiences. Had Grossman compromised on either of these fronts, this book would have been issued years earlier, but true to the book's message, its author refused to compromise, even if that meant that his book would never be published. That it has been published warrants our thanks to both its principled author and its publisher, who saw the promise in Grossman's deft handling of the splice between ideas and their impacts on life.

This Foreword could appropriately end here, but my own love for Spinoza leads me to extend it to point out the exalted character of this book's subject.

Spinoza's given name was Benedict, which is the Latinized equivalent of the Hebrew *baruch*, meaning blessing or benediction. (Latin was the intellectual language of Spinoza's Europe and the one in which he wrote.) This makes his name translate into English as Blessed Spinoza. No epithet was ever more appropriate, for as Bertrand Russell pointed out in his *History of Western Philosophy*, "Spinoza is the noblest and most loveable of the great philosophers." This is true, but it leads to what I have elsewhere dubbed the Spinoza anomaly, which is: Why is Spinoza so loved and respected but little followed? Today there are Platonists, Thomists, Kantians, and Wittgensteinians, but few if any philosophers who call themselves Spinozists.

There is an easy way to resolve this anomaly, which I shall note only to put it behind me. According to this superficial resolution, Spinoza is loved because his life was exemplary, and he is not followed because his metaphysics is thought to be mistaken. If he was not mistaken in trying to construct a metaphysical system in the first place, as many philosophers today would contend, he was clearly mistaken in the way he went about devising it. Given the excitement attending the birth of modern science in the seventeenth century, we can understand why the geometrical method excited him, but too much has happened in the three hundred years that have followed to allow us to take it seriously. Geometrics have become multiple, logic turns out to be dead-end in paradoxes, and all efforts to find bedrock foundations on which logic's ladder might be planted unshakably—foundationalism—have led to quicksand. Percepts shift with their contexts (Gestalt psychology), facts reflect the theories that sponsor them (science and cognition generally), and there appear not to be any elementary particles from which nature is constructed (particle physics).

I call the foregoing resolutions of the Spinoza anomaly superficial because they trivialize the truth component in what we esteem, a move that is particularly unseemly for philosophers. It assumes that the not-less-than-holy life Spinoza lived was unrelated to the truth he saw. (Not-less-than-holy; I will fill in that epithet. By birth a man in exile and by temperament a recluse, Spinoza showed not the slightest bitterness in the face of the centuries of persecution his people had suffered and his excommunication by his own Jewish community in Amsterdam. Whatever the matter at hand, he always brought to it a mind free of attachment to self, party, or nation.) Or, if we prefer to hew to the cognitive grounds for our admiration of him, it assumes that coherence alone suffices to win our respect, whereas outside the formal sciences we know that it does not suffice if it did we would honor paranoids, for their logic tends to be impeccable; it is their premises that are out of touch with reality. To reduce metaphysics to a game well played is to rob it (and ultimately all philosophy) of its basis and importance. The mind that is fed "wholly with joy...unmingled with sadness" (*On the Improvement of the Understanding*) is not a mind applauding a logical victory. We need an explanation of the Spinoza anomaly that avoids the travesty of disjoining the respect we accord a philosopher from the question of whether he was right.

I suggest the following. Philosophers sense that Spinoza was right, but do not follow him because they do not understand how he reached his conclusions. The arguments that carried him to them, while logically impeccable, have not delivered his conclusions to many other philosophers, which is another way of saying that they have not found them existentially compelling. This way of putting the matter may seem as paradoxical as the anomaly I introduce it to resolve, but of course it isn't. Right and left, our instincts for truth outstrip the reasons we adduce to justify them we always know more than we can explain how we know it. Insofar as we claim the opposite, we exhibit what might be called "the European mistake": the mistake of thinking that it is the role of the sage to explain things from zero, whereas in fact his vocation is first to see and then to cause to see; that is, to provide a key. The classic error of Western rationalism is to assume that metaphysical conclusions are no stronger than the arguments adduced to support them and that they collapse the moment weaknesses in those arguments are exposed, an exposure that is easily accomplished because the premises of metaphysical proofs invariably elude everyday consensual experience. The truth is the reverse. Rather than being the causes of certainty, metaphysical arguments are their results. This makes the certainty in one sense subjective, but at the same time it is objective if it prolongs realities that are independent of our minds.

In calling the mistake just cited Western, I mean, of course, that it is the recent Western mistake; our very word theory derives from *theoria*, a term originally drawn from the theater and implying vision. Like Plato, Spinoza saw something. Had his mysticism been ecstatic we might be inclined to say that he experienced something, but because it was immaculately intellective-gnostic, or jnanic as Vedantists would say, it is better to say that he saw, or perhaps sensed, something (saw captures the clarity of his controlling insight, sensed captures its intuitive character, the difficulty of conveying it to persons who have had no direct contact with it). A moment ago we were citing Gestalt psychology and particle physics to document the mind's inability to arrive at empirical indubitables. For the phenomenal world this is plain fact, awash as that world is in relativity and change in Maya, to reach again for a Vedantic term. But beneath this remorseless flux Spinoza detected something permanent. This is not the place to try to say what that something is the book does that better than I could. It is enough here to say that he saw as clearly as man ever has what Substance is and how it is related to accident, grasping at the same time that everything participates in both while being always accident in relation to the one and only Substance that empowers it. In doing so he understood the nature not only of authentic religion, but also of metaphysics in the etymological sense of that word. As for philosophers, they sense that he had hold of that meaning, however little they may be able to follow his approach to it or blaze an alternative route.

This is my suggestion regarding the Spinoza anomaly. Philosophers do not call themselves Spinozists because the way he articulates his insight is, for the most part, not the way they would do so; it is too colored by thought patterns of a bygone era. But metaphysical systems are not mirror images of reality; they are symbols—fingers pointing at the moon, as Ch'an Buddhists would say. And Spinoza's finger, we sense (many of us do, at least), was precisely and accurately angled. That is why we honor him. He points us toward truth of a mode that, to the degree that we succeed in embodying it, can free us as it freed him.

I speak of degree, and it is important to close with this, for truth that is as existential as the kind Spinoza was immersed in is not simply accepted or rejected; it is appropriated incrementally. Sufis liken three stages in the acquisition of gnosis to hearing about fire, seeing fire, and being burned by fire. Comparably, one can respond affirmatively to Spinoza by assenting to what he says, seeing what he saw, and being consumed by what he saw. George Eliot was onto these distinctions when she wrote, "Spinoza says from his own soul what all the world is saying by rote." And (if I may venture this conjecture) it was alertness to the importance of these degrees of assimilation that caused the author of this book to insist that it include the exercises he devised to knead Spinoza's outlook into the lives his students, if I may put the matter that way. He would prefer not to have his book published rather than to forgo the opportunity he saw to make Spinoza live in the lives of his students and thereby ennoble them.

Not many can rise to the point of being "burned" by Spinoza's vision, for it involves recognizing one's individuality as a cosmic accident. But Spinoza himself is living proof that it is possible to catch sight of something so majestic—a Good beyond all goods—that at the mere sight of it one loses personal desires, forgets oneself in its contemplation, and adds a new dimension to the treasures of the soul. Spinoza has been faulted because his *Deus sive Natura* (God or Nature) is impersonal—transpersonal would be a better word. His audience is a different breed, or again better, a level of the soul that everyone possesses but that is too deeply buried in most people for them to detect on their own. It is the level at which one glimpses the Absolute, that cold, remote, emotionless Beyond where nothing stirs, where there is no agitation, where there is only that immaculate, almost unreachable height of the aloneness of God.

On completing his second reading of Spinoza's *Ethics* Goethe said, "I have never seen things so clearly, or been so much at peace." Welcome, dear reader, to *The Spirit of Spinoza*. I know of no other book that rivals this one in its resources for helping you to make Goethe's words your own.

— Huston Smith, 2003

INTRODUCTION

Many years ago, when I was an undergraduate physics major at MIT, I heard a story about Albert Einstein. According to the story, when Einstein came to this country he was asked whether he believed in God. He replied that he believed in the God of Spinoza. Einstein's opinions carried enormous weight for me, and, even though I thought of myself as an atheist at the time, if Spinoza's God was good enough for Einstein, He was going to be good enough for me too. I resolved to investigate.

Flash forward fifteen or sixteen years. I am a recently tenured philosopher of science with a promising career ahead of me. There are two piles of books on my desk. The first pile consists of all the stuff I needed to read to stay current in my chosen field of specialization, a field which, as a graduate student and for many years thereafter, had been of great interest to me, but in which I was now loosing interest. The second pile consists of material that I had always wanted to explore, but never had sufficient time to delve into. For many months I hovered uneasily between the two piles, unable to muster the interest and motivation to read from the first pile, but feeling guilty for wanting to read from the second. I finally resolved the dilemma by realizing that my true commitment as a philosopher must be to my own real interests, wherever they may lead, and not to a sense of obligation to keep up with what had been my chosen area of specialization. What is the point, I thought, of having tenure if I did not use the freedom that comes with tenure to explore my true interests? The first book on the second pile was Spinoza's masterpiece, entitled simply, *Ethics*.

Spinoza came to my assistance right away. Many editions of the *Ethics* include a short, unfinished, early treatise by Spinoza, entitled "On the Emendation of the Understanding." In the first few pages of this treatise, Spinoza describes his own struggle between doing what is necessary to have a successful career in a socially sanctioned profession and seeking spiritual truth. "I perceived that if true happiness were placed in the former I should necessarily miss it; while if, on the other hand, it were not so placed, and I gave them my whole attention, I should equally fail." And Spinoza had much more to lose than just a "promising career." He had been an outstanding student, and his teachers believed he would become a great world-renown Jewish theologian, with fame and reputation equal to and perhaps surpassing that of Moses Maimonedes. For Spinoza, following his true interests meant, not only that he would have no such career, but also that he would be excommunicated from the Jewish community of Amsterdam. At this point in my own life, the example Spinoza set gave me much courage.

Around the same time difficulties in my personal life lead me to therapy. But once in therapy, I got "hooked" by the process, and for the next fifteen years or so participated in numerous workshops, growth groups, and training programs, beginning as a frightened participant and ending as an experienced group-leader. Like most intellectuals, I was, as they say, dead from the neck down. Not only was I not in touch with my emotions, but also I actively resisted becoming aware of them. I recall, with humor now, how long it took my therapist to get me to recognize the difference between a feeling and a thought. During this time period, I explored everything from Humanistic Psychology to New Age Spirituality. I found much that was just fluff in all of this, but I also found much more that was very useful. One thing is clear to me now: had I not explored my own emotional nature in some depth, I would have not been able fully to understand Spinoza. Or, to put it differently, my understanding would have been merely intellectual, not experiential.

In philosophy courses and textbooks, Spinoza is classified as a seventeenth-century rationalist philosopher, sandwiched between Descartes, who lived in the generation before Spinoza, and Leibniz, who lived in the generation after. This classification, although not without some justification, is very misleading. For Spinoza has much more in common with Eastern thought generally, and Buddhism in particular, than he does with either of the two aforementioned philosophers. The system of thought contained in the *Ethics* is a system of spiritual psychotherapy—*spiritual,* because its goal is union with God, *psychotherapy,* because the path to this goal lies through an understanding and transcendence of what the Dalai Lama (in his book, *Ethics for a New Millennium*) has called our "afflictive emotions." It is possible, Spinoza maintains, to live a life free from bondage to the afflictive emotions of envy, hatred, anger, depression, guilt, blame, anxiety, fear, and so forth; his entire system of philosophy is dedicated to freeing us from this bondage. Spinoza is not a mere metaphysician, lost in remote abstractions, but a very practical spiritual teacher whose aim, as he explicitly states, is to "lead us, by the hand, as it were, to a knowledge of the human mind and its highest happiness." (*Ethics,* part 2, preface).

The more deeply I penetrated into Spinoza's teachings, the more appreciation and admiration I felt. Not only is his system of thought intellectually elegant and beautiful, but also, it is immensely practical. Here is a philosophy that offers, not just moral platitudes, but practical guidance for living. His theory of emotions is not just some quaint, antiquated seventeenth-century theory, but timeless in the same sense that Buddhism is timeless. It is true, as I said above, that exploring my own emotions through therapy and groups helped me to understand Spinoza; but it is equally true that Spinoza's theory of emotions helped me to understand my own emotional nature. Moreover, Spinoza's theory explained to my satisfaction why therapy works when it does work, and also, why therapy doesn't always work.

However, it seemed to me that I was somewhat alone in my appreciation of Spinoza. On the one hand, those who felt themselves to be on a "spiritual path" and who were honestly struggling to rid themselves of the afflictive emotions could not avail themselves of the assistance offered by Spinoza because they could not penetrate the admittedly difficult seventeenth-century philosophical jargon in terms of which he wrote. On the other hand, professional philosophers, whose training might enable them to understand Spinoza, are, for the most part, caught up in the materialist and atheistic ideology that dominates academia today and are hence unable to comprehend fully a philosophy that aims at union with what they believe to be a non-existent God. Moreover, on the whole, academics lack the experience of working with their own emotions in a therapeutic context, and hence lack the personal data that is necessary to fully understand, appreciate, and benefit from, Spinoza's philosophy. Thus, those who can penetrate Spinoza's system of thought are not interested in learning from him personally, whereas those who might be interested in learning from him personally are not able to penetrate his system of thought.

The purpose of this book is to make Spinoza's system of thought accessible and available to those who can benefit from it. It is written as a sort of intellectual self-help book, self-contained, free from footnotes, and as much as possible, free from jargon. It contains many "exercises," integrated into the text, which invite the reader to apply the ideas under discussion to her or his personal life. Without such application, it is not possible fully to understand the ideas, any more than one could understand how to play tennis just by reading a book. Or perhaps a better analogy is that one does not fully understand a given scientific theory without spending some time in the lab. The laboratory provides the data that the given theory supposedly explains; it provides the evidence that supports the theory. So the laboratory of our personal lives constitutes the data that Spinoza's theory explains. Moreover, just as an adequate scientific theory not only explains its subject matter but also gives us some control over it, so also, an adequate theory of human emotions not only explains our emotions, but, through the understanding provided by the theory, gives us some control over them, so that even if not fully released from bondage, we suffer much less. So I urge the reader not to skip over the exercises, but to take the time to do the necessary self-reflection and introspection. Indeed, I think it would be more beneficial to do the exercises and skip the text, than to read the text and skip the exercises.

Spinoza, as I have said, is a spiritual therapist. But his system of therapy is embedded in a sophisticated theory of human emotions, which is itself embedded in a theoretical understanding of what it is to be a human being, which in turn is embedded in a theoretical understanding of God and the relationship between God and the world. Altogether, it is a system of thought that is both intellectually satisfying and emotionally healing. Reading this book will require some effort. Intellectual effort is required to grasp the concepts, and personal effort is required to do the exercises. It is my belief, and also my wish, that this effort will be deeply rewarding.

Twenty Years Later

This book was completed in its original form about twenty years ago. After several unsuccessful attempts to get it published, the book languished in a desk drawer for another ten years. It was eventually published by Susquehanna University Press in 2003, with the title: *Healing the Mind: The Philosophy of Spinoza Adapted for a New Age*. It has been "out of print" for several years and copies have been hard to find, and expensive when found. I am, to say the least, not aggressive when it comes to pushing or publicizing my own work, and this book might very well still be languishing in my desk drawer were it not for a "chance" encounter with the publisher of ICRL Press. On the one hand, it would never occur to me that a science press would be interested in the ideas of a historical philosopher. On the other hand, it perhaps should have occurred to me, as many scientists have found in Spinoza a philosopher whose ideas they can relate to. Spinoza's system of thought is a natural fit for those scientists and consciousness researchers who have come to the conclusion that (i) the consciousness we now experience ourselves as being is not produced by the brain, and (ii) the Source of the consciousness we experience ourselves as being is a consciousness greater than our own, and which also includes our own. This appears to be the conclusion that scientists are coming to, based on research on the Near-Death Experience, children with verifiable past-life memories, communications with deceased individuals under controlled laboratory conditions, electronic voice phenomena, psychic research in its various forms, including of course the impeccable research done at the Princeton Engineering Anomalous Research Lab. Spinoza, I believe, would welcome finding a home among such courageous scientists, and his system of thought provides an elegant conceptual framework for those scientists whose empirical research has lead them to the two conclusions mentioned above.

But as I have emphasized, Spinoza is more than a metaphysician; he is a spiritual therapist, and the personal guidance he offers for living one's life is unique in the history of philosophy. To merely study Spinoza as scholars do, without following him in one's personal life, is seriously to short-change oneself. To reach mid-life, let alone advanced years, without spiritual values that are applied to personal life is among the more unfortunate things that can happen to a person. For the "continuous and supreme joy" that Spinoza promises [in the Treatise on the Emendation of the Intellect] is psychologically achievable. Indeed, even short of attaining the exalted state of Blessedness, which consists in a conscious, continuous, and experiential "knowledge of the union which the mind has with the Whole of Nature," it is psychologically possible to become free from the various afflictive emotions, which freedom allows for great happiness, tranquility, and peace of mind. No goal is more worthy of a human being than this. In Spinoza's own words,

> ...a free man hates no one, is angry with no one, envies no one, is indignant with no one, despises no one, and is in no way prone to pride.... Furthermore, the free man has this foremost in his mind, that all things follow from the necessity of the divine nature, and that therefore whatever he thinks to be irksome and bad, and whatever besides seems impious, horrible, unjust, and base arises from the fact that he conceives the things themselves in a distorted, fragmented, confused way. For this reason he endeavors above all to conceive things as they are in themselves and to remove the obstacles to true knowledge, such as hatred, anger, envy, derision, pride, and other things of this sort. And so he endeavors, as far as he can, to do well and rejoice. (*Ethics*, part 1V, proposition 73)

For Further Reading

If the reader has any doubts concerning either the reality or achievability of the state of consciousness Spinoza calls "Blessedness," I urge her or him to consult the vast literature on the Near Death Experience. Tens of thousands of people have experienced this state of consciousness. Of course, they do not use 17th century philosophical jargon to describe their experiences, thank goodness, but even a cursory look at descriptions of Near-Death Experiences will convince the reader that they are experiencing the very same thing Spinoza's philosophy guides us towards: (i) identity with the Being of Light, (ii) an Unconditional Love so powerful that most NDErs do not want to return to their body, (iii) a felt sense of waking up to a Reality infinitely greater than what is experienced while embodied, (iv) and a sense of themselves as eternal. Spinoza would add that one does not need to first die in order to attain this state of consciousness. It is available to us now, even while still embodied. This is the universal testimony of all mystics, those who *have* attained Blessedness while alive. There are a number of contemporary spiritual teachers who, in their writings, talks, and workshops, exemplify the spirit of Spinoza. In particular, reading anything by Eckhart Tolle will deepen your appreciation of Spinoza's system of thought, and will greatly assist in applying that system of thought to your personal life.

— Neal Grossman, March 2014

WHO IS SPINOZA?

Baruch de Espinoza was born in Amsterdam in 1632, the son of Jewish refugees from the Portuguese Inquisition. His father was a prosperous merchant and Baruch was given the best education possible for a Jewish boy at that time. The rabbis who taught him, impressed with his intellectual gifts, had very high hopes that he would become a great Jewish rabbi and philosopher. These hopes were dashed when the young Spinoza began discussing ideas that were heretical to both the Jewish and Christian concepts of God and religion. In particular, Spinoza rejected the concept of a theistic God who creates the world out of nothing, in favor of the concept of a pantheistic (or pan*en*theistic) God who creates the world out of Himself. Confrontations with the religious authorities escalated, until he was finally excommunicated from Judaism in 1656, after which he changed his name to *Benedictus*.

For the next twenty years, until his death in 1677, Spinoza supported himself financially by grinding lenses, wrote down his philosophical views, and maintained a rich and extensive correspondence with many of the leading intellectuals of Europe. He was esteemed not only for his ideas, but also for the kind of person he was, and he warmly and graciously received many visitors into his home. Towards the end of his short life he turned down an offer for a professorship at the prestigious University of Heidelberg, as he did not wish to be held accountable for his thinking to any Institution.

Immediately after his death—probably caused by inhaling glass dust—other philosophers simply did not know what to make of his philosophy. He was referred to as "that God-intoxicated man" by one and as "that accursed atheist" by another. His writings fell into oblivion for about 150 years, until he was "discovered", not by philosophers, but by poets (Goethe, Coleridge, Wordsworth, Shelley, and others), who by temperament tend to be more sympathetic than philosophers to the *spirituality* inherent in Spinoza's system of thought. As Hegel wrote early in the 19TH Century, "To be a philosopher you must first be a Spinozist: if you have no Spinozism, you have no philosophy."

For those interested in a biography of Spinoza, I recommend *Spinoza: A Life*, by Steven Nadler, Cambridge University Press (April 2001).

1 METAPHYSICS

There are many ways in which a human being can live his or her life, yet it seems that very few of us are able to live in such a way as to enjoy true happiness and peace of mind. Spinoza asks whether it is possible to attain a state of mind in which one enjoys *continuous* happiness. Now, we are all familiar with *transitory* happiness—a happiness that lasts for a short period of time and usually arises as a result of a satisfaction of some desire. And most of us have also experienced occasional moments of peace of mind. Is there an upper limit to these fleeting experiences of happiness and peace of mind? Or can they be extended indefinitely until happiness and peace of mind completely permeate the personality, flowing continuously through one's mind much as the blood flows continuously through the body?

Spinoza affirms that such a permanent state of mind is possible, and this places him in the tradition of mystical philosophers, for only mystics believe in, and claim to experience, a state of consciousness in which one enjoys "supreme and continuous happiness." This state of consciousness ultimately consists, as Spinoza says, in an awareness of the union that exists between the individual human mind and the Mind of God.

Now if this is so—if our mind is already united with God's mind—then two questions immediately present themselves: (1) Why are we not *now* aware of our connection with God? and (2) How can we become aware of this connection? The answer to the first question involves a detailed analysis of the nature of the human condition, especially of human emotions and how our emotions limit our ability to understand; the answer to the second question involves a detailed therapy—that is to say, a practice, which when followed will allow us to overcome the limitations of our emotional nature and to experience ourselves directly as a "part" of the infinite Mind of God.

The uniqueness and elegance of Spinoza's system of thought consists in a derivation of a psychological theory, with its consequent therapy, from metaphysical first principles. The human being, after all, is a part of reality; hence any conceptual account or theory of human beings, whether of our physical nature (physiology) or our mental nature (psychology), must follow from, or be a part of, a more general theory of the nature of reality per se. By the term "metaphysics" I shall mean any general theory of the nature of reality. The "first principles" of Spinoza's metaphysics are extraordinarily simple and self-evident, although, like the simplicity of a Beethoven quartet, it takes some attentiveness to fully appreciate.

FIRST PRINCIPLES

Let us begin with where we are right now. We are beginning an inquiry into the nature of things generally (metaphysics) with the intention of applying what we learn to better understand ourselves (psychology), from which will arise, we hope, understanding, greater happiness, and peace of mind. How do we know that such an inquiry will bear fruit? Why should we believe that it is possible for us to understand the nature of things? Why should we believe that reality is intelligible?

We respond to this question by observing that a willingness to believe in the intelligibility of the world, which includes ourselves as a part, is a prerequisite to any inquiry into the nature of things. It would be quite irrational to attempt to figure out the nature of things, including oneself, without believing that the nature of things is such that it can be figured out. It would be absurd, for example, for someone to work on a jigsaw puzzle while believing that the pieces do not fit. Even an "I don't know whether the pieces fit" attitude is not fully rational because with such an attitude one is likely to give up at the first sign of difficulty. That is, with an agnostic "I don't know if the world is intelligible" attitude, when faced with something one doesn't yet understand one is likely to take one's lack of understanding as evidence that the world is unintelligible, rather than make the effort to change one's way of thinking about things. Only an initial faith in the intelligibility of the world, ourselves included, will provide the motivation necessary for pushing through our own limitations.

The title of one of Spinoza's works, "A Treatise on the Emendation of the Understanding," implies that our present mode of understanding is faulty and that the conceptual framework with which we approach the world is not adequate and needs to be "corrected," "mended," or "healed." This is not a matter of merely adding more "facts" or "information" to our present set of beliefs—it is a matter of radically changing and transforming the very process of understanding itself. I recognize that this is likely to be insulting to the ego, which always likes to believe that its present conceptual framework is perfectly adequate. This attachment of the ego to its present conceptual framework, however, is an impediment to growth and self-knowledge, for when confronted with a situation that the ego does not understand it will conclude that the thing in question is not intelligible and abandon the process of inquiry rather than conclude that it is the conceptual framework, the "mind-set," of the individual that needs to be emended. For example, Freud preferred to believe that women are mysterious and irrational (unintelligible) rather than believe that his conceptual framework was just not adequate for understanding women. Had he been less arrogant, he might have taken his inability to understand women as *his* inability (and made the effort to emend his own understanding). Instead, he took his inability to understand women as "evidence" that women are not understandable. Thus, a rational inquiry into the nature of things requires an initial attitude of faith in the intelligibility of reality, accompanied by an attitude of humility toward our present way of conceiving that reality.

I used the word "initial" in the above sentence because after one has approached things with this attitude one soon gains sufficient evidence to justify the initial faith. To refuse to taste the pudding until it can be "proven" that it tastes good is quite irrational, for the only "proof" possible lies in the eating. So when Spinoza says, in effect, that there is a better way of living in the world—a way that leads to continuous happiness, peace of mind, and social harmony—the only real proof that there *is* this better way lies in following the path he has indicated for us and finding out through our own experience whether this path leads to increased happiness and peace of mind. If so, then our own experience will constitute the "proof" that our initial faith—without which we would not be motivated to follow the sometimes arduous path—was justified.

Now, the belief in the fundamental intelligibility of reality has profound and immediate consequences. For it leads to what has been called a principle of sufficient reason: i.e. given anything that happens, anything that *is,* there is a reason why the thing has happened and why it is. We may not *know* what the reason is for a particular thing's existence or behavior, but that doesn't mean that there *is* no reason. The belief in the intelligibility of the world implies a commitment to believe that there is a reason or cause for everything that happens, and that this principle of sufficient reason applies to mental events as well as to physical events. A belief in this principle, as Einstein observed, is also essential for science. Can you imagine a scientist, when confronted with a specific phenomenon he doesn't understand, ever, under any circumstances, saying "well this must be one of those things for which there is no reason?" I think not. Rather, the scientific attitude toward such a phenomenon would be something like: "There must be a reason or cause for this phenomenon, even though I do not yet know what it is." The principle of sufficient reason is both a metaphysical principle and a methodological rule. As a metaphysical principle it asserts that everything that goes on within the world is causally linked with other things; as a methodological rule it guides us, when confronted with a situation we don't understand, to assume that understanding is always possible—that there is a reason why the situation has occurred that we do not yet know.

The principle of sufficient reason leads directly to the concept of God. The existence of God is the most obvious thing in the world, but its obviousness is hidden by our tendency to form mental images and then demand proof that our images correspond to reality. This tendency must be avoided; we will give several examples later on, taken from mathematics and science, that demonstrate our ability to understand many things for which we cannot also form an image in our mind. A brief example will suffice for now. It is obvious to our understanding that the set consisting of all the natural numbers (0, 1, 2, 3 . . .) has an infinite number of members, even though we cannot with our imagination picture all the (infinitely many) numbers. The fact that we cannot form an image of an infinite number of things does not mean we do not have an adequate understanding of the concept of infinity. It means only that there are some things we can understand but cannot picture. The concept of God is one of those things.

THE EXISTENCE OF GOD

The conception of God most prevalent in Western societies is highly anthropomorphic. "Anthropomorphic" means the unjustified projection of human qualities onto things that are not human. The Western concept of God—a concept invented by ancient desert tribes, refined somewhat over the years, and made intellectually respectable by Descartes—consists in forming an image of a being with human qualities. Some of these qualities are magnified indefinitely (God is all-*knowing*, all-*powerful*, all-*good*), while others are not (God is imagined to be emotionally affected by what we do—God is pleased or displeased with us in the same way in which *we* are pleased or displeased with others). When people, including philosophers and theologians, ask whether the existence of God can be proven, they generally mean to ask whether this image, which they have formed in their minds, can be proven to correspond to anything in reality—that is to say, to anything outside their imagination. The fact that this image of God has no existence outside of the imagination means not that God does not exist, but that the popular image of God is, like Santa Claus, a fiction.

So we must form a different, non-anthropomorphic conception of God—a conception from which God's existence will follow directly. Indeed, the fact that it is possible to doubt whether the Judeo-Christian concept of God exists is in itself a reason to question the adequacy of that particular conception. We seek a conception of God—a definition of God—from which her existence follows, in much the same way that the non-existence of married bachelors follows from the definitions of the terms "married" and "bachelor." This procedure is generally referred to as the "ontological proof for the existence of God"—the attempt to prove that the existence of God follows from the concept of God (or from the meaning of the term "God").

Such proofs have generally failed because philosophers have held on to an inadequate concept of God. A criterion for an adequate concept of God is that his existence follows immediately from the definition of the concept. We will give two definitions of "God" and then show that they are equivalent to one another—that is, that both definitions define the same concept. The reason for giving two definitions at once is that the first is logically more fundamental, but the existence of God is easier to see right away from the second.

(1) "God" = "independent being" or "a being the existence of which does not depend on anything other than itself."
(2) "God" = "the totality of everything there is" or simply "all-that-is"

God's existence follows immediately from the second definition, for anyone who claims to doubt whether God as so defined, exists, has simply not understood the definition. No one can doubt that everything which exists does in fact exist—that is simply a tautology. What, of course, is different here and which requires further elaboration is the "appropriateness" of defining the term "God" in this way. Therefore, we will discuss the more usual definition of God (definition 1 above) and show that it leads logically to definition two. For now, the reader should reflect that defining God as all-that-is does indeed necessitate the existence of God thus defined and that no other definition of God (that does not entail definition 2) has this consequence.

Before considering the first definition of God, I want to make very clear the immense difference between Spinoza's conception of God and the more popular Judeo-Christian conception of God. The difference between these two conceptions is most apparent when one considers the question: what is the relation between God, on the one hand, and Creation (or the World), on the other? The familiar Judeo-Christian view conceives of God as wholly other than the world, much as a sculptor is different from the sculpture he creates, or the watchmaker is different from the watch he makes. So God, like the watchmaker, is conceived as making the world, winding it up, so to speak, yet remaining *other than* and *external to* the created world. The Spinozistic conception of God, on the contrary, holds that the world is internal to God. This can be expressed in many ways: there is nothing but God, God creates the World out of himself, the World is a part of God, the World is a manifestation of God, nothing is external to God, God has no "outside," God is One with respect to which there is no other, all things are in God, or as St. Paul puts it, "in Him we live and move and have our being."

Thus, the physical universe as a whole may be thought of quite literally, as constituting the body of God, to which Spinoza gives the name *Extension*. Similarly, the mental universe as a whole (which includes our minds, but is not limited only to human minds) constitutes the Mind of God, to which Spinoza gives the name *Thought*. It follows from this that we ourselves, body and mind, are constituted by and form a part of the very fabric of God. The difference between these two conceptions of the relation between God and the world cannot be overemphasized. In the Judeo-Christian account, the human being is totally outside of God; the alienation of humans from their Creator is built into the very concept of God. In the Spinozistic account, the human being is intrinsically connected with God—the fact that most of us do not experience conscious awareness of our connection with God means, for Spinoza, not that this connection does not exist, but only that our present level of awareness is not sufficiently developed to experience the connection. Spinoza's philosophy aims at leading us to this experience.

We now return to the first definition of God. The concept of independent being is in itself fairly obvious: an independent being is one that needs no other being in order to exist; a dependent being is one that needs other beings in order to exist. How to apply this concept is less obvious. It is quite easy to see that nothing in the physical world satisfies the concept of independent being. Take our own body, for example. It came into being in time and hence its existence depended on things external to itself; moreover, once the body comes into being, its continued existence is dependent on things and processes external to itself. It would perish instantly if Earth lost its oxygen, if the sun became extinct, etc. But this applies to any and every object within the physical world. Every thing—from rocks to galaxies—comes into being in time and hence depends for its existence on those things and processes out of which it emerged.

It might be tempting to conclude, incorrectly, that since everything in the world is dependent on other things, then either (1) the concept of independent being is vacuous or (2) the concept of independent being refers to a being not in the world. But this is a false dichotomy, for it does not consider the possibility that the world as a whole might satisfy the concept of independent being. Let us now consider this possibility.

The so-called causal proof for the existence of God goes roughly as follows: we assume that every event has a cause. Take any event and call it A. A will have a cause, say B. But B is also something, so it too will have a cause, say C. The original version (Aristotle's) of this argument appeals to the intuition that this causal chain (...C→B→A) cannot extend indefinitely, and so there must be a "first cause" that sets in motion the whole causal chain and terminates in the event A (God → ...C→B→A).

Critics of this argument point out that the notion of an infinite causal chain, which extends without limit into the past and the future, is fully intelligible, and therefore the postulate of a first cause is unnecessary. That is, it could be the case, these critics argue, that the world consists of a series of events (objects, beings) each one of which depends causally upon some other(s) which depends causally upon some other(s), etc., and that there need exist no object nor being that is independent in the sense defined above. Notice that this criticism of the causal argument for the existence of God really rests on the claim that metaphysical conclusions (that there must be a "first cause") cannot be drawn from what we can or cannot imagine (an infinite series of events). It is true that we cannot imagine—that is to say, we cannot form a picture in our minds of—a world in which every event is caused by a preceding event which is caused by a preceding event ad infinitum, with no "first event" to set the whole thing in motion. But our inability to imagine such a world does not mean that we cannot understand it perfectly well.

For example, consider the set of all (positive and negative) integers:

$$I = \{...-3, -2, -1, 0, 1, 2, 3...\}$$

I is a set consisting of an infinite number of members, with no "first" member and no "last" member. No one can picture this set in its entirety, yet this set and all its properties is completely understood mathematically. This illustrates a general principle in Spinoza's philosophy: our ability to understand is not limited by our ability to picture, and vice versa. We can understand many things that we cannot imagine ("imagine" means here "to picture in the mind," "to form an image in the mind"), and conversely, we can imagine many things that cannot be understood. We shall come back to this later and illustrate it in detail. Now let us return to the causal argument.

So we have concluded that our inability to picture a world with no first cause does not mean that the world cannot be conceived in this way. Let us then conceive of such a world: $W = \{\ldots C \to B \to A \to \ldots\}$, a world in which everything that is depends upon something other than itself. Now, this conception of the world is supposed to show that the so-called causal argument for the existence of God fails—that the world could be an infinite series of dependent beings and therefore the concept of an independent being is not needed. We will show, however, that this conception of the world, far from rendering the concept of independent being unnecessary, actually requires it. For the very conception of the world as a series of dependent events makes it possible to talk about the *series* as a whole, in much the same way that one can talk about the *set* of all numbers. And just as the *set* of all numbers (I) has properties different from those of any of its members, so also the *series* (W) of dependent events will have properties quite different from those of any of its members.

In fact, a little reflection will show that W has all the properties usually associated with God. Clearly, W cannot depend for its existence on anything outside of itself because there is nothing outside of itself. Thus its existence depends only on itself and W satisfies the concept of independent being. Does W exist "in time" (temporal) or is W "outside" time (eternal)? Clearly, only individual members of W can be in time; W as a whole exists outside time, yet includes time within itself. Does W exist necessarily or contingently? Since there is nothing external to W, there is nothing upon which W's existence could be contingent; hence W exists necessarily. For the conception of W includes everything that is—past, present, and future, mental, physical, and anything else, if there be anything else. We have thus arrived at the concept of an independent being—a being that includes within itself all dependent beings, such as ourselves, a being whose existence is self-caused, eternal, and necessary. We cannot form an image of such a being, but we can understand the concept perfectly well.

Let us now return to the Judeo-Christian conception of God, contrasting it with the present Spinozistic conception. Under the Judeo-Christian conception, God is an independent being wholly other than the world or anything within the world. What is wrong with such a conception, and why is Spinoza's conception more adequate? In the first place, Spinoza's conception is simpler, for according to the Judeo-Christian conception, there is God *and* there is the world; whereas according to Spinoza's conception, there is only God (everything else being included in the Being of God). A deeper problem with the Judeo-Christian conception is that it is not fully consistent. For consider the following question:

does the fact of the world's existence, or the existence of anything within the world, have any effect on God? If we answer "yes" to this question, then God is no longer an independent being, since her nature is held to be affected by, and hence dependent on, the world.

For example, if God is thought to be "pleased" or "displeased" by anything we do, and if "we" are regarded as existing external to God, then God's "mood," so to speak, depends upon our actions (which are believed to be external to God), and hence God no longer satisfies the concept of Independent Being. So if God is to be wholly other than the world, and is also to be an independent being, then there can be no interaction between God and the world. Indeed, God cannot even be said to have knowledge of the world, because such knowledge would alter his state of mind, and hence his state of mind would *depend* on both the existence and the nature of the world. If, for example, we imagine that God created the world in Time, then God's state of mind would have to be different before and after the creation. Just as when we now perceive something that formerly was not present, and so our state of mind depends upon the object we see, so God, after creation, would "perceive" a world that was formerly not present; and hence, his state of mind would *depend upon* the existence of something external to her—the world.

Now it may be objected that one thing may be independent of another thing and still be affected by it, so that God could be affected by the world and still be independent of it. This is the more popular conception of "independent," and it allows us to think of ourselves as independent beings who are merely affected by, but not dependent on, our interactions with other beings and objects external to ourselves. But if we keep our understanding fixed on the definition of an independent being as a being whose existence and nature depend only on itself and on nothing external to itself, then it is quite apparent that only the world-as-a-whole satisfies this definition. For the contents of God's mind must surely be a part of his nature, and if those contents are different before and after the creation of the world, then so is God's nature different. Hence God's nature is made to depend on the existence of a world external to himself, and therefore God, conceived as wholly other than the world, cannot be regarded as an independent being—a being whose existence and nature depend only on herself.

Furthermore, it is difficult to understand why God, conceived as wholly other than the world, would ever create the world in the first place. The principle of sufficient reason tells us that there must be some reason why the world exists rather than doesn't exist, and that, since the world is not the cause of its own existence, this reason must be external to the world; that is, it must lie in God. But it is hard to understand why God would have any reason for creating the world. All the "reasons" usually given—that God was lonely, that he had some inner need or desire—contradict the concept of God as independent and self-sufficient and are merely anthropomorphic projections of the motivation we human beings have for doing things. And since God can have no reason for creating the world, the existence of the world appears arbitrary and without meaning.

A PRACTICAL APPLICATION

Much more could be said about these matters, but I do not wish to indulge in metaphysical excursions for their own sake, beyond what is necessary to develop a conceptual framework that satisfies the demands of reason for logical consistency and assists us in finding our way toward greater happiness, the latter being our main purpose. The framework that we have developed teaches us that the world and everything in it, including ourselves, is a manifestation and expression of the Nature of God; that everything that is, is internal to God; and hence, that every cell within our body and every thought within our mind are parts of the very being of God. We are thus quite literally sparks of divinity with a touch of amnesia (since we do not consciously experience our own divinity—our connection with God), and our purpose here on earth must be, as Plato might put it, to recollect the divinity we already are (for it is not possible to be without being a part of God). In this "recollection" lies our happiness. Spinoza's conceptual framework is most useful because it aligns our intellect toward this understanding (of the connection between ourselves and God) and contains specific practices—a therapy—for overcoming those parts of ourselves that create the illusion of separateness. The mere thought that we are "sparks of divinity," if kept before the mind will be useful in overcoming much negativity.

Since our aim is chiefly practical, we want to derive as quickly as possible some concrete guidance for the emendation of our understanding—or for removing obstacles and limitations to our own happiness, which is the same thing. Although we will discuss emotions in detail later on, it will be most useful here to give a concrete example of how the metaphysical conception of God previously outlined can be used to derive specific guidelines for treating dysfunctional emotions.

Perhaps of all the emotions that consume our mental energy, impairing our ability to understand and our capacity to feel joy, none is as debilitating as the emotion of guilt. Now guilt involves a feeling of regret for some past action of ours that we believe could have and should have been different. We may, for example, feel guilty because we lied to someone, or because we lost our temper, or because we failed to achieve the goals we set for ourselves. To be specific, let us consider the case in which a person feels guilty after losing her temper and speaking harshly to someone. The person, while feeling the guilt, torments herself by thinking, "I should not have lost my temper," "I should not have shouted," "I should have behaved differently." The belief that I should have behaved differently involves the belief that it was possible to have acted differently. But is this belief really so?

According to the principal of sufficient reason, for any and every thing or event—whether the event be a human action or not—there is a reason or cause why the event happened rather than didn't happen, and why it happened in the particular way it did, rather than in some other way. If the event in question be a human action, such as losing one's temper, then there is a cause why that action occurred, whether we know what it is or not. For the action to have been different, its cause would have had to be different. But the cause of any action must be another object, event, or action, which as such, must also have a cause—that is, a reason why it is what it is. For the cause of the original action to have been different, *its* cause would then have had to be different. We thus have an infinite regress leading ultimately to the totality of All-There-Is, or God. Since God is the cause of all things, for any particular thing to have been different, including human behavior, God herself would have to be different from what she is. But how is this possible? Could the totality of All-There-Is really be different from what it in fact is?

Well, the principle of sufficient reason tells us that for anything to be other than what it is, its cause would have to be different. But what could cause All-There-Is to be different from what it is? The answer is, of course, nothing, since there *is* nothing outside of All-There-Is. To put it simply, since any particular thing that is (including a human action for which one feels guilt) is a part of All-There-Is, for the particular thing to have been different, All-There-Is would have to be different. But since there is nothing outside of All-There-Is, there is nothing that could cause All-There-Is to be different. Therefore, All-There-Is is *necessarily* what it is and could not possibly be other than what it is, and this necessity extends in the minutest detail to each and every particular thing within the totality of All-There-Is.

Returning to our feeling of guilt that arises out of some past behavior of ours and involves the belief that we should have behaved differently from the way we did, once we understand that this belief rests on the belief that All-There-Is, or God, could have or should have been different—a metaphysical absurdity—then the feeling of guilt will subside. In the same way, it can be shown that many of our emotional responses rest on this false belief that All-There-Is could be different from what it is. Blaming another person for his or her actions involves the same metaphysical error as does the feeling of guilt—which latter is blame directed toward oneself rather than toward another.

The reader will no doubt have many objections to this, so habituated are we to those emotional responses, such as blame and guilt, which are based on the belief that a given thing could have been other than what it in fact is. We acknowledge that a logical demonstration is rarely sufficient to overcome an habituated response; therefore, we wish to do three things which will make our understanding more lively: (1) to begin a "practice," (2) to show more clearly the holistic nature of All-There-Is and what this implies for particular things (one implication being that a given thing could not have been other than it is), and (3) to show why it is that the mind tends to believe otherwise.

EXERCISE 1: Although the "practice" or therapy that Spinoza develops is based on his fully detailed theory of emotions, which we will present later, it is very important to begin the practice as soon as possible, even if its rational basis is not yet fully understood. So, consider some past behavior of yours about which you feel a little guilt. (It is better to begin with something that involves a little, rather than a lot, of guilt; practicing this exercise to remove little guilts will give you the strength to remove the larger guilt.) Let your attention go back and forth from the specific past behavior to the present feeling of guilt that arises as you recollect that past behavior. Now introduce the thought "this past behavior could not possibly have been otherwise" (you may play with different wordings for this thought, e.g., "if my behavior in that situation were different, then All-There-Is would have had to be different, which is absurd," or "my behavior followed from the Nature of God and could not have been otherwise," etc.). Even if you do not yet fully believe it, repeat this thought to yourself as your attention goes back and forth between the memory of the past behavior and the present feeling of guilt. Notice what happens to the feeling of guilt. Even if this exercise is practiced for only a few minutes each day, you will notice a substantial reduction in the intensity of your guilt feelings, and eventually they will subside altogether.

This exercise may also be used to alleviate feelings of hurt and anger that appear to be caused by someone else's behavior toward you. Let your attention alternate between the other person's past behavior and the present feeling (hurt, anger, blame, etc.) that arises in you when you recollect that behavior. (And, as before, it will be better to begin with a "little" hurt rather than a "big" hurt.) Now introduce the thought "this person could not have behaved differently" (or "this person's behavior was a direct consequence of the nature of All-There-Is" or "to wish that this person's behavior were different is to wish that God were different," etc. And again, as before, notice how the feeling of hurt or anger subsides as you repeat that thought. Many readers will no doubt resist attempting this exercise, or will attempt it only halfheartedly, so firmly habituated are we to the belief that such emotions (guilt, anger, etc.) are justified and appropriate responses to our own and other's behavior. We will show later that this belief is quite false and that these emotions are deeply harmful to the individual. For now, I urge the reader to practice these exercises daily in a spirit of playful curiosity. The proof of the pudding is in the eating—try it and see what happens.

THE WHOLENESS OF CREATION

We now return to the concept of All-There-Is. We wish to understand more deeply why it is that this concept represents a single, indivisible, individual whole, rather than a mere collection of parts. For example, one may form the concept of the set of all objects on my desk, but this set (consisting of papers, pens, mail, telephone, memos, books, etc.) is not a single individual—it is merely an aggregate of parts. By contrast, the set of all molecules in my desk, or the set of all cells in my body, is not an aggregate of parts but a single individual whole—the desk and my body, respectively. Why do we insist that God, defined as All-There-Is, is more like the set of all cells in my body than the set of all objects on my desk—that All-There-Is is a whole, and not a mere aggregate of parts?

Now although Spinoza believed, rightly I think, that the holistic nature of All-There-Is could be demonstrated "a priori," that is, from the very concept or definition of All-There-Is, he also believed that our minds are more likely to be convinced by "a posteriori" demonstrations, that is, by appeals to our own experience. We are fortunate today to have at our disposal a wealth of collective experience, namely science, that was unavailable in Spinoza's time. Many excellent books have been written by physicists that explain the revolutionary nature of the "new" physics, and the reader is strongly urged to seek out several of these books. We will use the results of quantum theory and modern cosmology—with just enough explication of the physics to render the concepts intelligible to the reader—to show that the physical universe (we here consider only the *physical* world; the mental world we will discuss later) is a single indivisible whole.

Holism and atomism

Let us use the term *holism* to refer to any metaphysical framework that holds that the world is a single, indivisible whole, not reducible to the sum of its "parts"; and let us use the term *atomism* to refer to any metaphysical framework that holds that the world is not an indivisible whole, but rather, is made up of and reducible to its parts—that the world is an aggregate of parts. Each framework carries with it an associated methodology, that is to say, a way of approaching any given problem. For example, if, as atomism asserts, the world really is made up of parts, then the right method of understanding any phenomenon is to break it up into its constituent parts. These "parts" will in turn also have parts, and this process of reduction continues until one has reached the ultimate parts. On the other hand, if the whole is more than the sum of its parts, as Holism asserts, then the correct method of understanding any particular thing involves finding a larger whole in which the particular thing is embedded. This larger whole will itself be embedded in a still larger whole, and this process of "embedding" continues until one has reached the "Ultimate Whole"—All-There-Is, or God.

The human body, for example, conceived *atomistically*, is made up of cells, so to understand the body one must understand the behavior of the cells. But cells are in turn made up of molecules, so to understand the cells one must understand the behavior of the molecules that constitute the cells. But molecules are made up of atoms, etc., and this process of division continues until one has reached the ultimate "building blocks" of the material world. On the other hand, the human body, conceived holistically, is in dynamic interaction with a larger physical ecosystem, without which the body could neither have been brought into being nor continue to be. Thus, to understand the body, one must understand the larger ecosystem in which the body is embedded, and which makes the continued existence of the body possible. This larger system—from which the body receives its food, oxygen, water, etc.—is embedded in a still larger system (Earth as a whole), which is embedded in a still larger system (solar system, galaxy, etc.), and this process of embedding continues until one has arrived at the ultimate ecological unit—the universe as a whole.

Now, both holism and atomism, considered as methodologies, are immensely useful and both can be employed simultaneously to understand any given phenomenon. A meteorologist, for example, to understand the weather, would need to know about both the nature of the molecules that make up the atmosphere *and* how the atmosphere interacts with the surface of the earth. However, holism and atomism, when considered metaphysically—as theses about the nature of reality—cannot both be true. For either the physical world is made up of ultimate parts, in which case atomism is true, or it is not made up of ultimate parts, in which case holism is true.

So, let us suppose for the moment that atomism is true—that the physical world is constituted by, or made up of, ultimate building blocks and that everything is explainable in terms of the nature and arrangement of these ultimate parts. What must these parts be like? First of all, these parts must be *simple;* for if they were complex, that is, if they were made up of anything, then they would not be ultimate but would depend upon the things out of which they were made.

More importantly, the ultimate parts must be *independent.* Now, by hypothesis, the ultimate parts cannot depend upon anything other than themselves, because there is nothing other than these ultimate parts; anything that is not itself an ultimate part is merely an aggregate of a certain number of such parts. Moreover, a given ultimate part cannot depend on other ultimate parts, for if it did—if **a** depended on say **b** and **c,** which in turn depended on **d, e,** and **f,** etc.—then one would no longer have an atomistic framework, since each part would depend on other parts which would depend upon still other parts, etc., and this results in each part depending on the totality of all parts, which is holism.

And finally, an ultimate part cannot be created or destroyed in time, for if this were to happen then, according to the principle of sufficient reason, there must be a cause for why the given ultimate part came to exist or ceased to exist, and the given part would then depend for its being on this cause and would not be independent. Keep in mind that according to atomism anything that is not ultimate comes to be in time as a result of the motion and arrangement of the ultimate parts that constitute the thing. But this could not account for how an ultimate part itself could come into being. Therefore, in any atomistic framework, the ultimate parts must be simple, independent, uncreated, and indestructible.

The demise of atomism

It is a remarkable and conclusive result of contemporary physics that there are not, nor can there be, any objects which satisfy the above conditions. The full story of this result, as mentioned, is explained by various physicists in numerous books on the subject, to which the interested reader is referred. We will here give a brief account of the story, in a way that will bring out its metaphysical aspects.

Consider the problem of change. Descartes considers this problem by discussing a ball of wax, which when heated, becomes liquid. How do we know that the liquid wax is the same wax as the solid wax, given that the two appear so different to our senses? How is it possible for something that is solid to become something that is liquid, or for something that is liquid to become something that is gaseous (water to steam)? Is it the same "thing," which is first solid and then liquid? Or has something that was solid changed into something else that is liquid? What does physics tell us?

First of all, physics tells us that solids, liquids, and gases are all made up of tiny particles called molecules, too small to be seen with the eye. These molecules are in a state of constant motion, and the amount of their motion depends on the temperature of the object. At relatively low temperatures, molecular motion is small, which allows the molecules to get close to one another, forming a solid. At higher temperatures, the molecules move too fast to get close to one another, but not fast enough to altogether escape from one another's company, and they begin to roll over one another. This comprises the liquid state. At still higher temperatures, the molecules move too fast to enter into any relationship with one another, thus forming the gaseous state. So given a change, say, of (solid) ice to (liquid) water to (gaseous) steam, we say (1) that the individual molecules that constitute the given piece of ice are the same molecules that constitute the water and the steam, (2) the degree of motion of the molecules determines whether the molecules arrange themselves in solid, liquid or gaseous form, and (3) this degree of motion is affected by the temperature.

The general, that is to say, metaphysical, structure of this explanation is as follows: given an observed qualitative change (solid to liquid), physics postulates the existence of something that does not change and explains the qualitative transformation (of solid to liquid) in terms of quantitative differences among the molecules. The intuition here is that the fact of qualitative change would be a deep mystery—it would violate the principle of sufficient reason—unless there were some cause for the change through which the change could be understood. And this understanding seems to consist in "seeing" that the qualitatively distinct solid and liquid are merely different manifestations, or different states, of the same underlying reality, namely the molecules that constitute them.

Now, continuing this line of reasoning, molecules themselves can undergo qualitative change. For example, a water molecule can, under suitable conditions, transform into molecules of hydrogen and oxygen. This transformation would be as mysterious as frogs transforming into princes if there were nothing that remained invariant under the transformation. So, as before, physics postulates the existence of something—atoms, in this case—that remain unchanged during the transformation and in terms of which the transformation can be understood. Thus, the atoms that make up the water molecule before the change are the very same atoms that, after the change, make up the oxygen and hydrogen molecules. The different compounds are merely different arrangements of the same underlying stuff (the atoms), and *that's* how it is possible for different compounds to change one into another.

Recalling the third criterion for "ultimate particles," one way of telling that the molecule is not an ultimate unit of matter is that a given molecule can be created and destroyed in time. That which remains invariant, that which does not change, during a given transformation, is more fundamental (more "basic," more "ultimate," more "real") than that which comes into being and/or passes away during the transformation. So, during the transformation of water into hydrogen and oxygen—$2H_2O \rightarrow 2H_2 + O_2$—we say that, *because* the atoms that make up the initial water molecules are the *same* atoms that make up the final hydrogen and oxygen molecules, (whereas the water molecule ceases to exist and the hydrogen and oxygen molecules begin to exist), that *therefore* the atoms are more fundamental objects than the molecules.

What about the atoms themselves? Do they satisfy the conditions for being an "ultimate unit" of matter? The answer is, of course, no, since they too undergo qualitative change. For under appropriate conditions, a given atom can transform into two or more other atoms (fission) or two or more different atoms can combine to form a single atom (fusion). Physics explains this transformation by postulating the existence of something that remains invariant as the atoms change, in terms of which the atoms themselves are defined, and in such a way that the possibility of such qualitative change can be understood. As everyone knows, the atom is defined in terms of the so-called elementary particles (neutrons, protons, electrons), and transformations among atoms are simply different arrangements of the same elementary particles. Thus, when a given uranium atom decays into two other atoms, the same protons, neutrons, and electrons that formerly constituted the uranium atom now constitute the two new atoms. During the transformation, the uranium atom ceases to exist, the other two atoms begin to exist, but the elementary particles remain the same. It is for this reason that the elementary particles are regarded as more fundamental than the atoms which they constitute.

What about the elementary particles themselves? Do they satisfy our criteria for being ultimate units of matter? The answer is, perhaps surprisingly, no, because every elementary particle can be created and destroyed, that is to say, they undergo qualitative transformations similar to (and in some ways more dramatic than) the transformations that occur at the atomic and molecular level. The elementary particles can transform not only into one another, but also into pure energy. To account for this change, we again postulate the existence of some underlying "stuff" that remains invariant as the particles undergo transformation.

It is at this point that atomistic methodology, which was so successful until now, breaks down completely. For it is not possible to regard this invariant underlying "stuff" as a still smaller particle. To be sure, physicists have tried to apply atomistic methodology to explain particle transformation, but the "quarks," which they postulate to constitute the particles fail to satisfy the conditions for an atomistic metaphysics. For one thing, the quarks also undergo qualitative transformation (both into one another and into other particles), and thus bring us no closer to the ultimate units of matter which Atomism requires. But more interestingly, quarks cannot exist separately—that is to say, quarks cannot exist apart from the particles that they constitute. Now a bunch of "parts" that cannot exist independently of the whole that they constitute are not really parts at all. The quarks, because they do not exist independently of the whole that they supposedly constitute, fail to satisfy the independence criterion (in addition to failing the criterion of permanence) for an atomistic framework.

So, back to our search for an underlying stuff or substance that remains invariant as the particles transform. This basic stuff, according to physics, is pure energy. Consider the following example: suppose we have an electromagnet and gradually increase the intensity of the magnetic field between the poles. When the intensity of the magnetic field reaches a certain level, electrons and positrons will be observed to emanate from the region of space between the poles. According to physics, before the creation of the particles the magnetic field contained a certain amount of energy. After the creation of the particles, the energy in the magnetic field is reduced by an amount equal to that required to create a particle ($E = mc^2$). Thus the total energy before and after the appearance of the particles is constant, and energy therefore represents a more fundamental level of being than do the particles. Indeed, the particle itself is a form of energy. And since particles make up atoms, which make up molecules, which make up everything else, the basic stuff, which constitutes the being of everything physical, is energy. Particulate matter is one form in which energy can exist; non-particulate matter, or "field," is another form.

Thus, we have shown that there are no viable candidates for the position of ultimate units of matter, and that every proposed candidate violates the criterion of permanence and/or independence. Physics also tells us—and I will merely state this without going into the details—that there can exist no object that is both extended (in space) and simple. Anything that occupies space cannot be simple; that is, it must have an internal structure, and so the concept of something that is "solid" matter through and through is vacuous, according to physics. So if there were to exist an ultimate unit of matter it could not have any extension in space.

Holism and quantum physics

I wish to turn now to the independence criterion and show that not only is the negative result (that atomism is false) true, but so also is the positive result that, according to physics, the material world is a single indivisible whole. Now, we all have a feeling for the difference between a "whole" (such as my desk, or my body) and a mere aggregate of parts (such as the objects on my desk). If we are asked to say what it is that makes one thing a unity and another thing an aggregate, we would probably say that spatial contiguity of the parts is necessary for something to be a unity. The molecules that constitute my desk and the cells that constitute my body are next to one another in space. On the other hand, if two or more things are, or can be, spatially separated—such as the objects on my desk—then that is usually sufficient to conclude that these objects do not form a natural unity but merely an aggregate of parts. It is a dramatic consequence of the quantum theory, however, a consequence initially discovered by Einstein, that spatial separation is not a sufficient condition for individuation. Let us explain.

Consider the following thought experiment: we get two identical movie cameras that we place at right angles to each other. They are each focused on the same live cat, and we begin and stop each camera at the same time. It is obvious that the films from the two cameras will look quite different from one another; when one shows the cat's head, the other will show the cat's side, and so on. Suppose we give our two films to someone who does not know that they are films of the same cat, taken simultaneously but from different perspectives. Could this person, by analyzing the films frame by frame, arrive at the conclusion that the two films are films of one and the same cat? The answer is of course, yes; there would be frame by frame correlations between the two films that would lead an observer to conclude that the two films are different perspectives of the same underlying reality—the cat.

Now the quantum theory predicts—and these predictions have been verified—that under certain conditions two spatially separated objects will behave as if they are different perspectives of the same underlying reality. That is, a "frame by frame" analysis will reveal correlations between the behavior of the two spatially objects; these correlations indicate that the two objects, which appear to be distinct, are really parts of, or aspects of, a single underlying unity. And this is what is meant when I said that spatial separation is not sufficient for individuation, for although the two objects (atoms, particles) in question may be very far apart spatially, they are not independently existing individuals, but are parts of a larger unity.

Now, under what conditions does this feature of quantum wholeness manifest itself? The conditions are simple: any two (or more) particles that interact with each other will exhibit this feature of wholeness and will continue to exhibit it even after the interaction has ceased. No matter how far the particles move away from each other spatially, they will continue to exhibit the kind of correlations that lead us to conclude that they (the particles) are not independently existing individuals, but are aspects, or parts, of a larger unity. This "larger unity" includes the two particles but has holistic features that cannot be explained in terms of two independently existing particles. These holistic features will continue indefinitely until or unless something external to the two-particle system interferes with it, destroying the unity. Summarizing, quantum theory shows that (1) any two or more interacting particles form a "whole" that is not reducible to the sum of its parts; (2) this whole persists even after the interaction has ceased and the particles have become spatially separated; and (3) this wholeness can be broken only if the system interacts with something external to it.

What can we conclude from this about the physical universe as a whole? According to modern cosmology, the universe is expanding. This means that in the past the universe was smaller, and the farther back we go in time, the smaller the universe gets. At the moment of the big bang, all the "stuff" (energy) of the physical universe is concentrated at a single point. Clearly at this time, and shortly afterward, everything is in very strong interaction with everything else. Therefore, at the time of the big bang, condition one above is satisfied, and everything in the universe must be regarded as constituting a "whole" that is not reducible to the sum of its parts. Furthermore, since there is nothing external to the universe, there is nothing that could break this wholeness, and so condition three can never be satisfied. Hence, according to condition two, this wholeness must persist even after the "parts" of the universe have become spatially separated. The entire physical universe is thus a single individual—a whole, a unity—not divisible into parts.

Recall our previous discussion of physics' unsuccessful search for the "ultimate" building blocks of physical reality. The intuition that guided us (from molecules to atoms to elementary particles) is that whatever is invariant under a given transformation must be more real than, or more fundamental than, those things that change, that either begin or cease to exist. Physics' search for ultimate units was unsuccessful because there is no particle that continues to exist under all transformations. The only thing that remains invariant under all possible transformations is the universe as a whole, for no matter what changes may occur within the universe, the universe always retains its unity as a single indivisible whole. It is thus the most fundamental reality, or I should say, the only fundamental reality, since there is nothing external to it.

I think this is sufficient to demonstrate that All-There-Is is a single indivisible Being, an Individual Whole, an organic Unity, and can in no way be regarded as a mere aggregate of parts. Yet, it must be admitted that when we look around us it certainly *seems* as if what we perceive is a bunch of disconnected objects. But from the fact that we do not perceive with our senses the interconnection between things, it does not follow that all things are not really interconnected. For, as we shall see later, our body, which itself is a part of the unbroken wholeness of Nature, has the ability, through its sense organs, to create images of things as if they were separate and distinct. So the fact that the world appears to us as if it were constituted by separately existing things, tells us more about the nature of our sense organs than about the nature of things as they are in themselves. Science, which transcends the limitations of human perception, aspires to gives us an understanding of things as they are in themselves, not merely as they appear to human beings. And according to this understanding, all things are interconnected in such a way as to constitute a single indivisible Being. Therefore, those who have been reluctant to embrace a holistic worldview out of fear that such a worldview is "unscientific" may now completely relinquish their fears. For holism is not only fully compatible with modern science, it is the only worldview that is.

This excursion into physics not only informs us about the nature of the world—that its nature is holistic, not atomistic—but also tells us something about the nature of the understanding itself. For, whereas sense perception always works in terms of concrete images of things, the understanding, if we take modern science to exemplify what it is to understand, works in terms of those features or properties that individual things have in common, and that remain invariant as the individuals themselves undergo all sorts of change and transformation. It must be emphasized that *methodologically speaking,* both atomism and holism can give genuine understanding of particular things, and science avails itself of both methodologies. Any finite thing is both constituted by smaller units and itself constitutes a part of a larger unit. The human body, for example, is constituted by molecules that exist both before and after the human body comes into and passes out of existence; the molecule is therefore a useful concept through which the body can be understood. (Molecules are common to all bodies and are invariant as individual bodies arise and perish.) But equally, the human body is a part of a larger ecosystem, (atmosphere, food chain, etc.), which it requires in order to maintain its form. This larger ecosystem is also (as were the molecules) common to all human bodies and invariant as individual bodies arise and perish; and hence, the human body can also be understood in terms of the role it plays—i.e., its function—within the larger ecosystem. From a metaphysical perspective, however, there is only one ultimate invariant, as we have shown, namely the Universe-as-a-Whole. For only God, or All-There-Is, is common to all things and remains invariant as individual things come into being and pass away. Therefore, from this ultimate perspective, God is the cause of things and is the ultimate "sufficient reason" through which all things must be understood.

THE CAUSALITY OF GOD

Divine necessity
We will elaborate on the claim that God is the cause of all things because we wish to remove from the mind the habit of thinking of God as a "remote" cause, as a Being who, so to speak, wound the universe up at some long ago time and then ceased to have anything to do with it. The concept of God we are here developing holds that the universe is a process of continuous creation—that God is eternally present to each and every thing there is. Let us then consider a particular thing, say, an individual human body, and ask, what is the cause of this body? Now this

question can be approached, methodologically, from many different perspectives, but each perspective ultimately involves the concept of God.

For example, if we proceed atomistically and attempt to explain the body in terms of the atoms or molecules that constitute the body, we are led to ask several questions.

1. For each atom in the body, there was a cause for its coming into being, and so to understand the body in terms of its constituent atoms leads us to ask for the cause of each atom. Now atoms in fact are created in stars, and indeed, the heavier elements (like iron) are created only in supernovas. So the existence of our body is intimately linked with the existence of supernovas in that were supernovas not to exist, our bodies could not exist either, and therefore an understanding of our bodies in this way involves an understanding of the forces that generate supernovas. But these forces have to do with the most general nature of matter, energy, space, and time, and therefore an understanding of any particular physical thing involves understanding the Universe-as-a-Whole.

2. If we consider the atoms that constitute our body, at a time after their creation but prior to their being organized in the specific arrangement that constitutes the given body, one can then ask, what is responsible for organizing and arranging all these atoms into the specific form of the body? (This, in philosophical jargon, is asking for the *efficient cause* of the body's existence). Since each atom in my body has a causal history, to understand the body in this way involves understanding the history of each and every atom in my body. That is to say, insofar as my body depends for its existence on the particular atoms that constitute it, it also depends for its existence on the physical laws and processes responsible for bringing each atom in my body into physical proximity with each other atom in my body.

For example, how did a specific iron atom, which originated in a supernova millions of years ago and light years away, get into my body so as to form a part of my body? Well, first of all it had to travel from the supernova in which it was made to Earth. But during the course of this journey it was influenced by many things (gravitational fields, electromagnetic radiation, space-time warps, and myriads of other particles). Had any one of these other things been different, that particular iron atom could not have reached Earth. Therefore, since an understanding of how that iron atom reached Earth involves an understanding of all the things that influenced it on its journey, and since an understanding of these other things involves an understanding of the physical universe as a whole, it is easy to see that my body (which is constituted of billions of atoms, each one of which came here from someplace else) depends for its existence on the whole universe.

3. It is a tribute to science (and to the power of the human mind that invented science) that it has shown us in great detail the why's and wherefore's of the interconnectedness of all individual things. This interconnectedness applies not only to the past with which our bodies' existence is connected, and depends on those processes that created and brought together the atoms that constitute it, but also to the present. That is, given that the atoms that constitute the body have been brought together so as to constitute the body, this set of atoms requires continuous interaction with the rest of the universe in order to maintain the form of the human body. For the atoms could not maintain the form of the body were the earth to cease to exist; Earth could not continue to exist were the Sun to cease to exist; the sun could not continue to exist if the galaxy were to cease to exist; but our own galaxy is interconnected with other galaxies, etc., and thus we see that the continued existence of our body involves the Universe-as-a-Whole.

It is clear, therefore, that the Universe-as-a-Whole, or All-There-Is, is necessarily involved in (1) creating the raw materials out of which our body is made; (2) organizing the raw materials into the form of the human body (or, to put it better, creating the body out of those raw materials); (3) continuously sustaining that form for as long as the atoms are arranged in that form; and eventually (4) destroying the body. Moreover, the very raw materials, the atoms that constitute our body, are themselves manifestations of an underlying and all-pervasive energy (Spinoza, writing before Newton, uses the term "motion and rest") that constitutes the very being of All-There-Is, or God, insofar as God is conceived physically.

Could it really have been otherwise?

Once the total dependency of the human body, indeed, of any given thing, upon God is understood, it follows that for any given thing to be or to have been different from what it in fact is, the totality of All-There-Is, or God, would have to be different from what she in fact is. But if God could really have been different from what she is, then there would have to be a cause or reason sufficient to explain why God is not in fact different from what she is. This "cause" cannot lie outside of God, for there is nothing outside of God. But to say that the cause of God's not being different from what he is lies inside of God, is to say that God contains within himself, within his own nature, the reason for being what he is, rather than something different. Therefore, it is absurd to conceive that God could possibly be other than what it in fact is, for God is what she is out of an inner necessity; and since everything that exists is caused by, depends upon, and is a part of, God, this divine necessity extends to all things whatsoever. Therefore we conclude that nothing could be or could have been other than what it in fact is (or was or will be).

Although this is all very clear and straightforward, we must nevertheless acknowledge that it is extremely rare for philosophical consideration to dispel deeply ingrained habits of thinking and the emotional responses that are consequences of those habits of thinking. As mentioned earlier, the emotion of guilt depends upon the (false) belief that a given past behavior of ours could have (or should have) been different, and hence to change that belief would destroy the emotion. As anyone who has been involved in therapy knows, our emotional patterns have a life of their own and actively resist any attempt to change them. Since the majority of our emotional patterns involve the belief that a given action of ours or another's could have been other than what it is or was, these emotional patterns will actively resist any effort to remove or alter the belief upon which they rest and will present to the mind many objections concerning the conceptions we are here presenting (e.g., "we can't have a moral world unless we can blame or praise people for their actions," "a world without free will is meaningless," "how can the evils of the world follow from God?," etc., etc.). Therefore, in addition to having shown the falsity of the belief that a given thing could have been other than what it is, we will now show why it is that most people not only hold this belief, but regard it as obvious and self-evident.

Now this belief is quite universal and appears in just about every known culture. Therefore, the conditions under which this belief is formed—that is to say, the psychological causes of the belief—must also be universal, a part of the "human condition."

The causes of this belief cannot lie in experience, for experience teaches us only what is, not what could be. Suppose, for example, I enter my office and observe a certain book lying on the left side of my desk. This experience tells me only what is—that the book is now lying on the left side of my desk. From this experience I have no basis for believing that the book could have been lying on the right side of my desk, so if, while observing that the book is in fact on the left, I also believe that the book could have been on the right, I am believing something that does not originate in my experience. Something must be "added" to my experience of the book as lying on the left in order to get the belief that it could have been lying on the right. This "something," according to Spinoza, is *imagination*.

Spinoza uses the term "imagination" to refer to any mental experience that involves an image. The term "imaging" would perhaps be more appropriate for contemporary readers, since "imaginary" has the connotations of "seeing something which isn't there." Nevertheless, we will retain Spinoza's usage, keeping in mind that by the term "imaginary" Spinoza means not only forming an image of something that isn't real, so to speak, but also forming an image of something whether it be really there or not. Thus, when the mind perceives a tree that exists, Spinoza would say the mind *imagines* (forms an image of) the tree. But the mind also imagines a tree when it forms an image of a tree that isn't there (hallucination); and it also imagines a tree when it remembers a past experience of perceiving a tree. The mind also has the power to imagine things that it knows to be contrary to fact, as when we form a mental picture of a winged horse, a Santa Claus, or, to return to our present discussion, of a book, which in fact is lying on the left side of my desk, as lying on the right side. But from the fact that we can form an image of something as being different from what it is, we cannot infer that the thing itself could have been different.

Suppose, furthermore, that yesterday the book was on the right side and that today, while perceiving the book on the left side I remember that the book was on the right side yesterday. The presence of this second image (representing the book on the right side) invites us to believe that *today* the book could have been on the right side. But clearly our experience tells us only that yesterday the book was on the right and today it is on the left; experience does not teach us that on either day the book could have been any place other than where it in fact was. Our tendency to think otherwise comes from (1) the ability of the mind to create contrary-to-fact images of things together with (2) the inability of the mind to find any reason why what it imagines could not be so. But it is quite obvious that neither our ignorance of why a given thing is and hence must be what it is, nor our ability to form an image of a thing as different from what it is, can in any way support the erroneous belief that a given thing could have been in any way other than what it is. One more example should suffice to remove any remaining doubt.

Suppose I toss a coin in the air and after it lands, but before you can see which side has landed up, I cover the coin with my foot. If I ask you whether it is possible that the coin landed heads up, you will say "yes"; similarly, if I ask you whether it is possible that the coin landed tails up, you will again say yes. Now what is meant by the term "possible" in this context? It cannot refer to the actual coin, since the coin has already landed and it is either (a) heads up—in which case it is not possible that it be tails up—or (b) it is tails up—in which case it is not possible that it be heads up. So if (a) has occurred, but you do not know that (a) has occurred, you will say that it is *possible* that the coin show tails up when I remove my foot. But the only thing you can mean by this usage of the term "possible" is simply that you do not know, that you are ignorant, which of the outcomes has in fact occurred. The mind will form two images, one representing the coin as landing heads up, the other representing the coin as landing tails up. The mind then deceives itself into believing that either of these images could really be the case; but actually only one of these images could really be the case and the mind does not know which of its images corresponds to the facts. Later, I remove my foot and you see that the coin shows heads up; now I ask you, could the coin have shown tails up? You will be tempted to answer "yes," but this error stems from the facts that (1) you recall the time when you did not know which outcome had occurred and (2) at that time your mind *imagined* two outcomes, one of which was in agreement with the fact, the other of which was contrary to the fact. But from the fact that we were once (or are now) ignorant of the true outcome, and from the fact that we did form, or are forming, or remember having formed, contrary to fact images of the outcome, it does not follow that the outcome itself could have been anything other than it was in fact. Therefore we affirm what is really a tautology, that everything is what it is and that nothing could have been other than what it in fact is. This "tautology" is an essential consequence of the metaphysics of holism and must be kept firmly in mind. It is a fairly simple matter to see the truth of this with respect to books and coins; it is somewhat more difficult to apply this truth to ourselves.

The illusion of free will
But yet, we human beings, body and soul, are a part of God, and for us to be different from what we are or to have been different from what we were (and this includes all our thoughts, feelings, emotional responses, behaviors, actions, etc.)

God herself would have had to be different, which is impossible (This does not imply, it should be noted, that tomorrow we will be the same as we are today.). For the same forces that produced the galaxies, stars, and planets also produced the human being, who is a part of nature and follows the natural order of things and is not an "exception" to nature.

The overwhelming tendency of human beings to believe that in a given situation they *could have* behaved differently from how they in fact behaved, or that they *could have* made a decision contrary to the one they in fact made, reflects a powerful egocentricism that claims that humans are exceptions to nature. Every action or behavior of our body and every thought or decision of our mind is an event within the natural order of things and hence it has a cause, which cause is also within the natural order of things, and that cause itself has a cause, etc. So if any given action or thought of ours were different from what it was, the whole natural order of things would have to be different. But this is absurd, since the natural order of things (the term "natural" is of course redundant, since the order of things could not be other than what it is) is a manifestation of the Nature of God, and it is impossible that God should have a different nature.

Indeed, if we pay but a little attention to the psychological process to which we give the name "deliberating," "choosing," "deciding," etc., we will easily see that this process in no way justifies our belief that in a given situation we could have "decided" to do something other than what we in fact decided to do. Let us consider a specific example of a so-called free choice. I am at an ice cream parlor and I have to decide from among, say, 20 different flavors. The psychological process of deciding involves representing to myself—that is, forming an image of, or simply, *imagining*—the tastes of the different flavors, observing my own reactions to these images, alternating back and forth among the taste images until I settle on one to which my own reaction feels most positive, at which point I place my order. Let's say I order chocolate. Why am I tempted to believe, after I've ordered chocolate, that I *could have* ordered coffee? For all my experience teaches me is that at one time I was deliberating and then I ordered chocolate. Experience does not teach me that the result of the process of deliberating on that particular occasion could have been anything other than what it in fact was. The temptation to believe otherwise arises, as before, from the fact that we now remember (after ordering chocolate) the sequence of images representing alternative flavors together with the fact that at that time we did not know which of the images would prevail and hence were "free" to imagine that an image, different from the one that did prevail, might possibly prevail.

But this sequence of images that represents what appears to be possible "choices" is itself determined by physiological and psychological causes (even though we may be ignorant of these causes), and the fact that these images present themselves to the mind cannot in any way support the belief that we could have made a "choice" different from the one we actually made. Every process of "deliberating," "choosing," "deciding," etc., has this structure: (1) a series of images, representing what appear to be different "possibilities," present themselves to the mind; (2) the mind alternates back and forth among the images, drawing perhaps further images (representing, say, consequences of each "possibility"); (3) eventually one of the images grows stronger and prevails; and (4) then the mind acts on the image that has prevailed. It does not follow from the fact that a series of images is presented to the mind and the mind does not know at the time which of these images will prevail, that an image that did not in fact prevail could have prevailed. Therefore, we affirm that everything that is—and this includes those mental processes referred to as "deliberation," etc.—is a part of the natural order of things that expresses a divine necessity and could neither be nor have been different from what it in fact is.

The importance of practice

It is not enough to give merely intellectual assent to this consequence of Holistic metaphysics; it must be applied on a daily basis to every emotional response, such as blame or guilt, which is inconsistent with this principle. For the reality of our day-to-day experience is primarily sensory and emotional. The sole purpose of metaphysics is to provide a conceptual framework in terms of which our day-to-day experience can be transformed in a direction of increased happiness and peace of mind. This transformation cannot occur unless one is willing to bring one's own emotional responses into harmony with one's intellectual understandings and this harmony cannot come into being without constant practice. The merely intellectual understanding—that, say, the emotion of guilt is based on the false belief that in a given past circumstance one could have behaved differently—cannot by itself remove such feelings of guilt, any more than one can learn the game of tennis simply by reading about it. What is required is to bring the intellectual understanding to bear on concrete instances of the emotion, so that each time guilt is felt the mind gently reminds itself of what it understands intellectually. This must be done over and over again, until the understanding of guilt so completely pervades one's being that the highly dysfunctional emotion is no longer a part of one's character structure.

EXERCISE 2: Each time a feeling of guilt or an impulse to blame another occurs, remind yourself that this particular feeling of guilt or this particular impulse to blame, insofar as these emotional responses involve the false belief that either you (in the case of guilt) or another (in the case of blame) could have acted differently in a specific circumstance, is out of harmony with what your mind understands to be true, i.e. that nothing could have been other than what it in fact is or was. This process of reminding will not instantly remove the feeling of guilt, any more than one or two practice sessions at the piano will make you a proficient pianist. But with even a little practice some progress will be noticed, and one will then have some positive reinforcement that one is on a path that *leads* somewhere, and that one is not engaging in mere intellectual mind games.

Indeed, this conception of philosophy as providing an intellectual map that leads somewhere and hence must be followed in practice if one is to get to where the map leads is essential for understanding Spinoza. For much of what passes for philosophy today *is* of the nature of an intellectual mind game—interesting, perhaps, like a crossword puzzle, but not intended to be relevant to one's personal life, and hence useless as a basis in terms of which to understand and improve the quality of one's concrete, daily emotional reality. But Spinoza's philosophy *is* intended to be relevant to daily living; it is thus impossible to understand Spinoza merely by reading his books, but only by applying his ideas to one's own personal life. Only in this way can the relevance be experienced. Let us briefly discuss this concept of philosophy as intellectual map in more general terms.

Suppose several people are walking in a forest and begin to realize they are lost. One of them formulates the question, "Where are we?" Someone else in the group responds, "You are right here." Now consider why this statement is not an adequate response to the question. First of all, it must be acknowledged that this response is absolutely and undoubtedly true, it is logically impeccable. But as true as it is, it is absolutely useless because it is of no help in getting out of the forest. Any adequate response to the question must involve a way of getting out of the forest. To be told that you are right here, even to be given a detailed description of the terrain visible from "right here," does not respond to the request, implicit in the question, for guidance on how to get out of the forest.

A *useful* response to the question would be in the form of a map that would include (1) a general description of the whole terrain and (2) an "X" marking the place where the people are presently. The second point is important. For in order that a map be useful to a given individual, the individual must be able to locate herself on the map. Now much of philosophy belongs to this "true but useless" category. For example, Descartes responds to the question "What am I?" with "You are a thing that thinks." But just as a person lost in the forest knows that he is "right here" before he asks "Where am I?", so we already knew we were a "thinking thing" before we asked "What am I?"; and thus Descartes' reply is as undoubtedly useless as it is undoubtedly true. For anyone who has felt in her soul the question "What am I?" is asking for an answer that can be used as a guide for living. If one also feels, however vaguely, that there must be a *better* way of living than the path of material acquisition and self-aggrandizement prevalent in society, then any intellectual map that is to be an adequate response to this question must show a path leading to this "better way" of increased happiness, fulfillment, etc. But for such a map to be useful as a guide it must make detailed and explicit contact with where one is at right now; that is to say, with one's present emotional reality.

Part of the intellectual map we are in the process of constructing includes the principle that nothing could have been otherwise. But this general principle remains useless until the individual applies it to his daily personal life. This process of applying a metaphysical principle to concrete daily life, whereby the later is transformed and the former more deeply understood, is the process of locating oneself on the map and using the map as a guide. If, as we follow the map, we find that the new terrain we experience is as described by the map, then we gain both greater trust in, and better understanding of, the map itself, as well as a "better way" of living our lives. We now proceed with a further elaboration of Spinoza's "map."

MIND AND BODY

So, what are we? We know thus far that whatever we are, we are a part of a larger Whole. But this by itself is not sufficient to distinguish the part of God that is a human being from any other part of God. We need a more detailed account of what it is to be a specifically human portion of the being of God. We all believe that we have a physical component (our body) and a psychological component (our mind). What is the relation between the two? Historically, there have been three major responses to this question.

1. There exists only the physical; what we call "mind" is simply the product of material processes occurring in the brain, and should those processes cease, our mind would also cease to exist. This point of view we will call "materialism."

2. There exists only the mental. That which appears to be physical, including our bodies, is simply an illusion created by a (not necessarily human) Mind or Spirit. We will call this view "Idealism."

3. There exists both the mental *and* the physical; the mental cannot be "reduced to" the physical and the physical is not an illusion created by the mental. It is this third position that Spinoza adopts, although, there are tendencies in his system toward Idealism.

Now it is interesting to note that Spinoza never gives any argument, or reason, for believing the third response rather than first. He assumes from the beginning that mind and matter are distinct kinds of substance, neither reducible to the other. Perhaps he didn't feel the need to give a reason for this because the people he was writing for already believed it. Today also, the great majority of people believe the third response, and not the first. Nevertheless, materialism has become intellectually fashionable, and our universities are overwhelmingly dominated by people who sincerely believe that their mind is solely a product of their neurons, that their consciousness will be totally extinguished when their body dies, and that anyone who believes otherwise has fallen prey to religious superstition. We, therefore, discuss briefly, and offer several considerations, why Materialism should be rejected.

Some considerations against materialism
I say "considerations" rather than "proofs," because, as history shows, any belief system may be clung to no matter what the evidence to the contrary may be; to those who are deeply wedded to materialism and whose whole life would be thrown in disarray should they come to believe in the existence of spirit, what I have to say here will not be convincing (for there is nothing that could convince such people). The following considerations, therefore, are addressed to those intellectuals who feel in their hearts and suspect in their minds that perhaps we are more than just bodies, and yet are hesitant to explore for themselves a non-materialistic framework because they fear ridicule from their friends and colleagues.

1. One consideration is a kind of argument from authority: many, if not most, of the creative geniuses of our culture—poets, novelists, artists, musicians, scientists and philosophers—have expressed strong beliefs in a spiritual dimension to reality. Of course, this is merely a consideration, not an argument, but is it not odd that our intelligentsia at best ignores, and at worst treats with scorn and ridicule, a worldview espoused by so many of our culture's acknowledged creative geniuses? Are these geniuses all soft-headed, mushy-brained, fuzzy thinkers? When Einstein wrote in 1936 that

   > ...everyone who is seriously engaged in the pursuit of science becomes convinced that the laws of nature manifest the existence of a spirit vastly superior to that of man, and one in the face of which we with our modest powers must feel humble. (M. Jammer, *Einstein and Religion: Physics and Theology*, 1999)...

   was he being soft-headed, uncritical? Why is it that almost without exception the great creative scientists of this century (Einstein, Schroedinger, deBroglie, Heisenberg, Pauli, Godel, Eddington, Bohm, Wigner, Margenau, etc.) ascribed to a spiritual worldview? And why is it that this fact is systematically ignored by most intellectuals?

2. A second consideration, which in my opinion is direct evidence for the survival of consciousness after the death of the body, is the phenomenon of the near-death experience (NDE). There is a growing body of data, collected by respectable physicians and psychologists, subjected to appropriate statistical analysis, that appear to rule out every attempt to explain (or explain away) the NDE and other such phenomena in physiological and/or psychological terms. To my knowledge, there is not a single researcher in the field who, as a result of his research, is not inclined to take the NDE at face value—that is, people really do leave their bodies during such experiences. One would think that intellectuals would undertake a serious study of this phenomenon, because the issue—whether consciousness can exist outside the body—is so important and so highly relevant for assessing life's meaning. And yet, like the bishop who refused to look through Galileo's telescope

(because he "knew" there could be no such thing as moons circling Jupiter), the intellectuals of our time generally refuse to look at what is at the very least strong *prima facia* evidence for the existence of consciousness independent of the body.

3. The third consideration involves the intuition that there are no rational grounds for suicide. A person who takes, or attempts to take, his own life, by that act demonstrates that his mind was unbalanced at the time. It does not matter what "reasons" he gives for committing suicide, because the reasons are themselves the product of an unbalanced mind. I believe this would be the attitude of all psychiatrists and therapists. I cannot imagine any circumstances under which a psychiatrist might say to a suicidal client, "Yes, you have good reasons to kill yourself. I agree that that's the rational thing to do." Now if the intuition that suicidal behavior is a symptom of mental imbalance is accepted, then I want to apply this intuition to collective behavior. For example, when the tragedy of mass suicide involving the followers of Jim Jones occurred in Guyana, no one argued that they had good reasons to kill themselves. On the contrary, everyone agreed that the fact of mass suicide was sufficient evidence for the claim that Jones and his followers were psychologically unbalanced.

    Cannot the same argument be advanced for Western civilization as a whole? For Western civilization is now actively contemplating suicide in two ways: (1) through global nuclear war and (2) through irreversible pollution and destruction of the environment upon which our existence depends. But isn't this insane? Suppose an anthropologist from another planet visits Earth after we self-destruct by means of nuclear war. What will he think? Will he think that we had "good reasons" to destroy ourselves, or will he automatically take the fact that we destroyed ourselves as proof that we had collectively gone insane? Would he not ask, "What did these poor deluded people believe, what did they value, how did they live their lives, how did they become so psychologically unbalanced that they could see no alternative to self-destruction?"

    I suggest that the materialist beliefs and values of our culture are leading directly to self-destruction and that these beliefs and values therefore may properly be called insane. As men and women of good conscience, we should not participate in a thought structure that is leading toward the annihilation of life on Earth, but instead explore, intellectually and personally, with our hearts and our minds, alternative thought-systems such as Plato's and Spinoza's, which provide metaphysical grounds for fostering, in ourselves and in others, life-supporting values and qualities such as cooperation, compassion, true generosity, genuine acceptance and appreciation of those who are different from us, and Universal Love.

4. For our final consideration, we will present a version of an argument first given by William James in his essay "On Human Immortality." This argument is among the masterpieces of philosophical reasoning, for it grants the materialist just about everything and yet demonstrates that there can be no compelling reasons for believing that spirit does not exist. Now the materialist believes that human beings are nothing over and above a physical body, which includes the brain, and hence, everything about us must be explicable solely in terms of the body. In particular, those aspects of ourselves we are in the habit of calling "mental" or "psychological"—e.g., thoughts, consciousness, awareness, etc.—must be produced by the body (since otherwise they would have a reality independent of the body, which is contrary to materialism). Since in this view the mind itself is produced by the body, specifically the nervous system, there can be nothing in the mind that is independent of our body, and our mind is thus a function of our body. To say that the mind is a function of the body means that there can be nothing in our mind that does not correlate with something or other in our body. Now although we have presented above some empirical reasons for thinking that this is false—i.e., people, in the near-death experience report a continuation of conscious experience even when the brain is not functioning, let us here assume that it is true. That is, let us assume a complete functional dependence of the mind on the body—that there is no thought, no perception, no feeling however subtle, that does not depend on the functioning of the brain. William James grants this, and then shows that this still cannot prove that materialism is true. What James says, in effect, is from the fact (if it be a fact) that our conscious experience is *totally dependent* upon our

nervous system, it does not follow that our consciousness is *produced* by our nervous system.

Consider, for example, a television set. Everyone will agree that the picture that appears on the screen is a function of the inner workings of the set. Every detail of color, shading, motion, etc., corresponds to something happening in the mechanism of the set, and nothing can appear on the screen that does not correspond to something in the mechanism. But yet we know that the picture itself does not originate in the mechanism of the set; it originates in the TV studio and is transmitted in the form of electromagnetic radiation to the antenna of our television set. The set itself is simply a receiver: it transforms the electromagnetic signals (which signals exist independently of any TV set) into the form of sound and light that we experience when we watch TV. The TV set does not generate or produce the signal (or information); it merely transforms ("transmits" is James' term) it from one form (electromagnetic) into another (visible picture). Thus it does not follow from the fact that there is a one-to-one correspondence between the picture and the mechanism of the set that the picture is produced by the mechanism.

Analogously, from the fact that our conscious experience is, or may be, a total function of the nervous system, so that nothing can belong to the former that does not have some counterpart in the latter, it does not follow that our consciousness is produced by, or originates in, the nervous system. It could be that our body is simply a mechanism that receives a consciousness that exists independent of the body and transforms it into the form we experience as "our own." The most neurophysiology can demonstrate is the wondrous details of the correlation between conscious experience and the brain. It cannot decide the issue between whether the brain produces conscious experience or whether the brain merely transforms consciousness from one form into another. Thus, neurophysiology is *neutral* with respect to this issue, and there are no scientific reasons for preferring a materialistic point of view over a non-materialist point of view. Once the reader sees that materialism is a non sequitur, that it does not and cannot ever follow from the facts of neurophysiology, he is then free to examine other philosophical perspectives concerning the nature of the mind and its relation to the body.

The relationship between mind and body

We now return to Spinoza's account of the mind and its relation to the body. Given that mind and body are distinct in kind— so that neither is reducible to, or explicable in terms of, the other, what is the relationship between them? Spinoza's response to this question is greatly different from what the majority of people believe. Most people believe that the mind and body interact with each other, that one can affect the other. It seems very obvious that a desire (which is in the mind) can cause the body to move; e.g., the desire to, say, take a walk causes the body to walk, or that harmonious sound waves striking the ear can cause the mind to experience beauty. Nothing seems more obvious than that the mind can affect the body and vice versa. Nevertheless, Spinoza denies that any interaction can occur, and the basis for his denial is very straightforward.

The common view, which Spinoza rejects, asserts

1. Mind and Body are distinct in kind, and

2. Mind and Body can interact with one another.

It is easy to see that these two statements are inconsistent; that is, they cannot both be true. For if we assume that mind and body are distinct in kind, then they have nothing in common (for if they shared anything in common, they would not be distinct in kind). But if they have nothing in common, then they cannot possibly interact with one another. In other words, what it means to say that two things can interact is that something from one affects the other, and therefore, that the two things must have in common the *means* by which they interact. But if they share in common the means by which they interact, then they cannot be distinct in kind. For example, when we perceive an external object, our body and the object interact—the same light that is reflected by the object enters our body through our eyes, and so that light is something that our body has in common with the external body. Our body and (any) external body are similar in kind; they are both made up of matter and it is because of this that one can affect the other. But consciousness, or mind, we are supposing, is not made up of matter; it is distinct from matter and therefore has nothing in common with matter, and thus cannot interact with matter.

I do not wish to belabor the point, but so habituated are we to imagining that (1) and (2) above are both true that the illogic of this position is apt to be difficult to see through. Let us consider two physical objects, A and B, and let us suppose that A and B interact with each other. There must then be some *means* by which A and B interact—e.g., they could interact through physical contact, gravitational attraction, electrical force, etc. When this is analyzed according to physics, it is apparent that every interaction between any two physical objects involves an exchange of energy, which energy is also physical, between the two objects. It is because A and B are both *physical* objects that they both have energy and have *in common* the energy that they exchange in order to interact. That is, the very same energy that, say, leaves A, is absorbed by B. But B is able to absorb this energy, and hence to be affected by A, only because B is of the same nature as A—that is to say, both are *physical* objects and energy is a defining characteristic of what it is to be a physical object.

If we now suppose that A is physical and B is not physical, then how is it possible for A to affect B? For since B is not a physical object, it is not characterized by physical energy (if it were so characterized, it would be physical in nature), and hence is not capable of being affected by A. Conversely B cannot affect A, since the only means by which A can be affected is by absorbing or "feeling" some physical influence; but if B could produce something physical that could then affect A, then B would itself have to be physical. Thus, summarizing, if two things have nothing in common, they cannot interact because in order to interact they would have to have in common the means by which they interact.

According to Spinoza, mind and body are distinct in kind, which means they have nothing in common, which in turn means they cannot interact with one another. How, then, can we explain the fact that mind and body *appear* to affect one another? For it certainly does *seem* to be the case that I can move my body simply by willing my body to move and that it is the mental *willing* that causes the physical motion of the body. If there is no causal connection between mind and body, then what is the explanation for the observed correlation between them? Spinoza holds that this observed correlation is to be explained in terms of a deeper underlying reality, namely God. The physical and the mental are qualitatively distinct aspects—"Attributes," in Spinoza's terminology—of God. Because they are qualitatively distinct, there can be no interaction between them; because they are aspects of the *same* God, there will be correlations between them.

I wish to present an analogy that I believe will assist the imagination in picturing what Spinoza has in mind. The analogy is meant to appeal to the imagination, and hence must not be taken literally. Let us imagine that God is standing in front of a large number of mirrors. Imagine, further, that each mirror is differently curved, so that God is reflected *completely* in each mirror, but since the mirrors are all different, the reflected images of God will all be different from one another. It is clear, in this analogy, that there can be no interaction between the different images of God, yet there will certainly be correlations between the images since the different images are reflections of the *same* God. Now, one of these complete reflections of God is the entire physical universe, the "body" of God. Spinoza calls this the Attribute of Extension. Our body is a part of this Attribute. Another is the entire mental universe, the "mind" of God, which Spinoza calls the Attribute of Thought. Our mind is a part of this Attribute. The relation between the mind and the body is simply that they are different reflections of one and the same part of God. The human mind is a part of God reflected in the mirror of Thought; the human body is the very same part of God, but reflected in the mirror of Extension.

A note on terminology: The most basic distinction in Spinoza's metaphysical "map" is between independent being and dependent being. Spinoza uses the term "substance" or "God" when referring to the former, and "mode" or "modification" when referring to the latter. Any dependent being, such as a physical object or a finite mind, *depends on* independent being; that is, it is included in the larger whole that is God. So by referring to a given object as a *mode* of God, Spinoza explicitly reminds us of the dependency of that object on God. An Attribute of God is a complete reflection of God; the Being of God expresses itself, or manifests itself, in an infinite number of qualitatively distinct dimensions, each one of which is called an Attribute of God. We humans are aware of only two: the physical (Extension) and the mental (Thought). Thus, in Spinoza's terminology, the human being is a mode of God. The human body is that mode of God expressed in the Attribute of Extension; the human mind is the same mode of God, but expressed, or manifested, in the Attribute of Thought.

Let us now examine several consequences of our analogy. As we have already indicated, the reason why the mind cannot affect the body and vice versa is that the mind and the body are different mirror images of the same part, or mode, of God. An image that appears in one mirror cannot affect an image that appears in another mirror. The reason why mind and body are correlated with each other is because they are both images of the *same* mode of God. This "correlation" is a very general feature of Spinoza's system and is not limited only to human bodies and human minds. Every physical object must have some counterpart in the

Attribute of Thought, because a physical object *is* a mode of God reflected in, or manifested in, the physical dimension; that same mode of God is also reflected in, or manifested in, the mental dimension. Thus, if we consider a given physical thing—whether it be a table, a rock, a star, or a magnetic field—that thing must have a counterpart, or correlate in the Attribute of Thought. Spinoza refers to this correlate as the mind of the thing, or the idea of the thing. This is why Spinoza is often regarded as a pantheist: there is nothing in the physical world that is not associated with mind or consciousness.

This is a feature of Spinoza's system that may be difficult for some people to accept, for our anthropomorphic tendencies make us uneasy with the notion that intelligence can manifest itself in nonhuman forms. But it is a consequence of our model that in the same way that there exist physical objects, or bodies, that are not human, so also are there mental objects, or minds, that are not human. It is, on this view, as absurd to believe that the human mind is the only kind of mind there is as it is to believe that the human body is the only kind of body there is. Moreover, since the human body is a part of a larger physical ecosystem (Earth), which is part of a still larger ecosystem (the solar system), etc., and this process of inclusion continues until we reach the physical universe as a whole, or the Body of God—so also, the human mind is a part of a larger *mental* ecosystem (the "mind" of Earth), which is a part of a still larger mental structure, etc., and this process of inclusion continues until we reach the mental universe as a whole, or the Mind of God. The human mind is thus a part of a larger mental reality, and our salvation or liberation consists in experiencing our connection with this larger reality.

Now, because each "mirror," or Attribute, is a self-contained whole, the manifestation of God in one mirror (say, Extension) can neither influence nor be influenced by God's appearance in any other mirror (say, Thought). So when we are considering the events occurring in a given mirror, we can explain those events only in terms of the given mirror. Each mirror is explanatorily complete and self-sufficient; the human body must be explained only in physical terms and the human mind must be explained *only* in mental terms. Thus every activity of the body—and this includes so-called purposive activity—has its cause and explanation solely within the physical world; and similarly, every activity of the mind has its cause and explanation solely within the mental world. Nevertheless, although mind and body do not interact with one another, there are structural correlations between them that are due to their being different images of the *same* mode of God, It is therefore possible to infer some things about one from knowing about the other. We have already given two examples of this: (1) from the fact that there are physical bodies that are nonhuman we infer that there are mental bodies, (or minds, or spirits) that are nonhuman; and (2) from the fact that the human body is a part of a larger physical system we infer that the human mind is a part of a larger mental system.

A third example is: (3) from the fact that the human body is composite to a high degree—being constituted by bodies (e.g., cells), which are themselves constituted by bodies (molecules), etc.—we infer that the human mind is also composite to a high degree, being constituted by thoughts that are in turn constituted by other thoughts, etc. Since our awareness does not extend to most of these thoughts, any more than it extends to most of the physical structures that constitute our body, it is appropriate to say that we are generally unconscious of most of the mental structures (thoughts, ideas, feelings, etc.) that collectively constitute our mind.

Finally, (4) from the fact that our body contains within itself other bodies—bacteria, viruses, chemicals—that do not have the same nature as the human body, and that some of these other bodies are harmful and some are beneficial, it follows that the human mind contains within itself other mental objects that do not have the same nature as our own mind, some of which may be harmful to us, others of which may be beneficial. These are some of the things about the nature of our mind that may be inferred from our knowledge of the nature of our bodies together with the general structural parallelism that holds between mind and body.

However, the similarities between the mental and the physical are structural only, for the Attributes of Thought and Extension are qualitatively distinct and have nothing in common. *Awareness* is a characteristic only of minds; *extension* in space and *duration* in time are characteristic only of material objects. The mind can, and does, experience spatial and temporal relations as long as it is associated with a body, but when it withdraws from the physical into itself, it experiences its own nature, i.e., consciousness per se, and this nature has nothing to do with time. For the Attribute of Thought is the Mind of God and contains within itself an awareness first of its own nature and second of the natures of all the other Attributes or ways in which the Being of God manifests itself. Space and Time pertain only to Extension, not to Thought or to any of the other dimensions in which the Divine Nature express itself. The Mind of God is eternal, that is to say, outside of time; and since the human mind is a portion of—a mode of—the Divine Mind, it follows that the human mind, in its essential nature, is also eternal. The human mind, however, has so thoroughly identified with the experiences of its body that it has forgotten its own essential nature and is unable to conceive of the possibility of conscious experience outside of time. Indeed, even God herself is pictured as existing in Time. It will be useful, therefore, to "stretch our minds" on this point, so that we become more open to the idea of (or at least the possibility of) non-temporal conscious experience.

SPACE, TIME, AND ETERNITY

In medieval days, a philosopher who wished to show that his ideas were intellectually respectable had to show that they were in agreement with the Bible. Today, agreement with science has replaced agreement with the Bible as the mark of intellectual respectability. And I think this indicates progress, because science does not limit itself only to what can be imagined, or pictured, but strives to attain an understanding of the common properties of things even when that understanding, as physics clearly shows, involves using concepts that cannot be pictured by the mind. We have already appealed to the authority of physics when we showed that holism is the only metaphysics in harmony with physics. We shall now appeal to physics to show that space and time, as *we* experience it, are not fundamental categories, even of Extension. That is to say, if we pose the question, is there anything "beyond" space and time, physics answers "yes."

The expanding universe and the limits of the imagination
Most of us are perhaps familiar with some of the ideas we wish to discuss. We have all heard about black holes and the expanding universe, but the philosophical significance of these concepts has not been fully appreciated. Let us first consider the fact that the universe is expanding; the galaxies are receding from one another. At earlier times, the universe was smaller than it is now, and because the rate of expansion is known, it is possible to determine the time at which the entire universe was contained within an infinitesimally small volume. This is the moment at which the "big bang" occurred. Although the fact that the universe is expanding is familiar to most people, what is not familiar is the fact that it is impossible to imagine, or picture, this process.

For the mind invariably pictures the material of the universe expanding *into* a pre-existent space, but this picture is false because space does not "pre-exist." There is no space external to the universe *into* which the universe expands, and yet the mind cannot visualize the galaxies flying away from one another without also (falsely) visualizing a space into which the galaxies are flying. An oft-used analogy invites the reader to picture the expanding universe analogously to an expanding balloon. The galaxies are analogous to dots placed on the surface of the balloon; as the balloon is blown up, the dots will appear to recede from one another. In this example, it is clear that the space between the dots on the surface of the balloon does not pre-exist, but rather comes into existence as the balloon is blown up. That is, if we consider a Time at which the distance between dots is, say, one centimeter, and a later time at which the distance between dots is two centimeters, and then if we ask where does this extra one-centimeter distance come from, it is clear that it does not pre-exist on the surface of the balloon, but comes into existence as the balloon is blown up. The increased distance between dots on the two-dimensional surface of the balloon comes into existence *because* the balloon is expanding into a three-dimensional space. Analogously, the increased distance between galaxies in three-dimensional space comes into existence *because* the universe is expanding into a higher dimensional space. Just as an expanding two-dimensional spherical surface *requires* a third dimension into which it can expand, so also an expanding three-dimensional space (or four-dimensional space-time) requires a fourth (fifth) dimension into which it can expand.

The expansion of the three-dimensional universe into a higher dimension illustrates two points: (1) the ordinary three-dimensional space of human sense experience cannot be all there is—there must be "something" beyond ordinary space; and (2) this "something more" cannot be imagined, since the human mind's ability to form images is based upon its association with the body's experiences in three-dimensional space. But as mathematics and physics show, the mind's inability to form images of higher dimensional spaces does not mean that such spaces cannot be understood. Ordinary three-dimensional space (and time also) must then be conceived as lying on the "surface" of a higher dimensional space.

These same physical facts (the expansion of the universe) also indicate that time, like three-dimensional space, cannot be the most fundamental level of physical reality. For time, like space, does not exist prior to the big bang, but comes into existence with the big bang. The human mind incorrectly imagines that the big bang occurred at some moment *in* time. But this picture falsely represents time as pre-existing prior to the big bang, whereas, according to physics, time, like space, originates in the same process that generates the big bang itself.

The emanation of the spatio-temporal order from its eternal source
Let us carry our analysis further. The principle of sufficient reason asserts that there is a cause or reason for everything that happens. The big bang is certainly a happening so there must be a cause or reason for it. But this cause or reason cannot

be something that is "in" time (or space), because time itself comes into existence with the big bang. Therefore, the cause of the big bang must be something that exists outside of time. If we agree to use the word "eternal" to refer to anything that exists outside of time (and this is Spinoza's usage) it is clear that the entire physical universe as we experience it—the world of things in space and time—depends for its existence on causes that are eternal. Furthermore, since the cause of the big bang is eternal, i.e. it is not a temporal process that begins to exist or ceases to exist in time, it follows that this cause exists "now," and not only at the moment, so to speak, of the big bang. Therefore, the spatio-temporal universe must be *continuously emanating* from its eternal cause.

We will now develop a model in terms of which this process of continuous emanation may be better understood. This model will also assist us in understanding the possibility of Attributes other than Thought and Extension. I should add that the model to be developed here is not, as yet, required by today's physics, but it is strongly suggested by it. We begin with the concept of a black hole. Imagine, if you will, a sheet of paper in which a hole has been punched. Although the hole can be located by an imaginary two-dimensional being residing in the paper and its size can be measured, the hole itself is quite literally a place where the paper is not. Similarly, although a black hole can be located in space and time, and its size and mass determined, the hole itself is literally a "place" where space and time are not. Now imagine two identical holes at opposite ends of a sheet of paper. If we are allowed to curve the paper, it will be possible to curve it so that the two holes coincide with one another. A two-dimensional space traveler could then cover the distance between the holes in an instant, by going through one hole and emerging from the other, rather than by traveling in the plane of the paper. Similarly, it is possible for two black holes to be connected, even though they are very far apart in space and time. A three-dimensional space traveler could cross that huge distance in an instant, simply by entering one black hole and emerging from the other hole with which it is connected.

This example again shows that space and time cannot be ultimate features of the world, even though we cannot imagine a world that is not "in" space and time. For it is theoretically possible to enter a black hole here and now and instantly re-emerge millions of light-years away, and millions of years in the past or future, thus bypassing the usual spatial-temporal connections. By "theoretically possible" I mean that physics provides us with the conceptual apparatus for *understanding* (but not for *imagining*) how this could actually happen. The fact that ordinary space-time connections can be bypassed, that under certain conditions one can get from here to there without traversing the three-dimensional space in between, means that there exists non–spatial-temporal connections between things (such connections are called "topological," in the language of mathematics).

According to prevailing physical theory, the entire world of three-dimensional space and time, together with the matter/energy that "fills" space-time, emerged from a "singularity," or black hole, at the moment of the big bang. One model of the universe holds that this process of expansion will continue until some maximum size is reached, after which the universe will undergo a process of contraction until it collapses back into a black hole, whereupon it will re-emerge, expand again to some maximum size, contract and collapse, etc., this process of expansion and contraction continuing forever. Let us call this model the Oscillating Universe Mode. The picture looks something like this:

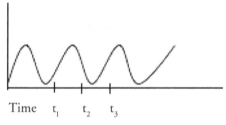

Time t_1 t_2 t_3

It should be obvious, however, that there is something wrong with this way of picturing an oscillating universe. For on the one hand we are picturing (imagining) these oscillations as occurring *in time,* with successive universes undergoing their cycles of expansion and contraction *one after the other.* But on the other hand, physics tells us that this picture is incorrect, because time does not exist within a black hole, and hence it is incorrect to picture these cycles of expansion and contraction as occurring in time. Time (and space) exist *within* a cycle, but not across the hole that connects one cycle with another; thus, one may correctly say that t_2 is later than t_1, but not that t_3 is later than t_2. The oscillations themselves occur in a higher dimensional space. Although this process cannot be pictured, a representation which depicts these universes as happening all at once is more accurate than the above representation which depicts them as happening "one after the other" in time.

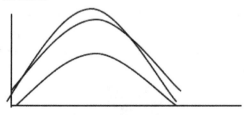

Our model, therefore, depicts physical reality as consisting of an infinite number of spatio-temporal worlds, all of which exist simultaneously in a higher dimensional space. I wish to suggest that this concept of parallel worlds be thought of as an *analogy* for better understanding the infinite number of Attributes, or ways in which God expresses himself. The analogy must not be taken literally, since all the (infinitely many) parallel worlds in our model exist *within* the Attribute of Extension. Nevertheless, our model is useful for showing how a given thing can simultaneously express itself in infinitely many ways. For just as in our model Extension expresses itself in terms of infinitely many simultaneously existing three-dimensional worlds, of which our world is but one, so also God expresses himself in terms of infinitely many simultaneously existing Attributes of which Extension is but one.

To develop our model still further, recall that we said earlier that a given black hole must be topologically connected (this means simply that the connection is not spatial-temporal) with another black hole. The two connected black holes must have identical physical characteristics (size, mass, rotation), since they are actually one and the same hole, even though there may be a large spatial and temporal separation between them. According to our model, the three-dimensional universe initially exploded out of a black hole and will eventually implode into a black hole. Since these two holes or singularities have identical physical characteristics (because the overall mass/energy and rotation of the universe remain constant), it is possible to identify the two holes. Thus, even though there appears to be a large temporal separation between the big bang and the final collapse, the black holes out of which and into which these two events occur are not two distinct holes, but one hole. But if the beginning of space and time (the big bang) is the same "point" as the end of space and time (the final collapse) then what is the status—the metaphysical status—of all activity that seems to be happening in between?

The logic here seems as paradoxical as it is straightforward; if what appears to be two distinct points are really one and the same point, then there can be nothing "in between" them, and whatever appears to be "in between"—the entire spatial-temporal world—has the status, metaphysically speaking, of an illusion. If the black holes marking the beginning and end of the spatial-temporal universe are not *two* holes, but one and the same hole, then the entire spatial-temporal world must be conceived as existing within, inside of, this hole. Thus, the entire world of space, time, and things in space and time is contained within an eternal object—that is, an object that is itself outside of space and time, and hence is continuously present to all spatial-temporal events that occur within it.

This is perhaps what Plato meant when he said that time is the moving image of eternity. Indeed, Plato, in his famous allegory of the cave, explicitly compares the three-dimensional spatial and temporal world to shadows that appear on the wall of a cave. Just as a shadow is a two-dimensional image of a three-dimensional reality, so the entire spatial-temporal world is a 3 + 1 dimensional image of a higher, eternal reality that is *continuously present.* This last point is important. The object must be continuously present in order to cast a shadow. So also, the eternal object—the black hole out of which and into which our world emerges and merges—must be continuously present in order that our world continue to exist. We must resist the notion of an "absentee Creator." For the cause of our world is not some Big Event that happened long ago and now no longer exists. Once it is understood that the cause is eternal—outside of space and time—then it is obvious that this cause must be continuously present and that our spatial-temporal world continuously emanates from its eternal source.

2 THE MIND

THE GENERAL NATURE OF SENSE EXPERIENCE

We indicated before that one of the reasons why we are not consciously aware of our connection with the whole of Nature has to do with sense experience, which presents to our awareness a world of seemingly separated and disconnected objects. Philosophers over the ages have been divided about whether our senses are like "windows" through which we experience reality directly, or whether they are more like "chains" which constrain the mind to experience a fragmented and truncated distortion of reality. Although common opinion holds the former, that our senses allow us to experience the world more or less as it is, the mystical philosophers such as Plato and Spinoza hold the latter view—that our senses represent to the mind a highly confused and inadequate image of reality.

Plato compares the world as it appears to our senses to mere shadows of "real" things, and says we are under the systematic illusion that the shadows are the only reality. In Plato's metaphor, our senses make it appear as if all we are is a body, since the consciousness that experiences through the body is not an "object" that can be perceived by the senses.

Thus, it seems to us as we though we are only a body. The mind, although independent of the body and eternal in its own nature, has so thoroughly associated itself with that portion of Extension that is its body that it has forgotten its own nature and is convinced that it *is* its body. For Plato, our happiness consists in "remembering" that we are not a material shadow, but a portion of a soul that has temporarily lost itself in a material form. It is much the same for Spinoza, except that his language is less poetic than Plato's. For Spinoza, our happiness, or Blessedness, consists in identifying with the Attribute of Thought and experiencing ourselves as such—that is, as a "portion" of consciousness that together with all other portions (some human, most not) collectively constitute the Mind of God—rather than identifying ourselves with, *and experiencing ourselves as,* that mode of Extension that we call our body.

Since sense experience is a major factor in creating and sustaining the illusion that our mind exists in isolation and separateness from other minds, and since this illusion of separateness engenders many emotions, such as fear, anxiety, and envy, which disturb our peace of mind and which we wish to overcome, it is necessary to discuss the nature of sense experience in some detail. It is important that the intellect be firmly convinced that much of what it thinks it knows concerning sense experience is not and cannot be true, for only then will the mind be open to an alternative account.

The myth of a homunculus

Popular opinion seems to hold that there is nothing mysterious about sense experience—that *seeing*, for example, is simply a matter of opening the eyes and observing what is objectively there. This view involves what has been called the myth of a "homunculus" (= "little man"), according to which our eyelids are like curtains or doors which, when open, allow the "little man" or "little person" inside of our skull to see what is there, and this homunculus is entirely passive with respect to the perceptions that it merely observes. This view is called "naive realism" in philosophy; it asserts that our mind/brain make no contribution to the perceptions that we have. For if the mind/brain were in any way involved in creating the sensory perceptions that it seems merely to have passively, then it could no longer assume that what it sees exists independently of its own nature.

According to Spinoza, sense experience is the result of an interaction between (1) something that exists outside of our body and (2) our body. Our body actively produces, or creates, a sense experience when acted upon by an external body, *but* the produced sense experience cannot be regarded as the same as, or in any way like, the external body involved in its cause. This is a very difficult concept to understand because the belief in a homunculus and its passivity with respect to what it sees is deeply rooted in all of us. For example, look at something—say, a tree. Do you not believe, while looking at the tree, that the tree exists as you see it and that you are not actively involved in creating the image of a tree, but are merely passively registering in your mind what is objectively there? This is the belief we have called naive realism, and it is this belief that, according to both Spinoza and contemporary neurophysiology, cannot possibly be true.

Generally though, it must be admitted that the body (and mind) does many things of which we are not aware. For example, we are not aware of how the body digests and assimilates food. While we are indeed conscious of certain sensations associated with the intake of food, such as hunger, satiation, indigestion, etc., these sensations by themselves tell us nothing about either the food we eat or the bodily processes involved in creating the sensations. Similarly, we are not aware of how the body absorbs oxygen, although we may be aware of certain sensations that accompany the process of breathing, such as increased energy if our respiratory system is functioning well and the air is good, or lethargy and tiredness if either of those conditions fails to hold. Might not sense experience work this way, too? Might not a visual perception be simply a sensation that accompanies the body's response to certain optical stimuli, analogous to the way in which satiation is a sensation that accompanies the body's response to food "stimuli," so that someone who thought that seeing was simply a matter of opening the eyes would be as naive as someone who thought that digestion was simply a matter of eating and respiration was simply a matter of breathing?

Structural parallels between mind and body

In order to discuss these issues more clearly, we will now develop some of Spinoza's terminology that pertains to sense experience. I do this with some reluctance, because I think that, generally speaking, special terminology obfuscates rather than clarifies, and is very widely used among intellectuals today to camouflage ignorance rather than express knowledge. Nevertheless, despite widespread abuse, a special terminology *can* be a very useful aid in both expressing and extending knowledge, as mathematics and physics demonstrate. Some of Spinoza's terminology we have already presented: the term "modification" or "mode" is used to refer to any "part" of any attribute of God. The terms "body" or "object" or "thing" are used to refer to any mode of God conceived under the attribute of Extension, that is, to any physical thing. The term "idea" is Spinoza's generic term that he uses to refer to any mode of God conceived under the attribute of Thought; that is to say, the term "idea" refers to anything mental, just as the terms "body" and "thing" refer to anything physical. The particular physical object that is the *human* body contains within itself many other bodies (cells, organs, molecules) and is itself contained within a larger body (the ecosystem within which the human body has its being). Likewise, the particular mental idea which is the *human* mind, contains within itself many other ideas (thoughts, feelings, emotions, perceptions) and is itself contained within a "larger" idea—a mental ecosystem within which the human mind has its being.

It must be noted that this usage of the word "idea" is quite different from that of ordinary discourse. In common usage, the term "idea" is used to refer primarily to certain mental objects or events which involve discursive, or conceptual, thinking and which occur within the human mind. According to common usage, it would be incorrect to use the term "idea" to refer to (1) an emotion or sense perception within the human mind, (2) the human mind itself, (3) any "parts" within the Attribute of Thought that are external to the human mind, or (4) any "parts" within the Attribute of Thought that contain the human mind within itself. As we have already discussed, however, the general parallelism that holds between the Attributes of Thought and Extension implies that there must exist the mental objects characterized by (1)–(4); and hence, in order to talk about them, it is necessary to have a generic term that can refer to any of these categories.

So, to detail the parallelism, under (1), cells and organs are examples of bodies or physical things that exist within the human body: a particular memory, emotion, or sense perception are examples of ideas or mental things that exist within the human mind. Under (2), the human body is itself a body, a pattern of organization that occurs within the Attribute of Extension. Similarly, the human mind is itself an idea—a pattern of organization that occurs within the Attribute of Thought. Common usage, by using the term "idea" to refer only to mental events occurring *within* the *human* mind and not to the human mind itself, presupposes that the human mind has a unique ontological status, or that it is an ultimate subject, and this involves a certain anthropocentric outlook. Under (3), a plant, a rock, another human body, a distant galaxy, are all examples of *bodies* that are external to our own body. To each of these bodies there must correspond an idea, or mind, that is external to our own mind. Under (4), the planet Earth is an example of a body that contains any given human body; but since the physical Earth is a mode of God projected into the Attribute of Extension, and since each mode of God is projected into all the (infinitely many, qualitatively distinct) attributes, it follows that there must exist in the Attribute of Thought an idea that is the mental counterpart of the physical Earth. The human mind is contained within this idea, which may be called the mind, or soul, of Earth. Yet another example of an idea or mind that contains within itself the human mind is the soul as conceived by Plato and Plotinus. The Platonic soul is an idea that contains within itself many ideas (or "lives," or personalities), all existing "simultaneously" (that is, outside of time) and of which a given human mind is but one of the many ideas contained within the soul.

We will thus use the term "idea" in this wider generic sense, and will qualify it appropriately when referring to specific kinds of ideas, such as those that occur within the human mind. One further point concerning this terminology needs to be emphasized. Ordinary usage tends to conceive of ideas as passive objects that require a mind to be aware of them. Spinoza emphatically warns against conceiving of ideas as "dumb pictures" that require a "self" or a "homunculus" to be aware of them. For Spinoza, the Attribute of Thought is intelligence through and through: *every* idea—not just the human ones—involves consciousness, awareness, and intelligence, although in varying degrees. There is no difference, in Spinoza's system, between an idea and a mind, and the two terms may be used more or less interchangeably.

It is interesting to note that one reason why most current philosophical and psychological theories of the human mind have been so unproductive—compared with, say, biological theories of the human body—is precisely because most such theories are highly anthropomorphic: they assume that the human mind is a fundamental entity and that it is the only kind of mind there is. This assumption is what makes a genuine scientific theory of the mind impossible. Consider how impossible it would be to have a truly explanatory theory of the human body if one assumed that the human body was a fundamental entity or that the human body was the only kind of body there is. True understanding of the human body is possible because modern biology defines the human body both (1) atomistically—in terms of other bodies (cells, molecules), some of which exist independently of the human body, *and* (2) holistically—in terms of the larger physical ecosystem in which the human body grows, is nourished, and eventually perishes.

Similarly, a truly explanatory theory of the human mind must *explain* the human mind in terms of something other than itself, and hence no theory that assumes there are no minds other than, or more basic than, human minds can possibly offer real understanding. Spinoza's theory offers real understanding because the idea that is the human mind is explained both (1) atomistically, in terms of other ideas that constitute the human mind, and (2) holistically, in terms of its place and function within a larger "mental ecosystem." And, just as practical guidelines for the care and well-being of the human body are a natural consequence of the understanding that biology gives us, so also, as we will see, very practical guidelines for the care and well-being of the human mind are a natural consequence of the real understanding that Spinoza's theory of mind offers us.

We now continue to develop Spinoza's terminology. We have seen that every "part" or mode within the Attribute of Extension must be associated with a corresponding mode in the Attribute of Thought. The idea that corresponds to a given physical thing Spinoza calls *the* idea of the thing. Now, to avoid confusion we note the following two points: firstly, it is very important to distinguish sharply between (1) *the* idea *of* a given thing and (2) an idea that a human mind may have *about* a given thing. The latter is an idea occurring internal to a human mind, whereas the former is totally external to the human mind. *The* idea of a given tree, for example, is as external to the human mind as the physical tree is external to the human body. What we see, or perceive, or experience when we open our eyes and look at a tree is not *the* idea of a tree, but an idea that exists within our own mind.

We shall elaborate on this later in this chapter. Secondly, it must be remembered that ideas do not exist in space and time and hence it must not be thought that, for example, *the* idea of a given tree exists only as long as the physical tree exists. Furthermore, although every physical thing that is continuous in space and time (such as a tree, a planet, a human body) has a counterpart—an idea, or mind— in the Attribute of Thought, it does not follow that every idea in the Attribute of Thought corresponds to a physical thing that is continuous in space and time. For example, the soul, as it is conceived by Plato (or any other reincarnation framework) is a complex idea, consisting of numerous ideas or minds, each of which corresponds to a distinct physical body or lifetime. Thus, the counterpart in Extension of the idea, which is the soul, is not a single human body continuous in space and time, but rather, a large number of human bodies, widely scattered in space and time.

The human mind is *the* idea of the human body, and yet, although we are the human mind, we are, at present, not fully conscious of *all* that we truly are. Just as the human body contains within itself numerous other bodies (cells, organs, etc.) of which we are not directly aware, and just as each of these other bodies has its own inner structure, and just as our body as a whole arises from the harmonious interactions of these constitutive bodies, *so also,* the idea of the human body, that is to say, the human mind, contains within itself numerous other ideas, or minds, of which we are not directly aware, each of which has its own inner structure and which collectively constitute the human mind through their mutual interactions. All this follows from the metaphysical fact that the human mind and the human body are one and the same mode of God, expressed *physically* as the human body and psychically as the human mind. This is why there must be a structural parallelism between mind and body: they are "mirror images" of one and the same mode of God. Thus, if the body has an inner structure, so must the mind; if the body is contained within a larger physical system, so must the mind be contained within a larger mental system, etc.

With this structural parallelism between mind and body, Spinoza has laid the metaphysical foundations for psychotherapy. For just as there are bodies (cells, organs) within our body (1) of which we are not aware *and* (2) upon the proper functioning of which our physical health in part depends, so also there are ideas within the idea that is our mind (1) of which we are not aware *and* (2) upon which our psychological health in part depends. This concept—that there exists within our mind ideas of which we are not conscious but which are causally active—is usually attributed to Freud, but we see clearly that this concept is a consequence of Spinoza's philosophy. It must be emphasized, however, that the ideas within our mind of which *we* are not conscious are not in themselves unconscious, for as modes within the Attribute of Thought—within God's Mind—they possess the consciousness, mind, awareness, and intelligence appropriate to their nature. Just as a given cell within our body does not depend upon *our* awareness for its existence and its physical properties, so also *the* idea of a cell does not depend upon our awareness for its existence and its mental properties (such as, intelligence, consciousness, etc.). To say of a given idea that *we* are not conscious of its existence is one thing; but to say that the idea itself is unconscious (until *we* become aware of it) is an anthropomorphic projection of grand proportions. The concept of an unconscious idea is really inconsistent in Spinoza's philosophy. For just as the properties of mass and extension are common to all physical objects, so also are the properties of intelligence and consciousness common to all mental objects. The concept of an unconscious idea is therefore a contradiction in terms. We shall discuss these matters in a later chapter when we shall treat more fully Spinoza's theory of emotions together with its consequent therapy. For now, let us return to the main subject of this chapter: sense perception.

The "illusion" of sense experience

The nature of sense experience is difficult to grasp, and of all the aspects of Spinoza's system is the one most often misunderstood. The difficulty is caused, not because Spinoza's analysis is especially complicated, but because, as mentioned earlier, we are under the powerful illusion that there is within us a homunculus—or that "we" are that homunculus—which merely observes what is objectively there. As a result, we tend to resist any analysis that suggests that the mind is actively involved in manufacturing the very perceptions that it, the mind, seems to be only passively "having." For the human mind strongly resists, as the history of psychoanalysis shows, any suggestion that it is involved in any process, or that things happening within it, of which it is not fully conscious. Again, look at some object, say, a tree. Do you not believe, while looking at the tree, that it exists objectively as you see it, that you are simply observing what is really there, and that your mind is not actively involved in creating the tree as you are seeing it? These beliefs must be unraveled so that we can understand our mind's role in generating the appearance of things, and why the appearance of things—that is to say, sense experience—is not, according to Spinoza, an adequate source of knowledge. And again, we will develop some more terminology.

Consider, as an analogy, a photograph. There are two very distinct ways in which one can describe the photograph. If, for example, you are showing a friend pictures you took while on vacation, your attention will be focused primarily on the content of the photographs: on the landscape and people in the pictures. On the other hand, if you are taking a class on photography, your attention will be focused primarily on the pictures themselves, rather than on their content. Your concern will be more with the kind of paper used, how the image was developed, exposure time, etc., than with what the pictures represent. Thus we may distinguish between (a) the content of a photograph—which may be a tree, people, etc., and (b) the photograph itself—which is a piece of chemically treated paper, exposed to light for a short period of time, and developed in a certain way.

Analogously, we will distinguish between an idea and the content of an idea. Every idea, of course, is a mode of thought—a portion of God's activity of thinking. But some ideas have for their content, not modes of thought, but modes of Extension. Sensation, sense perception, or sense experience, are ideas of this kind. The content of a sense perception may be a tree, a house, another person, etc., that is to say, a mode of Extension. But the sense perception itself is an idea, a mode of thought.

We need to be very careful here; for when we say, for example, that the content of a given photograph is a tree, we do not mean that an actual tree is *in* the photograph, but merely that the photograph represents, or depicts, a tree. Similarly, when we say that the content of a sense perception is a tree, we do not mean that that particular mode of Extension, which is the tree, is internal to our sensation. That would not be possible. Rather, the content of the sense perception is an image, or representation. The actual physical tree is *not* what we see and is *not* the content of our perception. And this is part of the reason why sense experience has the character of an illusion. For we *believe* that the tree exists as we perceive it—that the content of our perception is the tree—the actual mode of Extension as it is in itself.

Let us examine this further. Consider again a photograph of a tree. The physical tree is not "in" the photograph. This image, which represents the tree and which *is* "in" the photograph, is "made up of" the same material that makes up the photograph (the chemically treated paper). Consider now a sense perception of a tree. The physical tree is not "in" the perception. The image which represents the tree and which *is* "in" the perception, is "made up of" the same material that makes up the perception. But a perception is a mode of thinking; the image (of a tree) is a part of the perception and hence is also a mode of thinking. The content of every sense perception is internal to the perception; it is a part of a mode of thinking. And since every perception is internal to our own mind, it follows that the content of all our perceptions (everything we see) is really internal to our own mind, *even though* that content represents to us objects as external to ourselves.

Thus, what we see when we open our eyes and look is the content of our own mind. To believe that what we see when we open our eyes and look is something external to our mind is like believing that a real physical tree is "in" a picture of the tree. The picture may represent the tree, and the tree is causally involved in producing the picture that represents it, but the picture, as Spinoza might put it, does not express the nature of the tree. For the physical tree is three-dimensional; it is constituted by molecules of a certain kind; it has roots that sink into the earth; its leaves convert sunlight to sugar, etc. The "tree" in the photograph is two-dimensional; it has no "roots," its "leaves" do not perform photosynthesis, etc. There is quite a difference between the being of, or the nature of, the three-dimensional physical tree and the two-dimensional image that represents the (three-dimensional) tree. The image represents the tree but does not reproduce, or express, the nature of the tree. And so it is with sense experience. The images we see when we open our eyes and look represent external bodies to us, but they do not express or reproduce the nature of those bodies. There is at least as much difference between an external body and its image in sense experience as there is between a given thing and a picture of that thing.

The mechanics of sense perception
Any given sensation is our body's response to an external body or stimulus. It is certainly true that the sensation would be different if the external stimulus were different; but it is equally true that the sensation would be different if *our* body were different. We wish to show some of the ways in which what we see when we open our eyes and look—the visual appearance of things—depends on the nature of our own body, so that, if our body were different, and in particular, if the optical properties of our body were different, the visual appearance of things would be dramatically different, even though the things themselves remain the same.

In order for perception to occur there must be a physical interaction between the human body and an external body. The nature of this interaction is roughly as follows: (1) the external object either emits or reflects light, (2) this light then enters our body through the eye, whereupon (3) it interacts with certain cells in our retina, causing (4) signals or information to propagate along the optic nerve into the brain. It is (5) the brain's response to these incoming signals that generates, or correlates with, the sense experience of seeing the object. We will examine each stage of this process.

Stages (1) and (2): any given physical object, say, a tree, is constituted by a certain determinate molecular structure. Any light that falls upon this molecular structure interacts with it, and the reflected light is thus modified by its interaction with the tree. The light that is reflected by an object that appears blue to us, is different from the light that is reflected by an object that appears red to us. This reflected light then enters our body through the eye. It is important to emphasize that something external to our body (the light) actually enters inside our body—that our body is not passively isolated from the external world that it observes, but is actively involved in a determinate physical process. This process involves an external body, light, which is modified or affected by its interaction with the external body, and our own body, which is in turn modified or affected by the light, which was previously modified by (2). Now, since light is the means by which our body interacts with the external body, we must ask the question, what is the nature of light? What is the nature of that which actually enters our body?

Unfortunately, the word "light" is often used ambiguously. Sometimes it is used objectively to refer to that which enters the eye, and sometimes it is used subjectively to refer to the body's response to that which enters the eye. Objectively, light is characterized by wavelength, frequency, amplitude, etc.; subjectively it is characterized by color, hues, etc. Much confusion arises when we confound the two senses of the term; for example, (1) we think that when we have a sensation of blue the light that enters our body is itself blue, or (2) we think that the distinction we make between "visible" and "invisible" light has to do with objective properties of light (that "invisible" light is really invisible), rather than with the optical properties of our body. To avoid these and other confusions, we will use the term "light" in its objective sense only: to refer to any kind of electromagnetic radiation whatsoever. So, that which enters our eyes is electromagnetic radiation, characterized by objective physical properties, such as wavelength, which can be distinguished from the *subjective properties,* such as color, that characterize the body's response to the radiation that enters our eyes.

Now, the human body is sensitive to only a very small fraction of the full spectrum of electromagnetic radiation. The full spectrum consists of a wide range of wavelengths of light, from very short wavelengths (x-rays) to very large wavelengths (radio waves). All wavelengths are present to the human body—that is, *all* wavelengths of light actually enter the body through the eye, but the optical properties of the body are such that it responds only to light that lies within a very narrow range of wavelengths, roughly 4×10^{-5} cm to 8×10^{-5} cm. The cells in our retina are "hardwired" to respond only to light within this narrow range. In this respect, our body functions like a radio or television set; although all wavelengths of light strike the antenna, a radio or TV filters out all wavelengths except the one that corresponds to a specific station. *Moreover,* just as a television set transforms incoming radiation into a visible picture, so also the human body transforms incoming radiation into a three-dimensional picture that we call a sense perception. Thus, our body, far from being a window to the world—as the homunculus theory would have us believe—actually screens out most of the information that impinges upon it; each region of the spectrum carries information, but the optical properties of our body are such that it can be "tuned" to only a very small region of the spectrum. The visual appearance of things—what we see when we open our eyes and look—is our body's response to that very small region.

At the risk of repeating ourselves, we wish to emphasize this last point again. The body's involvement in producing the visual appearance of things is two-fold. *First,* the body, by means of the optical properties of the retina, tunes out all wavelengths except those that lie within a very narrow range. *Second,* the body, by means of the brain, responds in specific ways—specific to the human species—to that narrow range of wavelengths. One can imagine a species whose retinal optical properties are the same as those of human beings but whose brains process the information differently. The visual appearance of things would be quite different to such a species.

The dependency of the visual appearance of things upon the optical properties of the body

We are emphasizing that what we see when we open our eyes and look—the visual appearance of things—is *not* what is objectively "out there" but depends very strongly on the optical properties of our body. Let us now stretch our imaginations and consider how things might look to us if our body's optical properties were different. We will consider four cases.

1. Suppose our retina were hardwired to respond to light in a slightly different region of the spectrum. That is, suppose that instead of responding to light in the 4×10^{-5} to 8×10^{-5} cm region, it responded only to light in a slightly longer wavelength region, say 8×10^{-5} to 2×10^{-4} cm. How would things look? First of all, none of the familiar colors would be present to us. An object that looks green to us looks that way because our retina responds to radiation in the $4-8 \times 10^{-5}$ cm region. The color sensation of green is the body's response to radiation of about 5×10^{-5} cm. If, under our supposition, our retina does not respond to this wavelength of radiation, any object that emits or reflects light

of only this wavelength would look black to us. The familiar colors around us are not objective properties of things but are produced by our body, and if the optical properties of our body were different, the familiar colors would disappear from the visual appearance of things.

Secondly, under our supposition, our retina now responds to light in the infrared region, so that our body will produce color sensations in response to light in that region. Although we cannot possibly imagine what these new colors would look like (because our power of imagining colors is limited by the optical properties of the body), we can understand perfectly well that there could be beings whose bodies produce color sensations in response to light in the 8×10^{-5} through 2×10^{-4} cm region and that these color sensations would be as real and vivid to those beings as our color sensations are to us.

2. Suppose our retina were hardwired to respond only to light of large wavelength—say, 10–20 cm. How would things look? Well, as before, there would be totally different color sensations. But in addition, long wavelength light has different optical properties than light in the 10^{-5} cm region. In particular, light in the 10 cm. wavelength region can bend around corners, so that just as we can now hear around corners, we would be able to "see" around corners if our retina responded to light in this region. Just as we can now hear people talking in another room, because sound waves do bend around corners, we would be able to see people in another room. Moreover, just as we can hear someone whose back is toward us, because the sound waves bend around the body to reach our ears, so also we would be able to see the backside, in fact all sides, of any object. Although we cannot imagine what it would be like to be able to see simultaneously all sides of a given object, we can easily understand that there could be beings for whom, because of their bodies' optical properties, the visual appearance of things involves simultaneous perception of all sides of objects.

3. Suppose our retina were hardwired to respond only to light of very short wavelengths, say 10^{-10} cm. Electromagnetic radiation in this region are called x-rays, which have the well-known property of being able to penetrate the insides of objects. Thus, aside from having totally

different color sensations, we would be able to see into the insides of things. It is interesting to ponder that, for us, the visual appearance of a thing is generated by our body's response to light that is reflected by the outermost molecular layer, or the surface, of the given thing. But if our body could respond to x-rays, then the visual appearance of things would involve information coming from the interior of the thing. Although, as above, we cannot imagine what things would look like if we could see their insides, we can perfectly well understand the possibility of such experience.

4. Suppose our retina could respond to all wavelengths of light—from the shortest x-rays to the longest wavelengths. Aside from an infinity of color sensations, we would be able to see simultaneously the insides of any object and all of its outside surfaces. The full electromagnetic spectrum is present at every point in space, and so this information is always available. But our body, because of its optical properties, is able to utilize only a tiny fraction of the total amount of information available to it, and it is in response to this tiny fraction of the totality that our body produces the visual appearance of things.

We wish to call attention to the precise wording of the last phrase. For we are insisting that the visual appearance of things—what we see when we open our eyes and look—is an effect that is produced by the body in response to incident electromagnetic radiation. It is quite possible to conceive of a being whose body produces a *different* visual appearance in response to the *same* region of electromagnetic radiation. The optical properties of our body are such that all wavelengths of light are filtered out except those in roughly the 4–8×10^{-5} cm region. The visual appearance of things is constructed by the brain in response to this light. It is possible to conceive of a body with similar optical properties as our own (that is, a body whose retina responds only to light in this region), but whose brain processes the information differently from our own and hence constructs a different visual appearance of things than that constructed by our own brain. The situation here is analogous to the same power source, say, ordinary household electricity, producing different effects in different electrical appliances. The different effects (e.g., light bulb, toaster, radio) are due, not to a difference in input (which is the same for each device), but rather to the way in which the internal mechanism of each appliance processes that input to produce the desired output. Human sense perception is the brain's output, and it is quite conceivable that different organisms produce different outputs in response to the same input.

We emphasize this point in order to avoid the temptation to think that even though the optical properties of our body limits us to a small fraction of the electromagnetic spectrum, nevertheless, within this small fraction we see things as they really are. This is erroneous, for we have shown that even within this small fraction, what we see when we open our eyes and look is *not* what is really there, but rather, it is our brain's response to that which enters our eyes, and different brains with different internal properties could produce a very different visual appearance of things in response to the same input. Indeed, these considerations force us to conclude that even a being whose retina responded to the full electromagnetic spectrum could not be said to see things as they really are, for any sense experience of any being whatsoever is simply the bodily response of that being to some input, even if that input be the full electromagnetic spectrum. This is why Spinoza repeatedly tells us that sense experience indicates more about the nature of our own body than about any external body we seem to see.

A wonderful mystery

And now we are ready to raise a deeper question: if, as we have argued, the visual appearance of things is produced by our brain, how is it that what the brain produces is projected outside of our body? For what we see—the visual appearance of things—appears to us as external to our bodies. How is this possible? This question arises as soon as it is realized that what we have called the homunculus theory cannot be true; there is no "little man" inside of our heads who passively observes, through clear retinal windows, an objective reality external to itself.

For example, we experience the color green, which the brain creates in response to electromagnetic radiation reflected from the leaves of a tree, as lying outside of us on the surface of the leaves. The brain not only produces the color, but projects it outside itself. How does the visual information that exists inside our brain get projected outside our body, where we experience it? This is not an easy question to get a feeling for, and I urge the reader to go slowly at this point. The following train of thought is offered to assist the reader in getting a feeling for the question. (Notice, I did not say "in getting an answer to the question," for it is far more important to grasp the question, to appreciate its significance, and perhaps to experience some wonder, than it is to give a verbal answer.)

First, let us compare the sense of sight with the sense of touch. If a tactile stimulus is applied to our body, say our hand, electrochemical impulses travel along our nerves from the point of contact on the skin to the brain. The brain then processes this electrochemical input and produces the appropriate tactile sensation (hot, cold, soft, hard, etc.), which sensation is referred back to our hand. That is, we experience the tactile sensation as occurring, not in the brain, but at the point in our body that was stimulated by the external body. Although the mechanism according to which the brain projects tactile sensations outside itself and onto the point of contact may or may not be understood in physiological detail, the possibility of such understanding is straightforward; because every part of the body is connected to the brain and vice versa, it is clear that information can and does flow both ways, and thus, it is not unreasonable to suppose that some neurophysiological mechanism could account for the fact that tactile sensations are experienced at the point of contact, not in our brains.

But this kind of explanation fails in principle in the case of sight (and hearing). For in the case of sight, the point of contact between our body and the external world is our eye, or retina. The world "touches" us there in the form of electromagnetic radiation. The visual sensations that the brain produces in response to this input is projected, not onto the retina—the point of contact—but totally outside the body! Unlike tactile sensations, there is clearly no physical mechanism to explain how the brain projects visual sensation outside the body.

Let us develop this further. Suppose that at a given time, t_1, a match is lit. At a still later time, t_2, light from the match arrives at your eye and interacts with your retina. At a still later time, t_3, the electrochemical impulses generated by that interaction reach the brain. It is only at this time, t_3, or shortly thereafter, that we have the visual experience of seeing the lit match. It is only because the time intervals, t_2-t_1, and t_3-t_2, are so very small that we are prone to believe, erroneously, that our perception of the lit match occurs at the same time the match is lit. But the former occurs after t_3, whereas the later occurs at t_1. Suppose now that the time difference were a lot greater—that the intervals t_2-t_1 and t_3-t_2 were about one minute each. To make this thought experiment more dramatic, let us suppose that at 9:00 o'clock a very strong source light is turned on in an otherwise totally dark room. The light is left on for half a minute and then turned off. At 9:01 the light traveling from this source enters our eyes, and at 9:02 electrochemical signals traveling along our optic nerve reaches the brain. Until 9:02 the room appears totally dark to us, but for a half minute after 9:02 the room appears brilliantly lit, *even though the room is really in total darkness.* Moreover, to play with this example a bit, suppose that between 9:01 and 9:02—*after* the radiation from the light source has entered our body, but *before* the signals from the retina reach the brain—we change the position of our body, say, by turning around, or leaving the room. What we see at 9:02 will still be the room, even though we are no longer in it, and even though we close our eyes.

This example makes it abundantly clear that the visual appearance of things depends only on the state of our brain. It does not depend on where our body is, on the world around us, or even on whether our eyes are open or closed, except insofar as these latter are causally connected with the state of our brain. As Spinoza puts it, the mode of Extension that is correlated with a given sense perception, is not the content of the perception, but the state of our own body. A consequence of this is that there is no fundamental difference between a hallucination (seeing something that "isn't there") and so-called veridical perception (seeing something that "is there"), since in neither case is what is seen the same as that which is there. That is, even in veridical perception, what is seen is not what is there, but is the brain's creative response to what is there. Since, as we have shown, different creative responses to what is there are possible, the distinction between veridical perception and hallucination cannot be drawn on the basis of what is "really there." The basis, and it is a *fluid* basis, for drawing the distinction lies in the fact that most human brains are wired to respond in fixed and similar ways to a given input, whereas the brain of a person who is psychotic or schizophrenic, or under the influence of a psychedelic drug, responds differently. But what the psychotic or schizophrenic *sees* is no less real than what we see; in either case, what is seen corresponds with a given brain state; in either case what is seen is manufactured by a brain and projected external to itself.

We take the powers of the body too much for granted, do we not? We believe that digestion is simply a matter of chewing and swallowing our food, that walking is merely putting one foot after the other, that breathing is simply a matter of inhaling and exhaling, that seeing is simply a matter of opening our eyes. But as soon as we ask questions of detail—for example, what happens to the air after it is inhaled? How do the cells in the lungs absorb oxygen? What happens to the oxygen after it is absorbed?, etc.—the apparent simplicity of breathing disappears. For each question that is answered, many more arise. As we follow these questions and answers and questions again, we are led to greater understanding and deeper appreciation of the harmony and beauty of the laws and processes that govern the functioning of the body. And from this understanding and appreciation arises a sense of wonder and awe, of what Einstein refers to as a sense of the mysterious.

And nowhere is the mystery greater than in sense perception. For ponder, if you will, that the world you see when you open your eyes and look—this multicolored, three-dimensional world—is created by your brain and projected external to yourself. How does the brain accomplish this? How is this possible? Indeed, we must raise the question, *is this possible?*

Spinoza's metaphysical parallelism applied to the mystery of perception
As we have indicated before, once it is seen that there is no homunculus, no "little man" who sits inside our skull and passively peers through our eyeballs at an objectively given world, then it follows that the world we see when we open our eyes and look is, in a very real sense, our own creation. But this creation of ours, or of our brain's, is experienced by us as existing outside of ourselves, and so the question arises: how does this magnificent creation of ours—the three-dimensional, multicolored perceptual world—get to be outside of ourselves? And the answer we wish to suggest is that it doesn't. Although the perceptual world *appears* to exist external to our mind, it is really internal to our mind or consciousness. For just as the content of a photograph is internal to the photograph, so also is the content of any given perception internal to perception and hence, internal to the mind that contains that perception.

But, it will be objected, surely the objects I see are outside of me—the buildings, the trees, the clouds, the chair on which I sit, etc.—surely exist external to myself and not in my head. In order to avoid these and other such confusions, it will be helpful to apply several concepts and distinctions we have introduced earlier. Recall the parallelism that is a feature of Spinoza's metaphysics: for every physical object in the Attribute of Extension there exists an idea in the Attribute of Thought. Consider a given physical object, say, a tree. There exists, then, in the Attribute of Thought, a specific idea that corresponds with, or correlates with, the given tree. We may, for brevity, refer to this idea as *the* idea of the tree. (Our language, we note, provides us with a far richer vocabulary for referring to physical objects than for ideas, and this is why we are forced to identify the idea by referring to the object with which it is correlated, i.e., as the idea of *the tree*. To a mind that is not associated with a body, and which could experience ideas directly, there would be no need to refer to ideas indirectly. According to Spinoza's metaphysics, both the object and the idea exist in their own right, and one may equally use a given idea to refer to its associated object or a given object to refer to its associated idea. We must not allow the language to confuse us into thinking that physical objects are more fundamental than ideas.)

So we have (1) the physical tree, as it is in itself and (2) the idea of the tree, as it (the idea) is in itself. We also have (3) the human body, as it is in itself, and

(4) the idea of the human body, or the human mind. Now, as we have outlined above, sense perception involves an interaction between (1) and (3); specifically, electromagnetic radiation reflects off (1) and enters into (3). And thus we have (5) the affected human body, or the human body insofar as it has been modified, altered, affected, etc., by the light that has entered into it. And corresponding to (5) we must have (6), the idea of the affected human body, or the idea of the body insofar as the body has been modified, altered, etc.

Great confusion arises because we falsely believe that sense experiences gives us direct access to the physical world. The tree that we see when we open our eyes and look is not (1) the physical tree as it is in itself, but rather is part of the content of (6), which correlates not with (1), but with (5). This is why Spinoza says that a sense experience "involves, but does not reproduce" the nature of an external body. For (1) is causally involved in producing (5), but the idea that correlates with (5)—the visual perception (6)—does not reproduce the nature of the tree. As Spinoza says, a sense perception tells us more about the nature of our own body than it does about the nature of any external body; and this is because any sense experience is simply the idea in the Attribute of Thought that correlates with our body insofar as our body has been modified by means of interactions with other bodies. So, to answer the questions in the above paragraph, the physical tree (1) is not, of course, in our head (3), *but* the tree we are aware of in sense perception is part of the content of (6) and since (6) pertains to our mind (4), it follows that what we see when we open our eyes and look is necessarily a part of our mind. The fundamental illusion of sense perception is that it seems to us as if what we see is the same as what is "really" there. But this is to confuse (1) with (6), the physical with the mental, the physical tree with the content of an idea within our mind.

Thus, *everything* we see when we open our eyes and look is part of the content of our own mind; it is all internal to our own mind. The stars in the sky are indeed external to our body, but the images that represent or depict these stars to us in sense perception form part of the content of our mind. It should be noted that our own body is not an exception to this; that is to say, although our body is indeed a part of Extension, what we see when we look at it is *not* the body as it is in itself, but part of the content of an idea. Our senses create images of our own body in the same way they create images of other bodies, and all these images are part of the content of our own mind.

We wish to point out a further consequence of this theory. We noted above that (6) is a part of (4). As our body is modified, perturbed, etc., by its interactions with other bodies, so our mind is modified or perturbed, and these "perturbations of the mind" are what we call sense experience (together with memory and emotions). But since the major portion of our awareness, the conscious mind, is concerned with sense experience, memory, and emotion, it follows that there is a large part of our mind of which we are not conscious. It appears that the conscious portion of our mind is that portion of our mind that is correlated with that portion of our body which is affected through interaction with external bodies.

Let us make an analogy. Just as the light entering our eye is reflected from the outermost layer of molecules or cells of the things and people we see so that the resulting modification of our body is a response to the surfaces of things, so we may also say that the images which are the mental correlates of our modified body, and which represent those bodies to us, form only the surface of our mind. So the conscious portion of our mind, insofar as that portion consists of images, is merely the surface, so to speak, of a larger mental structure. Spinoza calls this portion of our mind "Imagination." Our full mind is *the* idea of our body (number 4 above), which is the same thing as God's idea of our body. If our consciousness could be made to extend to our full mind, our knowledge of ourselves would be as complete and perfect as God's. Spinoza gives the name Intuition to this kind of conscious experience in which our knowledge and awareness of things is as complete as God's. We will return to this later; for now, we note simply that we consciously experience only a small portion of our mind and that the concept, which is the heart of all systems of psychotherapy, that there exist within our mind mental structures of which we are not conscious yet which causally affect us, is a consequence of Spinoza's system.

Anthropomorphism and the imagination

It will be good at this point to pause and reflect about what all this means. As has been well known since Freud, the conscious mind, the so-called ego, likes to believe that it is in charge of things and actively resists any suggestion to the contrary. Spinoza's philosophy teaches us that this ego is an idea brought about, sustained by, and contained within a larger idea or psychological process. Both Freud and Spinoza believed that although we may resist becoming conscious of these larger psychological processes, it is nevertheless possible to do so. But Spinoza, unlike Freud, believed that the ego is ephemeral, that the core of our identity, our whole mind, is eternal, and that our consciousness can transcend the limitations of the ego and experience itself as the eternal idea it really is.

Now *resistance* takes many forms. In ordinary psychological terms, the ego actively resists bringing to awareness motivations and desires of which it is not conscious. In more spiritual terms, the ego, or Imagination, resists any suggestion that it is a part of a "larger" mind; it likes to conceive of itself not as a part of the natural order of things, which order includes Thought, but, as Spinoza puts it, as a "kingdom within a kingdom." This recalcitrance cannot be overcome by rational argument alone because our so-called reasoning process is almost always in the service of the ego and will not easily allow itself to be led to a conclusion that appears to undermine the sovereignty of the ego.

I use the term "easily" because, as the history of science shows, it not only *is* possible but has occurred; the worldview of modern science is far less anthropocentric than the worldview common a few hundred years ago. But science proceeds not by reason alone, but by reason together with experience. It is *because* science has allowed itself to *experience* domains of physical reality—the very large and the very small—that go beyond common experience, that it has been forced, so to speak, to develop new and less anthropocentric concepts. The term "forced" is appropriate here because every new concept in science, from field theory to kinetic theory to relativity to quantum theory, has been met with incredible resistance. The source of this resistance, I wish to suggest, is not only the usual conservative resistance to something new, but also involves the fact that this "something new" in science almost always involves a movement away from anthropocentricism.

Now, anthropocentricism usually connotes a view of the world that places human beings at the center of things. So a theology that attributes human emotions to God is anthropocentric, as is a theology that holds that God created the universe for the sake of human beings. But for Spinoza, any philosophy that takes the ego to be the only kind of mental activity that there is, is anthropocentric. The concepts with which the ego attempts to understand its experiences are extremely limiting, for they are all based, or run parallel to, the body's experience as a finite mode of Extension. Thus, anything of which we can form an image, whether it be in direct sense experiences or in concepts that represent a large number of sense experiences, pertains to the experiences of the body. And it is anthropocentric, according to Spinoza, to believe that the world can be understood through such concepts. Real understanding does not involve images. What Spinoza calls the Understanding, or "knowledge of the second kind," does not involve images and far exceeds the abilities of the Imagination, or "knowledge of the first kind."

Modern science, especially theoretical physics, is an example of this second kind of knowledge, for the "new physics" employs concepts that depict events and objects that cannot be pictured or imagined, but can be described mathematically.

Physics met tremendous resistance from both physicists and philosophers when it began introducing concepts that could not be imagined. And the source of this discomfort is the ego's, or the imagination's, insistence that all knowledge be represented in a form it can understand, that is, in the form of images and pictures. It is only the experience of new domains of reality that forced physics and physicists to overcome their resistance and to accept the fact that the universe, like our infinite set, can be understood but not imagined.

Now, in our analysis of sense experience, we are attempting to show that that part of our mind that pertains to sense experience—our ego, or Imagination—is (a) only a part of our mind even though (b) it is the only part to which our consciousness presently extends. As we mentioned above, the reluctance the ego experiences to this analysis is the same as that which it shows to *any* way of looking at things that displaces it from the center. This resistance can rarely be overcome by reason alone, but it can more easily be overcome if there is a willingness to experience something different, and that is why it is important to do the exercises in this book. To refuse to do these exercises because one is unconvinced of the argumentation is like refusing to taste the pudding because one is unconvinced by argument that it tastes good. In neither case is argumentation sufficient; but reasoning, together with a willingness to experience something different, may be.

 EXERCISE 3: So we suggest now another exercise that is designed to generate and enhance a feeling of wonder and awe about the illusion of sense perception. Begin by looking at some object, say a tree and noticing in detail its colors: the different shades of green on the leaves, the browns and grays of the trunk and branches, etc. Now, while noticing the colors as vividly and in as much detail as possible, introduce the thought that these colors are not features of the objects you are looking at, but are created by your mind. Hold in your awareness for as long as you can (up to several minutes, but even a few seconds will be beneficial) *both* (1) the vivid sensation of colors (which *seem* to reside on the surface of things) *together with* (2) the knowledge that these colors are produced by you. You might repeat to yourself slowly, and while looking at the colors, "these colors (name them—e.g., these shades of green, etc.) are created by my mind."

Now, whatever the mind produces must remain internal to the mind and hence the colors, which appear to be external to the mind, are really internal. Therefore, we introduce a third component to the exercise, (3) the knowledge that all these colors (and indeed, the entire visual field) exist within your mind. Hold the simultaneous awareness of (1), (2), and (3) for as long as you can. You might repeat to yourself a sentence like, "the colors I am now seeing are created by my mind and thus exist inside my mind" and/or "the colors that I am now seeing and that seem to exist independently of my mind are really internal to my own mind." If this exercise is done with full attention, a feeling of wonder and awe will begin to arise. This feeling is an example of what Einstein has called a "cosmic religious feeling." How wonderful (full of wonder) is this mind of ours, which not only creates the world we see, but also creates the *illusion* that this world exists independently of itself!

The inadequacy of imaginative experience

We have now developed enough of Spinoza's philosophy to explain and utilize one of the most difficult concepts in his system, one that is of immense importance in understanding the human condition. Spinoza classifies all ideas as either *adequate* or *inadequate,* by which he means something like complete or incomplete. Although Spinoza intends this distinction to apply to ideas, that is to say, to modes of substance conceived under the Attribute of Thought, it will be easier to explain and to develop a feeling for the distinction by first considering how it might apply to physical things, that is, to modes of substance conceived under the Attribute of Extension. It is possible to do this (to explain a distinction among ideas in terms of physical things) because of the structural parallelism that holds between Extension and Thought. Recalling the mirror analogy, it is easy to see that any structural property of modes within one Attribute will have its counterpart in all the other Attributes. We used this structural parallelism before, when, for example, we argued that just as our body contains within itself other bodies and is in turn contained within another body (ecosystem), so also the idea of our body (our mind) contains within itself other ideas (minds) and is itself contained within another idea (mind).

So, considering the Attribute of Extension, what is an inadequate, or incomplete, body? First of all, it is important not to confuse the complete/incomplete distinction with the independent/dependent distinction. All bodies are dependent, except for the physical universe as a whole, and similarly, all minds are dependent, except for the mental universe as a whole. Within Extension, all bodies are complete. Atoms, molecules, cells, dogs, cats, human beings, planets, galaxies, etc., are complete but dependent. A cell, for example, is a complete object, but the surface of the cell is incomplete; the surface has no existence apart from the cell of which it is the surface. More importantly, the cell interacts with its external environment at its surface, and so the physical shape of the cell wall, as well as the chemical reactions in the wall, involve and depend upon not only the cell itself but upon also all the other bodies with which the cell interacts. Hence the surface of the cell *considered in itself,* is an incomplete object.

Considered in itself, it is an abstraction; its nature is totally dependent on the cell of which it is the surface together with external bodies with which it interacts. The same holds true, more or less, for the surface of any object. The shape of our planet depends partly on geological processes going on within Earth and partly on collisions occurring between Earth and external bodies. That is to say, abstracting the shape of the planet from the planet as a whole and the external bodies with which it interacts, the shape of the planet is an incomplete object. We note, however, that even though it is incomplete, the surface of a body is still a mode of Extension and has all the physical properties relevant to being a mode of Extension.

Generally speaking, whenever two (or more) bodies interact, each will have some effect on the other. This "effect" is still a mode of Extension, but it is incomplete. If A interacts with B, then A will affect B and vice versa. The *effect* that B has on A—the *modification of A* due to its interaction with B—is, insofar as it is considered by itself, an incomplete object. Another way of putting this is that whenever two things (A and B) interact, they form a coupled system (A + B) and that this coupling constitutes a new "whole" in terms of which any modification of either component A or B has its being. Hence, the *modification of A* due to B, when considered by itself and apart from the whole system (A + B) in which it has its being, is incomplete. The quantum theory provides dramatic examples of this fundamental incompleteness of portions of interacting systems. In the examples we have been considering, the changes that each object induces in the other are incomplete when considered by themselves, but the objects themselves are complete. In the quantum domain, however, any two objects (A and B) that interact are incomplete—not just certain of their properties or changes that one produces in the other. Only the combined system (A + B) is complete and has its own identity.

We now apply these ideas to ourselves; we wish to know which of our ideas are adequate, or complete, or whole, and which are inadequate, incomplete, and partial. To anticipate the results, it will turn out that *all* sense perceptions are inadequate ideas, as are the great majority of our emotions. For in any perceptual context, some external influence enters our body and modifies it. Let "A" denote our body and "B" denote some external body, say a tree, which A is said to perceive. Light reflecting from the surface of B enters A through the eyes and produces electrochemical changes in the retina, which changes cause other changes, etc., until the brain itself is affected. Let M stand for the modification of the human body (A) caused by B. M depends on A and B—on the interacting system (A + B)—in just the way described above. For M depends for its existence not on A alone, nor on B alone, but on the dynamic interaction occurring within the coupled system (A + B). While this system exists, that is to say, while the human body is interacting with the external body, M exists and is a part of this larger system, as are the human body and the external body, respectively.

Again, while this interacting system exists, it constitutes a whole object, a larger body that contains within itself both the human body and the external body. This "larger body" (A + B) has properties, such as M, that cannot be understood in terms of A and B considered separately. Therefore, M is an incomplete object, and the idea that corresponds to M is necessarily inadequate (since M and its idea are the same mode of substance conceived under the Attributes of Extension and Thought, respectively). But the idea that corresponds to M *is* a sense perception. All sense perceptions (visual, auditory, tactile, etc.) arise from a coupling of our body with an external body. A sense perception is simply the idea that corresponds to how our body is modified while interacting with an external body. It is hence something that is occurring within the coupled system.

Let us summarize. A is our body, B is an external body, and (A + B) is the coupled system with holistic properties not reducible to the components A and B considered separately. M is a feature of this coupled system, and when considered by itself, apart from the system in which it has its being, it is an incomplete object like a shadow or the surface of a thing. Now each of these physical objects, A, B, (A + B), and M, have their associated ideas or minds. There is *the* idea, or mind, of A (which is our mind), *the* idea or mind of B, the idea or mind of (A + B), and the idea, or mind, of M. This latter idea *is* the sense experience that represents B to us as present. (We point out again that B as represented in the sense experience—in the idea of M—is not the same as the B that exists as an objective mode of Extension). This sense experience—the mind of M—is incomplete in the same way that M is incomplete. The complete idea, of which M is a portion, is the idea or mind of the coupled system (A + B). Just as A + B has holistic features not explicable in terms of the components A and B, so also the mind of (A + B) has holistic features such as the mind of M, that are not reducible to the individual minds of A and B, respectively.

Here's another way to understand the sense in which the mind of M is inadequate or incomplete. Any sense experience involves a coupling of our body with an external body; what we see when we open our eyes and look is something internal to the coupling. For example, when we see a tree, we experience a consequence, an effect, of the coupling, but not the coupling itself. A direct experience of the coupling itself—as God, so to speak, might experience it—would involve an awareness of the total system A + B. What we experience in sense perception is an effect that arises because of, and internal to, the coupling, but which we experience as if it existed independently of this coupling. When we open our eyes and look, we believe that what we see exists independently of ourselves, rather than that what we see arises from and is internal to a temporary coupling between our body and some external body, neither of which we perceive adequately. Therefore, all sense experience, as well as memories of past sense experience and emotions that involve sense experience—in short, all ideas belonging to the Imagination—are inadequate.

RELATIONSHIPS AMONG MINDS

The concept of a "larger" mind
All mystical philosophers have held that sense experience has the character of illusion and unreality. This is not to denigrate sense experience so much as to direct one's awareness to the existence of a realm of being (the Forms for Plato, Spirit for Hegel, intuitive knowledge or adequate ideas for Spinoza) that offers us a vastly superior experience of knowledge, love, joy and peace than is available to us through Imaginative experience. For our whole mind *is* an adequate idea—it is a part of the eternal and infinite Mind of God. But we do not presently experience ourselves as the eternal mind that we are. What we experience as if it were our whole mind is merely that portion of our mind which has associated itself with the body's experience and, indeed, not the whole body's experiences (e.g., our awareness does not extend to, say, interactions between cells) but only that portion of the body's experiences that pertain to its interactions with external bodies.

Thus our false identity, our *persona,* or personality, (or, in Spinozistic terms, our imagination) is constructed out of a series of temporary couplings between our body and external bodies; our personality is not our true, or whole, identity. It is that portion of our mind which has associated itself with (or, is the idea of) the series of effects that the series of temporary couplings have had on our body.

The *illusion* pertains to the fact that this portion of the mind generally believes itself to be the whole of the mind and is ignorant of its connections with the rest of its mind. To a mind that experiences itself as part of the eternal Mind of God, there is no illusion because, when associated with a body, it would experience its personality as a portion of itself and, conversely, its personality would know experientially that it is a portion of this larger mind.

A familiar analogy may be helpful. A person who is dreaming is said to be deceived because he is not aware that he is dreaming and takes the contents of his dream to be physically real. In lucid dreaming, however, the dreamer is not deceived because the true nature of his experience—that it *is* a dream—is present to his awareness. Another analogy: a person watching a movie can become so deeply engrossed in the story of the movie that she "forgets" that she is really sitting in a movie theater watching a movie. On the other hand, a movie critic watching the same movie remains somewhat detached, since he has to pay attention to facts *about* the movie (the directing, the acting, the casting, etc.), as well as facts *within* the movie's story. The difference between (1) remembering that it is a movie while watching it and (2) forgetting that it is a movie while watching it is like the difference between the enlightened person who *"remembers"* that she is a portion of a larger mind even while participating in imaginative experience, and the rest of us who are so absorbed in imaginative experience that we have "forgotten" our real identity.

Spinoza, in *his* explication of the nature of the mind, realizes that many of his readers will balk at these concepts and come up with many objections that will delay progress. He urges his readers to hold their objections until they have read the whole of his work, and, I might add, have practiced some of his exercises. He realizes the enormous difficulty in even considering, let alone accepting, the concept that our personality is part of a larger mental structure in a way similar to the way a cell in our body is part of a larger physical structure. The ego is threatened and insulted by the notion that it may be like a cell in someone else's body. But of course, the cell is not in "someone else's body"; it is in its own body and the cell contains within itself, in its DNA, the knowledge of the whole body. Nevertheless, Spinoza does not elaborate very much, especially when compared to other mystical philosophers, on the relationship between our personality, or ego, the imaginative part of our mind, and the "larger mind" or the (adequate) idea of our body *in which* our personality has its being. Nor does he say very much about direct relationships between and among *ideas* independent of the body.

This last omission has no doubt occurred to the reader from our earlier discussion of perception. For in sense perception, the human body, A, is coupled with an external body, B, resulting in a modification, M, of the human body. This is a description of what happens under the Attribute of Extension. We then made the correlation that what we see when we open our eyes and look—the conscious sense experience—*is* the idea of M; it is what's happening in the Attribute of Thought when our body is in the state M. But clearly, the idea of M—the sense experience—cannot be *caused* by M, since there is no causation across the two Attributes (recall the mirror analogy). The cause of the idea of M must lie in the Attribute of Thought and must involve the relationship between the idea of our body, A, and the idea of the external body, B. It must be possible to say how the mind of A interacts with the mind of B to form the mind of the coupled system (A + B) in which the mind of M, the conscious sense experience, has its being.

Perhaps Spinoza's reluctance to talk about such things is due to the precarious religious and political times in which he lived; perhaps he felt that delving into complex metaphysics far from the experience of the imaginative mind would detract from his eminently practical goal of helping the reader attain the state of conscious union with God. His tactic seems to be that since (a) we are much more familiar with bodies than with minds and (b) the "order and connection of bodies is the same as the order and connection of minds," it is therefore possible to (c) infer the relationships among minds by examining the relationships among the bodies that are associated with them. It is not until the very end of his *Ethics*, where he discusses human immortality, that he talks about mind in itself, independent of the body and its personality. This is a very useful tactic and one that we follow in this book. Nevertheless, we feel it will also be useful, and interesting, to say something about these "larger minds," their relationship to the personality, and the possibility of direct communication between minds (telepathy).

An example of direct communication between minds
We take our cue from one of the very few passages where Spinoza explicitly talks about these things. A friend of his had written Spinoza about an experience that today would be called precognitive: he (the friend) had heard sobbing sounds that seemed to be coming from his healthy son and that were identical to actual sounds the son later made when he (the son) died (Collected Letters, #17). Spinoza's explanation of this is instructive. Recall that the imagination (or ego, or personality) is that (inadequate) portion of our whole (adequate) mind that is associated with the temporal experiences of our body. This "whole mind" may be referred to by many different names, such as "the idea of the body," "God's

knowledge of the body," "soul," "higher self," etc. The "whole mind" is, of course, fully conscious, and what we experience as our own consciousness is merely a portion of this larger consciousness.

It follows, therefore, that our present consciousness, the imagination, although usually affected only by external things, as in sense experience, may at times be affected directly by the larger mind in which our present consciousness exists. In Spinoza's own words, "the effects of the imagination arise from the constitution either of the body or of the mind." By "effects of the imagination," Spinoza means any sense experience, whether visual, auditory, or tactile. But whereas "none of the effects of the imagination which proceed from corporeal causes can ever be omens of future things... [those] effects of the imagination or [those] images which have their origin in the constitution of mind can be omens of a future thing because the mind can confusedly be aware, beforehand, of something which is future" (Letter #17). This is possible because the *whole* mind, or *soul*, is eternal, that is to say, has its being outside the confines of space and time. The imagination is that portion of the whole mind that is associated with the body's experiences *in* time, but this portion of the mind, because it *is* a portion of the whole mind, can be affected by this larger whole, which exists outside of time and which is not limited by time.

Spinoza continues, addressing the experience of his friend. "To take an example like yours, a father so loves his son that he and his beloved son are, as it were, one and the same [a]. According to what I have demonstrated on another occasion, there must be in Thought an idea of the son's essence, its affections, and its consequences [b]. Because of this, and because the father, by the union he has with his son [c], is a part of the said son [d], the father's soul must necessarily participate in the son's ideal essence, its affections, and consequences [e]. Next, since the father's soul participates ideally in the things which follow from the son's essence, he can sometimes imagine something [f] of what follows from the son's essence as vividly as if he had it in his presence." We comment on the above.

[a] This may be taken literally. In the Attribute of Extension—in the physical world—one speaks of physical forces such as gravity, electromagnetism, etc., as causing interactions, couplings, binding, etc., among physical objects. In the Attribute of Thought—in the mental, or spiritual, or idea world—the force that binds mental objects, or minds, together is *love*.

[b] By "idea of the son's essence" is meant the soul of the son, and this idea, or soul, exists in the Attribute of Thought, or in the Mind of God, and is eternal and not a part of the temporal order. By "affections" (of the soul) is meant those properties or characteristics of a given soul that differentiate it from other souls. For just as all modes of Extension—all physical things—are unique and individual, so also all modes of Thought—ideas, minds, souls—are unique and have their own individual characteristics. By "consequences" of the soul is meant those things that are produced by, or generated from, or caused by, or follow from, the nature of the given soul. But we must be careful not to interpret this temporally. For just as the smoothness of a table is produced by, or caused by, or is a consequence of, the arrangement of molecules that constitute the table, *and* the smoothness exists simultaneous with, not later than, its cause, so also the consequences of a soul exist simultaneous with and internal to the soul. Among the consequences occurring within the son's soul is the idea of, or knowledge of, the death of the son's body. For the knowledge of both the birth and the death of a given body are equally present to the soul, since the latter is not bound by the temporal order of things.

[c] This, as with [a], should be taken literally. Through the power of love, the mind of the father is united with, or joined with, the mind of the son.

[d] We thus have a coupled mental system containing the respective souls of father and son. The soul of the father is a part of, or participates in, this coupled system.

[e] Therefore, because the father's soul participates in this coupled system (in the Attribute of Thought), it has access to all the consequences that follow from the nature of the son's soul, including the idea (in the son's soul) of the death of the body with which a portion of the son's soul is associated.

[f] This knowledge that the father's soul has about the son's death is, generally speaking, not available to the imaginative portion of the

father's mind. We must recall that the human condition is such that the imaginative portion of our whole mind, the personality, has separated itself from the whole mind which, metaphysically speaking, is impossible, and hence falsely believes itself to be the whole mind. Occasionally, however, information from the whole mind can penetrate the illusion of separation. The imagination then translates this information into images with which it is familiar, such as visions or audible sounds.

Thus, in this single example Spinoza establishes the possibility of direct communication between ideas, or minds, independent of the body (the communication between the father's soul and the son's soul) *and* communication between a whole, or adequate, idea and a portion of itself (the communication between the father's soul, or whole mind, and its imaginative portion, or ego). Spinoza also believed that visions and prophecy as reported in the Bible were cases of this latter kind, where the imagination is stimulated directly by the soul. It should be noted, however, that the imaginative portion of the whole mind is highly conditioned by its association with the body's experiences and will invariably translate and distort communications from the whole mind into symbols with which it is familiar.

So, for example, a vision of say, the Virgin Mary is most likely to occur only to a Christian and a vision of Lord Krishna only to a Hindu. For in either case, the vision is a symbolic representation, in terms the culturally conditioned (imaginative) mind of the recipient can understand, of entities and structures existing in the Attribute of Thought. Both of the above visions, for example, could be but different representation of the same spiritual principle: the power of love, which binds all minds together into a single mind—the Mind of God. A less extreme example, but one very common in contemporary spirituality, concerns psychic phenomena and mediumship, or channeling. The psychic receives, from his or her whole (or higher) self, impressions that the imaginative portion of that self experiences in the form of visual pictures, words, feelings, etc. And a medium apparently is able to act as a conduit for other minds—either its own higher self or that of some other spiritual agency. We may thus define psychic phenomena generally as any imaginative experience brought about by the larger mind of which the imagination is a portion, or by other minds with which the whole mind of the recipient is in communication.

Reincarnation

Let us give another example of direct relationship among ideas. Spinoza never, to my knowledge, discusses reincarnation, yet his system can easily be extended to cover this possibility. For those readers who are familiar with and believe in the concept of reincarnation, it will be useful to see how this concept can be mapped onto Spinoza's system. For those readers who are unfamiliar with the concept and/or believe it to be a mere superstition, it will be useful to see how this concept is an easy and natural consequence of the system of thought we are now developing. First, however, we shall clear away several popular misconceptions associated with the concept of reincarnation. For both those who believe and those who do not believe can hold the same erroneous concept, just as both the atheist and some religious people can hold the same erroneous concept of God—as a super authoritarian male—the former denying and the latter affirming the actual existence of such an imaginary being. The errors involved in popular conceptions of reincarnation have to do with the limits of imaginative experience, so that we (1) confuse the personality with the soul and (2) confuse duration (or time) with existence or eternity. Let us elaborate.

1. Most people believe that the concept of reincarnation involves the belief that they have lived before and will live again. But it is easy to show that this cannot be literally so. The statement "I have lived before" or "I have had many past lives" cannot be true if the word "I" is taken to refer to the present personality. Why is this so? Consider, if you will, a series of so-called past lives,

    $$x_1, x_2, x_3, x_4, x_5$$

    For simplicity, we limit ourselves to five "lives" and assume that x_3 is the present life and, in the popular way of speaking, x_1 and x_2 are "past lives" of x_3, and x_4 and x_5 are "future lives" of x_3. But—and now the error in thinking about reincarnation this way becomes obvious—all these lives are on a par, so that x_3 may equally be regarded as a "future" life of x_1, or as a past life of x_4. That is to say, if x_3 is my present life, it makes no more sense to think of x_1 and x_2 as "my" past lives any more than it does to think of myself as a future life of x_1 and x_2. For "my" generally refers to the personality, and the personality comes into being and perishes with each particular body, so that the individual personalities of x_1, x_2, etc., are as different from one another as are the respective bodies and cultures into which these bodies are born.

What does make sense is to think of these different personalities as being portions of a larger entity within the Attribute of Thought. This larger entity we will call the soul. Thus, instead of imagining that x_1 is a past of life of x_3, we shall conceive of x_1 and x_3 as belonging to the same soul.

2. Now this series of past lives is usually imagined as existing within a temporal order, that is x_1 "lives" before x_2, who lives before x_3, etc. But this cannot literally be the case. Indeed, all theories of reincarnation, from Plato to Hinduism, occur within a metaphysical framework that denies that time is fundamentally real. The notion that x_1, x_2, ... is a time-ordered series is merely a picture formed by the imagination to assist it in talking about such things. But this picture of a "soul" that migrates (or transmigrates) from life to life—one *after* another in a temporal sequence—cannot possibly be the case, for this picture confuses the soul with the personality (and we have shown that the personality does *not* reincarnate) and makes the soul a prisoner of time.

From the soul's perspective, *all* lives, x_1, x_2, ... exist simultaneously. It is only the imagination, or personality, which, unable to picture anything greater than itself, pictures the series of lives as temporally ordered and imagines the soul to be some itsy-bitsy thing that flits from life to life. It is this highly inadequate picture that invites such confused questions as, where is the soul when it is not inhabiting a body? (as if the soul needs a body in order to exist), or do more souls exist now than in the past? (since there are more people living now than before). But these and other such paradoxes can be avoided if it be remembered that the Attribute of Thought exists in its own right and is independent of time, and that the soul is a mental structure that has its being eternally in the Attribute of Thought and is not dependent for its being on either personalities or bodies.

We now define the concept of soul in terms of Spinoza's system of thought. Let "x" refer to a particular human body. X is a mode of Substance, or God, conceived under the Attribute of Extension. By the expression, "idea of x," we mean that same mode of Substance conceived under the Attribute of Thought.

The imagination, or personality of x, is a portion of the idea of x; it is called *inadequate* because it is only a portion of, not the whole, idea or mind. When applied to physical things, Spinoza's holism means that any given physical thing, such as x, is part of a larger physical thing, e.g., the earth, which is itself a part of a still larger physical thing, etc., and this process of holistic inclusion—wholes within wholes within wholes—continues until one has arrived at the ultimate physical whole, Extension Itself, or the Body of God.

But this same process of holistic inclusion must also govern the Attribute of Thought. Thus, any given idea is included within a larger mental structure, which is itself included within a still larger mental structure, etc., until one has arrived at the fundamental mental structure, the Attribute of Thought, or the Mind or Idea of God. Now, if we begin with the idea of x, a given human body, then this idea must be included within a larger idea or mind. This larger mental structure will contain within itself ideas or minds in addition to the idea of the given human body (that is what is meant by calling it a "larger mind"). And some of these additional ideas may have, as their respective counterparts in Extension, other human bodies. These ideas or minds, then, including the given mind, all belong to the same "larger mind," which we may call the soul.

Thus, the soul is one step higher than the human mind in the mental hierarchy of holistic inclusion that culminates in the Mind of God. For just as between the human body and the whole physical universe there are intermediate levels of physical organization (human body, Earth, solar system, galaxy,...), each level of which includes preceding levels, and which has holistic features not reducible to the preceding levels, so also between the human mind and the Mind of God there are intermediate levels of mental organization, and so we define the soul to be a level of mental organization one level up from the human mind.

Even though "past" and "future" have meaning only with respect to imaginative experience, such experience, however, is nevertheless the basis of the human condition; and hence, it will be useful to retain these terms as long as we keep in mind (1) that the present personality is a unique product of this present life and cannot have lived in the past—that is to say, it is not the personality that reincarnates; and (2) the soul exists outside of time and hence does not reincarnate either, if by "reincarnate" is meant a temporal process of taking on one life *after* another in time. We may continue to use the terms "reincarnation" and "past lives," if only to remind ourselves that our present personality is an inadequate portion of a whole mind (the idea of the body, higher self, etc.), which in turn is contained within a still larger mental structure called the soul; and that this soul contains within itself other whole minds, fragments of which constitute personalities like our own that may exist in the past or future *relative* to our present personality.

The mind of the earth
We wish to give one more example, or set of examples, concerning relationships among ideas. We first remind the reader that the mental universe—the Attribute of Thought—is every bit as rich and varied in structure as is the physical universe. Just as there are an infinity of physical things, with a rich infinitude of possible relationships among them, so also there are an infinity of mental things, or minds, that are interconnected with one another in an infinity of possible ways. Hopefully, by now the reader has shaken free from the anthropocentric view that only humans have consciousness, or that consciousness needs a body or brain in order to exist. Nevertheless, because (1) the human condition is deeply associated with the body and (2) the imagination can picture bodies and their relationships *much* easier than it can picture minds (including its own), it will be useful to proceed by first (3) discussing certain relationships among some physical things and then infer (4) that there must be a structurally similar relationship among their ideas or minds. This is the procedure that we (and Spinoza) followed in our discussion of sense perception.

Consider then the relationship that holds between an insect colony and the individual members of that colony. It is obvious that the colony as a whole is the fundamental unit of the species, not the individual insects. The individual insect behaves more like a cell within a whole body than like an autonomous organism. Just as the cells within an organism such as the human body do not exist independently of the organism, but rather are produced by the organism as a whole, so also individual insects do not exist independently of the colony to which they belong, but rather are produced by the colony whose purposes they serve. If this relationship is conceived in the Attribute of Thought, then the minds of the individual insects will be related to the mind of the colony in the same way that the bodies of the individual insects are related to the colony as a whole. The mind of the colony could be thought of as a "group mind," although it would perhaps be more accurate to conceive of the individual insect minds as "partial minds," since the latter minds are like thoughts in the mind of the colony in the same way that individual insects are like cells in the body of the organism.

Indeed, we could have used the relationship between the cells of an organism and the organism to infer what must be true structurally in the relationship between the minds of the individual cells (i.e., their ideas in the Attribute of

Thought) and the mind of the whole organism. But the relationship between insect and insect colony illustrates another point we have urged before: that spatial contiguity among "parts" is not a necessary condition for those parts to constitute, or belong to, a larger, organic whole. For, just as the body of an organism (and we include an insect colony as a kind of organism) has holistic properties not reducible to its cells, so also the mind of the organism has holistic properties not reducible to the minds of its constituent cells.

In nature there are many examples of co-evolution of organisms so dependent upon one another that neither could have come into being or continue to exist without the other. For example, there is a particular species of orchid that can be pollinated by *only* one species of wasp, which in turn can obtain nectar from *only* that species of orchid. It seems clear that neither species could have come into being without the other; that is, what comes into being is the total system, orchid and wasp. This total system forms a unity, a single organism, of which the orchid and the wasp are components. If we let "A" stand for the orchid, and "B" stand for the wasp, then A and B exist, not in their own right, but as portions of the whole organism (A + B), in much the same way that a stomach and kidney, say, exist only as portions of a larger whole. Any conceptual account, say, of the forces that bring a particular stomach into existence must involve the organism as a whole, which includes the kidney as a necessary part. Similarly, any account of how a particular member of that species of orchid comes into being must include the larger organism (A + B) in which the orchid has its being, and hence, as Spinoza would put it, the orchid can neither be nor be conceived without the wasp. One may be tempted to object that an orchid can be conceived without the wasp, since one can see an orchid, describe its characteristics etc., without mentioning wasps. But this is to confuse the imagination with the understanding. We can indeed picture the wasp without the orchid, but this picture is produced by the imagination, which is simply the body's response to external stimuli. The imagination, as we know, represents to us external things inadequately, as if they existed separately and unconnected. But science transcends the limitation of sense experience by giving us understanding, which consists in the knowledge of the connections that exist between and among all things. The scientific understanding of the orchid as a species must include the means by which it propagates from one generation to the next. No individual orchid comes into being except from a seed, and no seed comes into being except as a result of cross-pollination by a particular wasp; and thus, the conception of one involves the conception of the other. Their ideas, therefore, involve one another. That is, the idea of the wasp and the idea of the orchid are portions of the larger mental structure that we may call the mind of (A + B). In general, whenever two (or more) organisms form a tightly coupled system such that one can neither be nor be conceived without the other(s), then the individual minds of the organisms are portions of the mind of the whole system.

Since all living things are coupled with other things, both living and nonliving, this line of reasoning leads very naturally to the Gaia Hypothesis: that the earth as a whole is a single living organism with holistic features not reducible to the individual life forms that exist on the planet. This single living organism will therefore have its own individual consciousness, which we may call the "Mind" (or "Spirit" or "Idea" or "Soul") of the earth and *in which* the minds of particular things, including humans, have their being. It may be noted that even so-called inanimate things, such as mountains, rivers, and forests, have their associated ideas or minds that participate in the consciousness of the earth as a whole.

And this, incidentally, is what nature religions mean when they speak of the spirit of a particular mountain or river. For every ecosystem has its own idea (or mind or consciousness), which idea is a portion of the Mind of the earth in the same way that the mountain, river, or forest is a portion of the Body of the Earth. And, as we have shown, it is occasionally possible under some circumstances for the human imagination to be directly affected by the idea, or spirit, of a particular mountain, river, etc., since all minds, like all bodies, are interconnected. So, when people such as mystics, poets, and shamans, report speaking directly to a tree, a river, a mountain, etc., there is no reason not to accept such reports at face value, for the general possibility of such communication is a natural consequence of the system of thought we are here developing.

3 DESIRE AND EMOTION

THE NATURE OF DESIRE AND INTENT

We return now to a discussion of the human condition, for "of the infinitely many things [which] follow from [God, we wish to concern ourselves primarily with] only those that can lead us, by the hand, as it were, to the knowledge of the human mind and its highest blessedness" (*Ethics,* part 2, Preface). Implicit in this passage is the claim that we presently lack the knowledge of the human mind; and since the human mind is what we truly *are,* it follows that we are largely ignorant of our true nature. And this is because our consciousness is focused almost entirely in imaginative experience—in that portion of the whole mind that follows, as it were, the body's experiences. It is as if we are watching a movie and have become so involved in the action on the screen that we forget that we are really sitting in a movie theater. So caught up are we in the imagination—in the body's experiences—that we have forgotten our true identity as an eternal mode of Thought, as part of the infinite Mind of God. Regaining this "knowledge of the human mind" requires, for Spinoza, an understanding of the structure of the imagination and its power over us. We turn, therefore, to a discussion of human emotions.

Understanding the emotions

Spinoza begins his analysis of human emotions by noting that most people seem to believe that emotions lie outside the domain of rational thought and are intrinsically incapable or unworthy of being understood. Indeed, the terms "emotional" and "rational" are often opposed to one another. Although it is true that a person while suffering the effects of a strong emotion is not likely to be capable of rational thought, it is also true that emotions, like everything else in nature, can be rationally understood. For human emotions exist as modes of Thought within the Imagination, just as their corresponding bodily states exist as modes of Extension within the body, and so, like anything else in nature, they have definite structures and causes that can be described and understood. To believe that emotions are intrinsically irrational—i.e., not capable of being understood—is to believe that emotions lie outside of the natural order of things. But this is absurd, since everything that exists has its being within the natural order of things. Furthermore, the belief that emotions are irrational serves the purpose of preventing the believer from inquiring into the nature of his own emotions, since no one attempts to understand that which is believed to be not understandable.

We often speak of "irrational feelings" and "irrational desires." Perhaps it is jealousy, or a compulsion, or a fear of criticism, or guilt. The reader will have no difficulty identifying a number of such feelings, desires, behaviors, etc. The question we must ask ourselves is, what do we mean when we call such feelings (desires, behaviors) "irrational?" We cannot mean "not capable of being understood," because a feeling, e.g., jealousy, is something real, and its physiological correlates in the body are measurable. Rather, what we mean is something like: "this present feeling (desire, behavior, etc.) is not congruent with, does not fit in with, how I think I should feel," or more simply, "I do not understand my present feelings." Instead of referring to such feelings and behaviors, whether our own or others', as irrational, it would be far better to say "I do not presently understand why I'm feeling this way" or "I do not understand why she is behaving in that way." For above all, we must affirm and re-affirm to ourselves the fundamental intelligibility of all things. To believe that we human beings, or parts of ourselves, are irrational and not capable of being understood is to believe that we, or parts of us, are outside the natural order of things. But this is impossible, since nothing exists outside the natural order of things. This is a very important point, and we suggest another exercise to reinforce these ideas:

> EXERCISE 4: Think of a feeling (or desire or behavior) that you experience from time to time and that you are in the habit of thinking is irrational. Now, while still thinking of this feeling, introduce into your mind the thought that this feeling exists as a part of nature, that nature is fully intelligible, and hence, that this feeling can be understood, even though you do not presently understand it. (For if you did understand it, you could not consider it to be irrational.) Tell yourself also that you are willing to accept the idea that there are many things pertaining to your own mind that you do not presently understand, in the same way that there are many processes that occur within your body that you do not understand.

Having affirmed to ourselves that emotions are capable of being understood, we must now elaborate more on what it is to understand. According to Spinoza, the human mind has available to it three distinct modes of consciousness: (1) Imagination, (2) Understanding or Reason, and (3) Intuition or mystical insight. *Imagination,* as we have said, is that part of our mind that pertains to sense experience, emotions, and memory. What Spinoza calls *intuitions,* or *intuitive knowledge,* involves the conscious awareness of our mind as a part of the Mind of God, and it is in this awareness that salvation, or blessedness, consists. The *Understanding,* or *Reason,* is the vehicle that takes us out of our Imagination and brings us to this awareness. Now, we have already contrasted the understanding with the imagination, e.g., when we argued that science and mathematics offer us many examples of things such as infinite sets, quantum processes, and relativistic effects, which can be understood but not pictured or imagined. But in all these examples, the things to be understood are physical, parts of Extension. Can the Understanding be applied to the mental? Or, to put it another way, is self-knowledge possible? And of course, the answer to this question must be a resounding "yes."

But of what does this self-knowledge consist? To get a feeling for the answer to this question, let us ask the same question with regard to our body: of what does the understanding of the body, or any of its parts, consist? To be specific, we consider a part of the body, say the heart. In general terms, an understanding of the heart involves (1) knowledge of its constituent parts—the cells and tissues—and how those parts combine and interact so as to form a single organ; (2) knowledge of the function the heart performs within the larger whole (the body) in which it is a part; (3) knowledge of how the heart is connected with other parts of the body; and (4) knowledge of the forces (such as diet) that help or hinder the heart in performing its function. Although this "list" could probably be expanded, and most certainly be elaborated upon, it is clear that an understanding of a given thing, whether that thing be a part of our body or a part of our mind, involves knowledge of its component parts, knowledge of its function within a larger whole, and knowledge of its connections to other things.

We note three further characteristics of the understanding: first, it is not "all or nothing," so to speak. Biology, for example, has given us much understanding of how the body works, but no one would claim that it is complete or total. Thus, we may understand a thing partially, or in some respects but not in others. Second, the understanding always involves what Spinoza calls the common properties of things. For example, although every human body is individual and unique, the understanding of the body through biology makes no reference to any individual body, but instead explains the body in terms of characteristics that *all* bodies have in common, e.g., cells, internal organs, etc.

Third, and most important for our purposes, a consequence of understanding a thing is the acquisition of a certain power over the thing. When we understand that water is made up of hydrogen and oxygen, we have the power to create water (by combining the two gases) and to destroy it (by causing the water molecule to disassociate into its constituent parts). The more science understands the human body, the more is it able to specify what will strengthen it and what will weaken it. The knowledge of how to maintain a *healthy* body is thus a practical consequence of the endeavor to understand the body. So also, the knowledge of how to maintain a healthy emotional state of mind is, we claim, a practical consequence of the endeavor to understand our emotions. To the extent that we can understand our emotions we will have a knowledge of how to overcome dysfunctional emotions (e.g., envy, hatred, guilt, etc.) and how to strengthen and foster within ourselves those emotions that are conducive to our well being (e.g., self-respect, empathy toward others, love).

Indeed, as we have implied earlier, many philosophical and psychological theories are quite useless because they do not teach us how to live. A philosophical theory of the mind, or a psychological theory of the personality, that does not have practical consequences for living one's life is not only useless as a guide for living, but also cannot offer us any real understanding into the nature of the mind or personality. This is because to understand a thing is to know something of the forces and causes that produce and sustain the thing, and to the extent that we know these forces and causes are we able to gain, if not total, at least some partial control over that thing. To understand the nature of hatred, say, must necessarily involve a knowledge of the forces and causes that produce and sustain that emotion, and to the extent that we can affect those forces and causes are we able to master the emotion. A "theory" of, say, digestion that did not have as a consequence practical knowledge of what helps or hinders the process of digestion could not be said to offer any real understanding of how digestion works. Similarly, a "theory" of the mind, of the personality, or of the emotions, whether philosophical, psychological, or spiritual, that does not have as a consequence practical knowledge of how to live, cannot offer us any real understanding of our own nature. Such a theory is at best mere description; at worst it is empty verbiage.

The metaphysics of desire

At this point it will be good to remind ourselves of the metaphysical system developed in part I, for we wish to understand ourselves in terms of this system.

1. God or Substance is a Single, Indivisible, Being consisting of infinite Attributes.

2. Each Attribute is a way in which the Divine Being manifests its nature to Itself.

3. Our body is a mode, or part of God manifested in the Attribute of Extension (the Body of God); our mind is that same mode of God manifested in the Attribute of Thought (the Mind of God).

4. Thus, everything our body (mind) does is done within The Body (Mind) of God.

5. It is in the Nature of God, or Substance, to exist, and this Existence contains within itself the being of all things, including ourselves, that exist within God.

6. Therefore, each thing exists according to a certain divine necessity, or according to God's will. But in using the expression "God's will," we must take care not to think of God anthropomorphically—as having a will in the same way we believe ourselves to have a will. God's *will* and God's *nature* are one and the same thing. For everything that is, follows from or is a part of, God's nature or will.

7. So our body and our mind, and each part of our body and mind, including the imaginative part of our mind, exists as a consequence of God's Will and forms a portion of the fabric of that Will or Nature.

Now each thing, in whatever Attribute, experiences God's Will that it exist as an *endeavor*, or effort to persevere in its own being. The human body experiences this endeavor in the form of instinctive impulses to maintain itself, e.g., the so-called fight or flight response, as well as the immune system as whole. The human mind experiences this endeavor generally as a desire to be. Since, as we will show, happiness is strongly connected with this desire, we may say that God's Will that the mind exist is experienced by that mind, and each portion of that mind, as a desire to be happy and to pursue those things that it (the mind) believes will bring it happiness. Thus, our desire to be happy—and this includes transitory desires for those things that we rightly or wrongly believe will bring us happiness—is nothing but the subjective experience of God's Will that we exist, or of the Laws of Nature according to which we are produced and sustained.

It is easier for us to understand this with respect to the Attribute of Extension. Any physical thing, including our own body, is a focal point, a coming together, of various components. This "coming together" is *caused*; that is to say, it is a lawful process governed by physical causes that both produce the thing *and* hold it together as a single thing. It is not enough to conceive of the causes of a given thing as merely producing the thing, which, after being produced, exists by itself. This is like the Judeo-Christian conception of an absentee God who creates the world and winds it up, so to speak, but subsequently plays no further causal role in sustaining it. For Spinoza, the world is a manifestation of the very Being of God, or to put it another way, the world is continuously in the process of being created by God.

Applying this to our own body, it is not sufficient to conceive of the cause of our body's existence as having merely produced the body, as, for example, when we conceive the cause of our body's existence to be the coming together of a sperm with an egg. We must also conceive the cause of the body's existence to involve those forces, both internal and external to the body, that make it possible for the body to continue to exist on a moment-to-moment basis. One example of the former kind of cause or force is the body's immune system, which when weakened results in illness and death; an example of an external force is anything external to the body without which the body could not exist: food, water, oxygen, the earth, the sun, etc. For our body would surely perish were the sun to cease to exist, or even slightly change its output of energy. But—and this line of reasoning should be familiar by now—the sun's nature and continued existence depends upon the galaxy as a whole, which in turn depends on its relationships with other galaxies, etc., and this process of holistic embedding continues to the entire physical universe. Thus, the physical universe as a whole—or God insofar as God is conceived as constituting the physical universe—is causally involved in the continued existence of each thing. Hence, we may say that our body is *continuously created* by God.

And the same is true for our mind. We must resist the habit of thinking that God *created* the world; rather, God is actively *creating* the world, both mental and physical, *now!* Our mind—both the eternal "whole mind" and its imaginative portion, which follows the body's experiences in time—is a portion of God's mind *now;* it is continuously created by the Mind of God. The imagination's, or the personality's, subjective experience of this moment-to-moment creative force is in terms of moment-to-moment desires. Our desires are the means by which our personality endeavors or strives to persevere in its being, in the same way that the immune system is the means by which our body endeavors or strives to maintain *its* being.

Let us express these ideas using Spinoza's own words. He reminds us that

> ...individual things [and that includes our body and mind] are modes by which God's attributes are expressed in a certain and determinate way, i.e. things that express, in a certain and determinate way, God's power, by which God is and acts. And no thing has anything in itself by which it can be destroyed, *or* which takes its existence away. On the contrary, it is opposed to [that is, it actively resists] everything which can take its existence away. Therefore, as far as it can, and it lies in itself, it strives [or endeavors] to persevere in its being. [Furthermore]...the power of each thing, *or* the striving by which it [either alone or with others] does anything, or strives to do anything—i.e., the power, *or* striving, by which it strives to persevere in its being, is nothing but the given or actual essence of the thing itself. (*Ethics,* pt. 3, propositions 6 and 7)

A little later, Spinoza introduces the terms *will, appetite,* and *desire:*

> When this striving is related only to the mind, it is called *will;* but when it is related to the mind and body together, it is called *appetite.* This appetite, therefore, is nothing but the very essence of man, from whose nature there necessarily follows those things that promote his preservation. And so man is determined to do those things.
>
> Between appetite and desire there is no difference, except that desire is generally related to men insofar as they are conscious of their appetites. So *desire* can be defined as *appetite of which we are conscious.* (*Ethics,* pt. 3, prop. 9)

We could, of course, have interchanged the terms *desire* and *appetite* and then define appetite as a desire of which we are not conscious. The exact terminology does not matter; what does matter is the concept that there are motivational forces acting within us of which we are not conscious. Part of Spinoza's therapy involves becoming conscious of *all* motivating forces acting within us, as well as becoming conscious of the causes of those forces. (By "motivating force" I mean simply a desire, an appetite, a willing or decision to do something.) These motivational forces, conscious and unconscious, constitute (or follow from) or express, our essence, which in turn follows from (is an expression of, is a part of) God's being or power. This metaphysical understanding—that our desires are not opposed to God's Nature but are ultimately *an expression* of the Divine Nature and are what they are *because of* that Nature—is so important that we make it into an exercise.

EXERCISE 5: Consider several of your desires until you find one that makes you feel a little uncomfortable or guilty—perhaps it is a desire for more status or money, or for unhealthy food, or a wish that someone else should not succeed, or a behavior pattern you wish to change. While keeping this desire in your awareness, remind yourself of the metaphysical context in which this desire arises. Tell yourself that this desire is a part of your mind's striving to persevere in its own being, that this striving is a part of your very nature, which in turn, is ultimately a part of the Divine Nature. For "*everyone exists by the highest right of nature, and consequently everyone, by the highest right of nature, does (and desires) those things that follow from the necessity of his own nature*" (*Ethics*, pt. 4, prop. 37, note 2, Author's italics).

Now, of course, any given desire with which we are uncomfortable is accompanied with another desire—a "second-order" desire—to remove the given desire. For example, a person who desires to smoke may also desire not to have the desire to smoke. These second-order desires are very important, and we shall discuss them at length in the next chapter. The purpose of the above exercise is self-acceptance, that is to say, acceptance of our present condition. For we are prone to believe that although God may have created our mind, she did not also create the desires and emotions within our mind. And this is to believe that we are an exception to nature—a "kingdom within a kingdom," as Spinoza puts it—rather than an intrinsic part of the natural order of things, whether that order be conceived as Mind or as Body.

Indeed, to believe that our mind is a part of the Mind of God but that the desires and emotions within our mind are not, is as absurd as believing that our body is a natural part of the physical universe, but that the cells and molecules within our body are not. To the extent that we do not accept our present desires and emotions, to that extent we falsely believe ourselves to be sinful—that is, not part of the natural order of things. Self-acceptance is the first step in the process of self-transformation. To begin to move toward self-acceptance we must (1) bring awareness to the ways in which we do not accept ourselves and (2) gently remind ourselves of the metaphysical context in which we have our being. That is the purpose of the above exercise.

It will also be good, at this point, to begin to cultivate an attitude of Socratic ignorance toward our own mind. Spinoza repeatedly tells us that although we are conscious of our desires, we are not, generally speaking, conscious of the causes of our desires. We waste enormous amounts of energy inventing all sorts of rationalizations and justifications for wanting what we want; we invent elaborate personal ideologies, for example, which we then believe to be the reason why we want what we want and do what we do. But these "personal ideologies"—these stories we tell ourselves and others about what's good and what's bad, about right and wrong—are themselves the *effects*, not the causes, of our desires and emotions. A few simple examples will make this point clear.

1. A wealthy person who is greedy tells himself that poor people are lazy, and hence, because they are lazy, he deserves to keep his money to himself. But really his beliefs about poor people are caused by his greed, not vice versa.

2. A person who fears that others will harm her tells herself that people are mean, selfish, untrustworthy, etc., and justifies her fear by this view of human nature; but really, this view of human nature is created by the fear, which is then projected outward.

3. A man who beats women tells himself that women deserve it or that they enjoy it, and this ideology about women justifies his actions to himself. But really, the ideology is produced by the same violent impulses that lead to the actions in the first place.

4. A person who seeks power and status tells herself that she is better than others, and hence deserves the status she seeks. But really, what she tells herself—what I am calling the "personal ideology"—is produced by the desire for power and status, *not* the other way around.

Now for most of us, our projections or personal ideologies are not so obvious; otherwise we would see through them more easily. This is because we usually have conflicting desires and emotions. The greedy man may also feel compassion toward others; a seeker of power may believe both that she is better than and worse than others, etc. Nevertheless, the structure is the same, namely, that our rationalizations and justifications, our projections and our personal ideologies, are effects and consequences of our desires, appetites, and actions, not their causes. Spinoza's therapy involves learning to separate our desires from their often elaborate rationalizations. The truth is that we are for the most part ignorant of the causes of our desires and actions, and we must learn to accept this ignorance in order to bring our desires into full conscious awareness. For it is through our desires and appetites that we are most immediately connected with the creative forces that sustain our being. Therefore, justifications, ideologies, and beliefs about the way things are or should be, are obstacles to self-knowledge, insofar as they prevent us from knowing how we truly feel and what we truly desire. "From all this, then, it is clear that we neither strive for, nor will, neither want, nor desire anything because we judge it to be good; on the contrary, we judge something to be good because we strive for it, will it, want it, and desire it" (*Ethics,* pt. 3, prop. 9, note).

Determinism and the illusion of free will
We have discussed appetite and desire; what of the will? According to the metaphysics developed in part I, there is no such thing as "free will" in the sense that expression is usually meant. For what is the "will," or "decision-making process," supposed to be free from? Just as it would be absurd to suggest that our body, or any part of it, is "free from" other bodies and forces within the Attribute of Extension, which bodies and forces create, sustain, and constitute the body we call our own, *so also,* it cannot be the case that our mind, or any part of it, is "free from" other minds and (mental) forces within the Attribute of Thought, which minds and forces create, sustain, and constitute the mind we call our own.

For our mind is a part of the Mind of God, which is Single, Indivisible, and Whole; and this means that any mind, such as our own, within God's Mind is intrinsically connected with other such minds. So in no way can we, or that part of us called the will, be "free from" the Mind of God through which we are continuously created and sustained. The fact that we are ignorant of our connections with other minds and psychic forces, which minds and forces causally affect what we call our "decisions," does not mean that these connections are not there. To believe in free will is to believe that such connections do not exist, and no one tries to become aware of that which she believes does not exist. Seen in this way, the belief in free will is a hindrance to self-knowledge, since it prevents us from inquiring into the causes of our desires, our actions, and our so-called decisions.

Nevertheless, although the above ideas are quite obvious, the belief in free will—the belief that we are unconnected with anything outside ourselves—is so deeply ingrained in us that it is important to examine this from the perspective of our own subjective experience. So we ask, what is the nature of the *experience* to which we give the names "deliberating," "decision-making," "choosing," and which we believe proves or requires the existence of a "free will"? Let us pursue this question in the context of an exercise:

EXERCISE 6: Consider a recent experience of yours in which you made a decision or a choice. And to keep things simple (so that the dynamics of the decision-making process may more easily be seen), consider an experience that is not emotionally charged, such as deciding what to eat at a restaurant or choosing which movie to see on a Saturday night. Suppose there are three alternatives, A, B, or C, from which you have to choose. Consider the alternatives *concretely*, that is, fill in specific names—of movies, of foods, etc.—for A, B, and C. Note that toward each alternative you feel some desire, for if there is no desire then it is not a real alternative. Now, what is the actual psychological process you experienced and that resulted in your making a choice, say B? Was it not something like the following?

First your awareness moves from one alternative to the other—you find yourself thinking about A, then B, then C, then back to A again, etc. Next you visualize, or imagine, consequences of each choice. You imagine what A would taste like, how you would feel while eating B, how your stomach might feel after eating C. This process of imagining the consequences of each alternative affects how you feel about, your desire for, each alternative, and eventually your desire for one, say, B predominates over your desire for the others. This experience—of your desire for B predominating over your desire for either A or C—is what is called the *decision* to do B rather than A or C, or *choosing* B over A or C. The reader is urged to examine a number of personal examples of "choosing," and to consider carefully whether what is called "choosing" or "decision-making" is simply another name for the psychological process whereby our desire for one thing predominates over our desire for other things.

We must resist the tendency to think of desires as passive, as having no power of their own and hence requiring a "will" to "choose" among them. For desire is our very essence, our "striving to persevere in our being," our basic motivational force. Our desires often compete and conflict with one another, and the strength of any desire may fluctuate widely. What we call a "choice" is simply the predominance of one desire over others, and what we call "deliberation" or "decision-making" is, at its best, a psychological process that allows us to discern which alternative we more truly want, which desire is stronger at the moment. There is, therefore, no need to postulate the existence of a "homunculus" that picks and chooses from alternative courses of action; our subjective experience does not require, and our holistic metaphysics precludes, the existence of a homunculus.

At any rate, we cannot "choose" among competing desires unless we first have the desires. But do we "choose" which desires to have? For that matter, do we "choose" which thoughts come to our awareness—or do our thoughts just come to us? I think a little introspection will show that our thoughts simply come to us, just like our speech. For when we begin a sentence, we are not consciously aware of how it will end, unless we are delivering a speech. Even the thought that says "I choose B, rather than A or C" simply comes to us; we do not "choose" that thought. Indeed, if you do believe that you chose the thought that says "I choose to act on desire B," do you also choose the thought that says "I choose the thought that says 'I choose B'"? Clearly, we experience no such psychological process, which involves an infinite regress. But isn't it equally absurd to believe that your so-called free will chooses B but does not choose the thought that says "I choose B," since the so-called choice can't be made without the prior thought?

The mental activity we call thinking is a far less voluntary process than we would like to believe. This is a very important issue, and so we propose an exercise to help the reader gain a deeper insight into her own thought process. The reader will discover that thinking is a fairly automatic process that we do not "choose" which thoughts to think and that in a real sense there is no "I" (homunculus) that thinks its thoughts; rather, thoughts flow through our minds in the same way that blood flows through our veins.

EXERCISE 7A: Let us first attempt to choose a thought and see if we can think it. So pick a simple thought (e.g., "2 + 2 = 4," "my name is ___," "tomorrow I have to do the laundry," etc.). Now, having picked a thought, see if you can hold that thought in your mind for a full minute, and notice what happens. You will notice that your mind wanders, that is to say, other thoughts intrude and displace the intended thought. So your subjective experience is something like this: you begin with the intended, or chosen, thought. A little later—in a few seconds—you become aware of other thoughts together with the intended thought. These "other thoughts" just come, they are not "chosen." A few seconds later, you become aware that the intended thought has disappeared; this awareness, that you have not been thinking the intended thought, in effect reintroduces the intended thought, and the process begins again. The reader is urged to repeat this exercise over and over until she realizes how little control she has over her own thought process.

EXERCISE 7B: If there exists an "I," or a "homunculus" that "chooses" its thoughts and has any power to control them, then, in addition to being able to decide *what* to think (Exercise 7a), it should be able to decide *whether* to think. That is to say, if thinking was merely an activity of the mind and the mind exerted a free will over its thoughts, then the mind should be able to "choose" whether or not to engage in the activity of thinking. Try it. Try, even for a few seconds, to not have any thoughts. You will see that this is virtually impossible.

EXERCISE 7C: For imaginative thinking—and that is all we are concerned with here—thought and language are very intimately connected. We can hardly have a thought without also having the words we would use to express that thought to another. Speech, like thinking, is much less voluntary than we would like to believe. To see this, observe yourself while engaged in normal conversation with a friend. Do you consciously choose the words as they (or before they) tumble out of your mouth? I think not. Notice also that when you begin a sentence, you have no idea how it will end, no idea which words will be used to complete the sentence. Yet, without any conscious planning or control, the sentence is completed, and usually grammatically too. Our body, it would seem, produces speech as automatically as it breathes and digests its food!

Hopefully doing these exercises will induce a sense of awe and wonder with respect to the dynamics of our mind, in the same way that a little knowledge of biology can induce a sense of wonder at the rich complexity of our body. Hopefully, also, these exercises will serve as a correction to the erroneous belief, deeply ingrained in Western culture, that there is an "I," a "homunculus," which is independent of its thoughts, over which it exercises a certain control, or "free will." On the contrary, our personal identity, our feeling of "I-ness," is itself a product of, or created by, this flow of thoughts, which is why we cannot control, direct, or stop the thoughts that race through our mind, determining us now to this action, now to that action. We hasten to add that this is true only for the imagination—or ego, or personality—that portion of the whole mind which follows the body's experience. The mystical experience, which Spinoza calls "intuitive knowledge," does not involve this "flow of thoughts." Indeed, many meditative practices involve exercises that aim at stopping the flow of thoughts. But the "I" of imaginative experience, which is our present experience, cannot, as these exercises have demonstrated, stop or control this flow of thoughts, because the "I," is itself an effect of this flow, not the cause.

We now recapitulate the argument against free will. First we said that in order to choose among competing desires or courses of action we must first have a thought that tells us to make a particular choice (otherwise the action is mechanical, not deliberative). Next, we asked whether this thought that directs us to make the choice—or announces to us the choice we make—is itself freely chosen. For if this thought is not freely chosen, then the choice it tells us to make cannot be the result of a free will. We then urged, both from experience (exercises 7a, 7b, and 7c) and from reason that this thought is not freely chosen. The argument from reason involves an infinite regress and proceeds as follows:

1. Let A, B, and C stand for the alternatives.

2. Making what we call a choice involves having the thought "I choose, or want, or prefer *A*." Call this thought "thought A."

3. If this thought is freely chosen, then it is chosen from among other thoughts, such as "thought B" and "thought C."

4. Making a choice as to which of these thoughts to have involves having *another* thought which says "I chose, or want, or prefer thought A. Call *this* thought the "thought of thought A."

5. We repeat the process with this "second-order" thought. For if *it* is freely chosen, it must be chosen from among other such thoughts, the "thought of thought B" and the "thought of thought C." The choice comes into our awareness as a third-order thought which tells us, or

informs us, which of the second-order thoughts we want. But then if this third-order thought is freely chosen, etc., etc., involving us in an infinite regress.

No, we experience nothing like this; there is no psychological process of "choosing" which thoughts to think. What we call a choice, or a decision, is nothing more than the desire itself insofar as that desire is conceived under the Attribute of Thought. We choose neither our desires, nor which from among our desires to act upon. For, to consider the latter case, what we call a choice from among our desires is the same as saying that one of our desires (the one we "choose") is stronger than the others, and we are thus determined by the stronger desire, which our mind experiences as choosing the desire. In Spinoza's own words:

> So experience, no less clearly than reason, teaches that men believe themselves free because they are conscious of their own actions, and ignorant of the causes by which they are determined, that the decisions of the mind are nothing but the appetites themselves, which therefore varies as the disposition of the body varies. For each one governs everything from his emotions: those who are torn by contrary emotions do not know what they want, and those who are not moved by any emotion are easily driven here and there.
>
> All these things, indeed, show clearly that both the decision of the mind and the appetite and the determination of the body by nature exist together—or rather are one and the same thing, which we call a decision when it is considered under, and explained through, the Attribute of Thought, and which we call a determination (of the body) when it is considered under the Attribute of Extension. (*Ethics,* pt. 3, prop. 2, note)

Now, it is not my intention to plunge the reader into despair by pointing out that we do not consciously control what we want, what we speak, and what we think. It is not, after all, as if someone else, outside of us, controls our desires, words, and thoughts. Consider the following analogy: each atom inside our body was produced outside of our body—in stars. These atoms are brought together and held together in the specific form of our body by natural forces and processes occurring within the Attribute of Extension; our body, indeed, is created and sustained by these forces. Yet, we do not think the body is something "less" because it does not itself produce the atoms that constitute its being—or because it is an effect of a much larger physical process that brings the atoms together so as to constitute the human form. So also, the imaginative mind, the ego, is not "something less" because it does not produce the ideas (thoughts, desires, emotions) that constitute its being. The ego is created and sustained by psychic, or psychological, forces and processes in the same way that the body is created and sustained by physical forces and processes.

But when we say that the individual is an effect of forces *larger* than herself, we do not mean *external* to herself. Just as the body is not external to the atoms that constitute it, so also our mind is not something external to the ideas that constitute it. Rather, it is a temporary form assumed by those ideas in accordance with psychic law, that is to say, in accordance with the Attribute of Thought. Part of the purpose of the above exercise was to convince the reader that our mind as we consciously experience it is an effect of mental processes larger than, but not external to, itself. For if this were not so, why can we exert so little control over what we think? Why can we not stop thinking altogether?

Wholistic embedding and the metaphysics of choice

Although the above considerations should be sufficient to dispel the ego's feelings of inadequacy and insignificance (for, if anything, the imaginative mind is far more significant and wondrous than it conceives itself to be), I would like to point out, and partially develop, another way of looking at this. After all, the world is such that it can be viewed in many different ways, and each way of viewing the world—each "ism" (e.g., determinism, "free-willism," holism, atomism, etc.) can either be used to promote self-understanding, or abused to prevent self-understanding. A belief in free will, for example, can be used to empower an individual to follow her "better" desires and impulses ("I *choose* to quit smoking"); or it can be abused as a way of avoiding self-knowledge ("I don't care why I smoke; I just *choose* to smoke"). Similarly, determinism can be used to promote self-understanding ("I am *determined* to smoke by forces that I do not now understand; perhaps if I were to gain some understanding of these psychological and physical forces, I would have enough power to stop smoking"); or it can be abused as a way of denying the need to change ("I am *determined* to smoke, so why bother trying to understand why.").

Spinoza's system of thought is rigorously deterministic insofar as it is applied to the human condition. Yet, there is a complementary way of looking at things, consistent with Spinoza's metaphysics, but more in accordance with humanistic ideals of free will and choice. For it must be remembered that God is completely free, and this divine freedom extends throughout the whole Being of God; and since everything that exists, including ourselves, exists within the Being of God, it follows that there is nothing that is not free.

Consider, a person moves his arm freely. How should we conceive the motion of the cells that constitute the arm? Shall we say that each individual cell, being part of the arm, is constrained to move in a manner determined by the motion of the arm as a whole? Or shall we say that since the arm moves freely and the cells collectively constitute the arm, that the cells also move freely? Either way of describing this situation is fine; what would not work, however, is if a given cell regarded itself as intrinsically unconnected with and separate from other cells and the arm of which it is a part. This is the view that most people who believe in free will have in mind, the view that forms an essential part of Western religions, for the concept of sin depends upon the concept of free will, which in turn depends upon the concept of a self, a homunculus, that exists separate from its Creator. But there can be no such thing as freedom from the forces, physical and psychic, that create and sustain us. For we are, in body and in mind, a manifestation of those forces.

Nevertheless, these forces, being an expression of the divine nature, are essentially free; and *we,* being an expression of these forces, participate in that freedom. However, as long as we do not directly experience ourselves as an expression of these forces—as long as we do not experience our connection with the whole of Nature—we remain unconscious of our essential freedom. According to Spinoza, our freedom, or liberation, or salvation, consists in a conscious awareness of the union that exists between our mind and the Divine Forces that continuously create us. But yet, our metaphysical status—that our mind is in fact united with the Mind of God—does not depend upon our awareness of that status, although our happiness does. Hence, in a very real sense, we may regard ourselves as completely free, and everything that happens to us is the result of a "free choice." For if we could but experience the identity between our self and the forces that are creating our self, we would experience our lives, down to the tiniest detail, as a free and necessary expression of our innermost nature. *Free,* because there is nothing that could constrain the divine nature; but also *necessary,* because the divine nature cannot be other than what it actually is.

Now, to pursue this line of reasoning, if we are to regard everything that exists as free (since every thing is a part of and an expression of, the Divine Being who is free), there must exist a conscious experience of that freedom. Clearly, the Attribute of thought, that is, the Mind of God, experiences itself as free. But within the Attribute of Thought, different modes, or minds, experience themselves as partly free and partly not free. The human mind, for example, experiences itself as free with regard to some of the circumstances of its life and not free with regard to other circumstances. We experience our freedom when we "choose" which of our desires to follow: what to eat, where to live, with whom to associate, etc. But we do not believe that we freely chose our body, our sex, or our parents. But yet, the fact that we are born to one set of parents rather than to another—or that we are of one sex rather than the other, or that we grew up in one geographical location rather than another, etc.—these are not things that merely "happen" to us, but rather are consequences of the Divine Nature that freely and continuously manifests itself.

Therefore, there is a level of consciousness, a mind within the Attribute of Thought, for whom the above facts are experienced as conscious choices, in a way similar to how *we* experience what to have for dinner as a conscious choice. This larger mind is, of course, the soul in which we have our being. For just as a great work of art is produced as a free spontaneous expression of the artist's creativity, so also an individual human mind is produced as a free spontaneous expression of the creative forces within the soul. But since the human personality is obviously strongly conditioned by environmental forces (parents, culture, etc.), it follows that the soul, in "choosing" to manifest a portion of itself in the form of a specific human personality, must also choose the environmental conditions that will produce the given personality. Therefore, the fact that we have certain parents rather than others is experienced by the soul as a "free choice."

This way of looking at things raises many questions concerning the nature of the soul's experience of its freedom and the nature of relationships among souls, the answers to which we could not possibly begin to imagine. But this should no longer surprise us, since, as physics has shown, we cannot imagine—that is to say, we cannot form an image of—the full complexity of relationships that obtain among modes of Extension, although we can understand these relationships with ever increasing degrees of sophistication. Similarly, we cannot expect to be able to form an image of the full complexity of relationships that hold among modes of Thought, whether the mode in question is our own mind, or thoughts within our mind, or the larger mind (the soul) within which our own mind appears as a thought.

Nevertheless, certain things that we can understand but not imagine follow generally from our holistic metaphysical framework, and especially from what we have called the principle of holistic embedding. According to this principle, any given mind is embedded, or contained within, a larger mind that is itself contained within a still larger mind, etc., until one has arrived at the Mind of God, which contains within itself all individual minds. To the Mind of God everything whatsoever is "free," since there is nothing outside of itself that could in any way limit or constrain it. To minds within the Mind of God, some things are experienced as free and some things are not. Therefore, if there is some thing or some event that a given mind experiences as not free, it follows that the given mind must be embedded in a larger mind that experiences the given state of affairs as freely chosen.

Applying this to ourselves, there are many facts about our lives that we do not experience as free choices: our body, our parents, our sex, our talents, etc. Hence, our mind must be embedded in a larger mind that does experience these facts as a free choice. But it must be remembered, this larger mind is not something external to, or alien to, the nature of our own mind, any more than the cells in our body are alien to the nature of our body. Thus in no way can we regard ourselves as helpless victims of the choices of an alien intelligence; nor can we regard ourselves as victims in any sense—whether of fate, of circumstances beyond our control, of our parents' errors in raising us, etc. For the same soul that manifests a portion of itself as our identity also arranges the conditions and circumstances required to create that identity.

Our true freedom, or salvation, as we have said, consists in experiencing ourselves directly as a portion of a soul—or as Plato would put it, in remembering the soul that we truly are. As a step toward freedom, it is important to accept full responsibility for every fact and detail concerning our lives. In the absence of the direct experience of union with God and as a step toward that experience, we may intellectually identify with our soul—that is to say, with the creative forces within the Attribute of Thought of which we, the personality, are an effect. This "intellectual identification" is an example of using our *understanding* (knowledge of the second kind) as a stepping stone to spiritual insight (knowledge of the third kind). So, when we say to ourselves (as in the following exercise) "I chose my parents," we do not mean literally that the personality we now experience ourself to be chose its parents; that would be absurd, since the personality is a consequence of parentage. Rather, we mean to identify with the larger mind *in which* our personality is embedded, and *for which* the fact of our parentage *is* experienced as a choice. The following exercise will no doubt require considerable suspension of disbelief.

> **EXERCISE 8**: With eyes closed, simply repeat the sentence "I chose my parents" to yourself for four or five minutes. Notice your resistance to this idea. Does it irritate or anger you? Does your mind flood with a thousand and one reasons why, if it were a "choice," you would never have chosen the particular individuals who are your parents? As these and other objections race across your mind, remind yourself of the metaphysics involved: (1) God, or the Mind of God, is completely free; (2) all minds exist within the Mind of God; therefore, (3) for any and every state of affairs there must be a level of consciousness—an intelligence, a mind—that experiences that state of affairs as a free choice. (3) is simply a consequence of (2)—all things are in God—and (1) God is free. When we apply this consequence to our own lives, it means that every aspect and detail of our life, whether it be our parentage, our relationships, or even a physical illness, is experienced as a free choice by a larger mind in which our own mind is embedded. Using what I shall call the "language of choice" reminds us of this and helps us to align, intellectually, with the creative forces in the Attribute of Thought within which we have our being.

Using the language of choice, however, should not deceive us into thinking that the mind has "free will," in the sense imagined by Descartes and others. For, as we said earlier, the kind of experience we call a "free choice" is simply following a given desire or intention and each desire and intention is in turn caused by other mental causes, which are in turn caused by still other minds, etc., and this process of holistic embedding terminates in the Attribute of Thought as a Whole, which alone is free. Thus, when we say that the soul experiences the fact of our parentage as a free choice, we do not mean that the soul has a "will" that is independent of its connections with other mental structures within the Attribute of Thought. We mean only that the soul experiences something like a desire or intention to manifest a portion of itself in the form of a particular human personality. But this does not mean that the soul's desires do not themselves have causes, for as we have said, all things except for the Divine Being are caused—that is to say, all things are intrinsically connected to other things, and souls are no exception to this rule.

Nevertheless, until we attain the state of conscious union with the larger mind, or soul, of which we are a part, this identification with the "choice" of the soul is only intellectual, not experiential. For in the absence of the experience of union, what the soul experiences as a desire or choice, *we,* the personality, experience as a constraint or determination. The act of intellectually identifying with the soul's perspective, however, can fundamentally alter our *attitude* toward what we experience as our constraints. If the various constraints and difficulties of our lives are in fact desired for us by the soul, then the question immediately arises, why? For what purpose? That is to say, instead of assuming that the circumstances of our lives over which we have little or no control are the result of Cruel Fate or Blind Chance, we now assume that such circumstances are caused by a Purposeful Intelligence. Hence, whenever we come up against some obstacle in our lives, we do not lament, as does the victim of Fate or Chance, "Why is this happening to me?" but instead, reminding ourselves that what *we* experience as an obstacle the *soul* experiences as a choice, we ask simply "what is the purpose of this experience?" or "what can I learn from this?"

Psychophysical parallelism, causation, and purpose
At this point there are likely to be many objections, for here we are treading close to the so-called problem of evil: if everything is ultimately the result of a Divine Intelligence, why is there so much misery and suffering in the world? How could such things be the outcome of a *desire* on the part of our soul or on the part of a benevolent God? What grand "purpose" is served, say, by a soul incarnating into a genetically deformed body? It would seem better to believe that this world is the result of Blind Chance or Man's Evil rather than the result of Divine Purpose.

Although we will discuss such questions later, we note for now that many people would rather think about the world's problems than their own, and use such questions as an excuse to avoid responsibility for their own lives. We are urging a reversal of this habit of thinking. For peace and harmony will not be brought into the world by those who are not at peace within themselves; therefore, the first responsibility of anyone who sincerely wishes to alleviate the suffering of the world is to alleviate his own suffering as much as possible. For how can one who does not know how to alleviate his own suffering possibly know how to alleviate the suffering of others? Freedom from suffering comes through understanding, and understanding is facilitated by the attitude that there is purpose to our lives—to *all* aspects of our lives—and that these purposes are intelligible and can, with practice, be understood. We thus invite the reader to "try on" the attitude of purpose and to apply it to the details of his or her life.

EXERCISE 9: Select any aspect of your life that you do not experience as a "free choice" (e.g., your body, a difficult relationship, your work situation, etc.). Now remind yourself that it is no accident that you have the particular body, relationship, boss, etc., that you have and that, if it's no accident, then it must be "on purpose," so to speak. Then ask yourself, why did the larger mind of which I am a part desire this particular body, that particular relationship, etc. We do not, of course, necessarily expect a concrete verbal answer to these questions, although in time such an answer may come. But we do expect to feel a little differently, more positive and more accepting toward uncomfortable circumstances in our lives.

It is good to remind ourselves over and over again that in Nature nothing happens fortuitously—nothing happens that is not the result of some cause. When we conceive of Nature *physically,* under the Attribute of Extension, we conceive of these causes in terms of physical, including chemical and biological, forces. When we conceive of Nature *mentally*—under the Attribute of Thought—we conceive of them in terms of mental or psychic forces, that is, in terms of desire, intent, and purpose. For what we experience as our desires (including intentions and decisions) are, as we have previously shown, the forces with which we endeavor to persevere in our own existence. And any circumstance that pertains to our lives that we do not consciously experience as a choice or a desire—and this includes the fact that we exist as the unique body and personality that we are—*is* experienced as a choice or desire by another mind.

Let us dwell on this a little longer. Recall that the Divine Being, God, or Substance, manifests itself in infinitely many ways; each such manifestation is called an Attribute of God. Of the infinitely many Attributes that exist, only two are familiar to human experience: Thought and Extension. It may be helpful to recall our earlier metaphor in which we picture God standing in front of an infinite array of different mirrors, each of which reflects the entire Divine Being. Because each mirror (Attribute) is *distinct,* and because each mirror reflects Substance *completely,* it follows that any occurrence, or mode, in a given mirror, or Attribute, is explained or caused by other occurrences or modes in the same Attribute. There can be no causal influences from one Attribute to another.

Philosophers for ages have wondered how something mental can cause something physical and vice versa; how can there be an interaction between mind and body. Some, like Descartes, give up on the problem and conclude that it is one of those mysteries that we humans cannot hope to grasp. Others, like the materialist philosophers who dominate the academic scene today, also give up on the problem and conclude that minds do not exist (or to put it more charitably, that what we call conscious experience is entirely produced by the brain). For Spinoza, the mental and the physical are distinct manifestations of a single Divine Being and there is no causal influence from one to the other. The consequences of this metaphysical picture, when applied to ourselves, are enormous.

Consider that the question (1) "what is the cause of my body's existence and nature?" is totally different from the question (2) "what is the cause of my mind's existence and nature?" Even though the mind and body of a given human being are manifestations of one and the same mode of God, they are distinct manifestations, one occurring in the Attribute of Thought, the other in the Attribute of Extension. So when we are considering ourselves as body and ask questions concerning its cause, the explanations must be in terms of other bodies, that is, in terms of other modes within the Attribute of Extension (such as inherited genetic structure, nutrition, etc.). But when we are considering ourselves as minds and ask questions concerning *its* cause, the explanation must be in terms of other minds, that is, in terms of other modes or ideas within the Attribute of Thought. Now, within the Attribute of Extension we say that one thing influences or produces another through physical causes; but within the Attribute of Thought, one mind (or thought, or idea—these terms being used equivalently) influences or produces another through mental or psychic causes. Although mental causes are as varied and diverse as are physical causes, we may conceive of them all as a form of intent or desire.

We hasten to mention here that each idea within the Attribute of Thought *experiences* desire and intent differently, each according to its own nature, so that, say, the desire of a soul to manifest a portion of itself as a human personality is a different kind of desire than the desire of a human personality to become a lawyer rather than a doctor. Just as we recognize that *appetite* is common to all living bodies while also recognizing that each body experiences its appetites differently—so that the appetite of an insect for food and sex differs from that of the lion, which differs from that of the human, etc.—so also we may characterize the creative activities of modes of Thought as preceding from intent or desire, while recognizing that the intent of one mind differs from that of another.

It follows then that since our mind is not the cause of its own existence, the cause of our mind's existence is the desire or intent of another mind. And, we note again, this other mind is not really "other"—that is, it is not something with respect to which our own mind is external any more than the genetic code that produces our body is external to the body it produces.

So when we say that we—our mind—exist "on purpose" rather than by accident, we mean simply that our existence as the unique individual personality that we are, is desired, is wanted, is intended, by the larger mind in which we have our being. And we have every right to take comfort in this and to use this knowledge as an antidote to feelings of loneliness and despair. This is in part what Spinoza means in the passage already quoted: "everyone exists by the highest right of nature."

It should be apparent by now that Spinoza's views concerning the relationship between our mind and our body are very different from those of the culture at large, and this difference cannot be overemphasized. It is commonly believed, for example, that the cause of a perception of a thing—which perception is necessarily *mental*—is the *physical* thing itself. It is believed that the cause of our body's walking in one direction rather than another is our decision or intent to go one place rather than another. But both these beliefs are false, since they both involve the belief that there can be causal influences from one Attribute to another. Spinoza himself is very much aware of how deeply ingrained is this belief that body and mind causally interact with each other and addresses many objections against his view that they do not. We will consider one such objection, which goes as follows.

An objection to parallelism, and Spinoza's reply

It is difficult to believe that the great creative artistic works of human beings could be produced by the body alone without direction from the mind. For example, if we consider a beautiful painting, then according to Spinoza, since the painting is itself a physical object, its cause must also be physical, that is, it is produced entirely by the motions of the artist's body. That is, the mind of the artist (which includes her ideas, intentions, deliberations, etc., about what and how to paint) has nothing to do, causally, with producing the painting. In Spinoza's own words, "they will say, of course, that it cannot happen that the causes of buildings, of paintings, and of things of this kind, which are made only by human skill, should be able to be deduced from the laws of human nature alone, insofar as it is considered to be only corporeal; nor would the human body be able to build a temple, if it were not determined and guided by the mind" (*Ethics;* pt. 3, prop. 2, note).

There are three components to Spinoza's reply: [1] "But I have already shown that they do not know what the body can do, or what can be deduced from the consideration of its nature alone, and [2] that they know from experience that a great many things happen from the laws of (corporeal) nature alone which they never would have believed could happen without the direction of the mind—such things that sleepwalkers do in their sleep which they wonder at when they are awake." Moreover, [3] "I add here the very structure of the human body, which in the ingenuity of its construction, far surpasses anything made by human skill." Let us elaborate.

1. Many animals build very complex structures—termite mounds, spider webs, beaver dams, bird nests, etc. The more we study these structures, the more amazed we become at how sophisticated they are. Termites, for example, not only regulate the temperature of their environment to within a fraction of a degree, but also farm a species of fungi that they feed to their larvae and which fungi grows nowhere else. This, by any definition, is "purposeful behavior." (Unless of course, one defines purposeful behavior to be something of which *only* humans are capable. But such a definition would be extremely anthropomorphic and would beg the question at hand.) And yet we do not believe that the termites' conscious intent is required in order to explain how they build the structures they do. Although scientists may not fully understand how termites do what they do, they—the scientists—believe that termite behavior results from instinct rather than from conscious intent. Now, of course, the term "instinct" begs many, many questions and is often used to create the impression that we understand something that we don't. To say that the beaver builds its dam *by instinct* or that the spider spins its web *by instinct* is to convey no understanding whatsoever about how beavers build dams or spiders spin webs. Nevertheless, the term "instinct" reflects a commitment to searching for the causes of such purposeful behavior solely in the physical world, without resorting to nonphysical elements such as the conscious intent, or the mind, of the animal.

   To be sure, there is in the Attribute of Thought, an idea, a mind, that is to say, a conscious experience, that runs "parallel" to the bodily behavior of a given termite (beaver, spider, etc.), and this "conscious experience" may be called the *mind* of the given termite (beaver, spider, etc.). But this mind is not causally involved in producing either the animal or its behavior.

So it is with human beings. Our body does many things that fall under the category of "purposeful behavior": it prepares food, builds shelters, walks in one direction rather than another, reads books, converses with others, and, yes, builds temples. And for each of these behaviors there is a conscious experience (such as desire, intent, emotion) in the Attribute of Thought, which runs parallel to the behavior. Yet, as with other animals, the conscious experience is not the cause of the body's behavior. All these various bodily behaviors exist in the Attribute of Extension and must therefore be explained solely by physical causes. If the beaver can build a home for itself and its young by "instinct" alone, why cannot we?! This is what Spinoza means when he says we "do not know what the body can do."

2. We may add to Spinoza's example of the sleepwalker a kind of case that is well known today, namely, that the body seems to function at its best when the conscious mind makes no attempt whatsoever to control its movements. Athletes, musicians, martial artists, actors—performing artists of any kind—know that their bodies function maximally, and are capable of amazing feats, in those moments when their mind is totally able to let go of its incessant efforts to control and manipulate the body. During such moments ("peak experiences," as the psychologist Abraham Maslow calls them) we move outside the limitations of the personality and become a detached observer. The mind experiences itself as merely observing, or witnessing, what the body is doing *by itself,* as it were. Although according to Spinoza the mind *never* controls the body, during peak experiences we become aware of this, and this awareness is accompanied by an almost ecstatic delight and joy. Would it not be wonderful if this awareness could be enjoyed continuously?!

3. The more we learn about the human body through science, the more we are able to appreciate the complexity and harmony of its construction. Indeed, any organism, even a single-celled bacterium, is orders of magnitude more complex than any action or behavior the organism does. Nothing the human body does, including the building of temples, even remotely approaches the structural complexity of the body itself. And yet we have no trouble believing

that the body is a part of the physical world, that it evolved naturally in accordance with and as a consequence of physical laws, and that the explanation for its structure must be found in the physical world—in the Attribute of Extension. But is it not strange to believe both (a) that a structure as complex as the human body can come into existence without the guidance of a mind, but (b) that a structure as relatively simple as a temple cannot come into existence without the guidance of a mind?

We also note that there are many examples of purposeful behavior *within* the body, which behavior we do not deem necessary to explain in terms of a mind. For example, when a foreign bacterium enters our body, white blood cells mobilize to attack and destroy the invader. The behavior of the white blood cells is as purposeful as anything the human body does as a whole. We say that the white blood cells mobilize "in order to" and "for the purpose of" repelling the invader and protecting the body. Yet we believe that every aspect of the behavior of white blood cells can be explained in physical terms. We do not believe that the purposeful behavior of the blood cells requires a mind to direct it.

To be sure, there exists in the Attribute of Thought an idea or mind of each individual cell. But the idea or mind of a given cell is not the cause of its physical behavior. The cause of a cell's behavior is to be found in its inner structure and in its relationships with other physical things, even though there is within the Attribute of Thought a conscious experience that correlates with the cell's behavior. Is it not odd to believe that the purposeful behavior that occurs within the body (and we could add examples of this without limit) does *not* require a mind to guide it, but that the purposeful behavior of the body as a whole—such as walking one way rather than another, building a temple, etc.—*does* require a mind to guide it? Consistency demands that we commit ourselves to conceive the human body in the same way we conceive all other bodies: it is a mode of Substance, a part of God, insofar as God is considered to have manifested herself as the physical world. Hence, everything about the body—its cause, its internal structure, its behavior—must be understood solely in physical terms.

All this follows quite straightforwardly from Spinoza's metaphysics. For if Thought and Extension are qualitatively distinct, they can have nothing in common, and if they have nothing in common, they cannot interact. Our body is a part of God insofar as God manifests as Extension; our mind is the same part of God insofar as God manifests as Thought.

So, if it is the case that there is no interaction between mind and body, what then *is* the relationship then between the (mental) decision to walk one way rather than another and the body's actual (physical) walking one way rather than another? It is rather simple. At the moment we become (a) aware of our decision, the body, especially the brain, is in (b) a state of readiness to direct the muscles to move the body. (b), not (a), is the cause of (c) the body's walking in whichever direction it walks. (a) and (b) occur simultaneously; indeed, they are *one and the same* mode of the Divine Being manifested in the Attributes of Thought and Extension, respectively. We fall into the error of believing that (a) is the cause of (c) because we are generally conscious of (a) and (c), but not of (b). But clearly, any motion *of* our body, whether it be walking down the street, eating dinner, or building a temple, is caused *by* our body together with external stimuli acting *on* our body, and *not* by the awareness (which may take the form of a decision) that may accompany such motions.

Furthermore, if (a) is not the cause of either (b) or (c), then, conversely, neither (b) nor (c)—both of which are physical—is the cause of (a), which is mental. If it is asked, well then, *what is* the cause of (a), of my awareness of what my body is doing, the answer is the same as the answer to a similar question we discussed earlier concerning sense perception. For if, as we there concluded, the cause of a given sense perception is not the physical object that appears within the perception, then we can ask, well, what is the cause of my perception? In both cases, awareness and perception are modes of Thought and hence are caused by other ideas within the Attribute of Thought. Although these "other ideas" are generally unknown to our mind—or to the imaginative portion of our mind—it is nevertheless possible to discuss them. In our discussions of emotions to follow, we will give some clear examples that exhibit this structure—examples of modes of thought, or emotions that seem to be caused by events within the physical world but which, upon analysis, are seen to be caused by other ideas within our own psyche. Most systems of psychotherapy rest on this principle.

Dreaming, a context that exhibits the causal structure of Spinoza's psychophysical parallelism

Nevertheless, the illusions of sense perception are very difficult to penetrate, and so we offer the following analogy. Let us suppose you are having a dream, and in the dream you are walking along a path which at some point divides in two; you pause for a moment to "decide" which path to follow—we'll call them A and B—and then you begin walking along, say, path B. As you continue along, B you meet someone who engages you in philosophical conversation, and in particular, she asks you *why* you are walking along path B—that is, she asks you what is the cause of your body's walking along B rather than A. Not suspecting you are dreaming, you will respond with something like the following: "I'm now walking along B because when the path forked I *decided* to take this path," or "I *thought* this path would be the more interesting one," or "I *wanted* to walk this way." That is, you would say that the cause of your *body's* behavior (walking along B) is something in your mind (a decision, thought, desire, etc.).

But now, when you wake up, your analysis will be completely different. First of all, you would probably resist answering the question on its own terms. For once awake you realize it was all a dream and that your body did not "really" walk along B. Nevertheless, it certainly seemed to you at the time that your body was walking along B. Indeed, while dreaming we tacitly make the same sort of division into mental and physical as we do with our experiences when awake. Under *physical* we put our body, its behavior, and anything and all things that seem to originate *outside* of us: the paths A and B and anyone we meet along the path. Under *mental* we put anything that seems to be *inside* of us: thoughts, emotions, decisions, etc. Yet, when we wake up, we know that however we may analyze our dreams, it is certainly not the case that our *decision* to walk along B causes the body to walk along B, any more than, say, the fear that seems to be caused by a monster who chases us in some dream is actually caused by the monster. For in each case, I think we would want to say that both the inner *and* the outer—the fear *and* the monster, the decision *and* the body's behavior, are different aspects of the same underlying reality.

Dreaming then provides us with a context in which what seems to be a causal relationship between inner and outer experience—while dreaming it seems to us that the "inner" fear is caused by an "outer" monster and that the "outer" motion of the body is caused by an "inner" decision of the mind, etc.—is, upon awakening, seen to be not causal at all. Rather, one and the same state of mind of the dreamer produces both inner and outer. The fear and the monster are different projections of one and the same state of mind of the person who has the dream.

Now, in waking life we make the same distinction between inner and outer experience, calling the former mental and the latter physical. By denying that there is any causal influence from one to the other, Spinoza is saying that they are different projections, different manifestations, of the same underlying reality. This underlying reality is, in Spinoza's language, a mode of God, which, when projected into the Attribute of Thought, is experienced as fear, decision, etc., and when projected into the Attribute of Extension is the state of our body that corresponds with fear, decision, etc.

This analogy may be pushed a little further. We have already referred to the state of consciousness known to psychologists as *lucid dreaming*. The physiological indicators (brain wave patterns and rapid eye movements) show that during lucid dreaming the person is both awake *and* dreaming. Subjectively, this state is experienced as dreaming while at the same time being completely aware that one is in fact dreaming. The goal of Spinoza's system of therapy is to attain an analogous state of mind, which he characterizes as "blessedness," "union with the whole of nature," "intuitive knowledge," "intellectual love of God," etc. It is a state that, following our analogy, we may call lucid waking, in which we are fully conscious of our true identity as spirit and of our connections with the larger mind in which we have our being. It is a state of mind that is accompanied by intense delight.

THE DEFINITION OF EMOTIONS

We now return to Spinoza's account of emotions. Earlier we said that *desire*—whether it be an appetite of the body or a decision of the mind, and whether it be conscious or not—constitutes our very essence. It is the sole motivational force by which we are what we are and do what we do. Our desires are, in a manner of speaking, our temporal subjective experience of God's "will" that we be what we are and do what we do. Now, the human experience of desire shows us that our desires are highly determined by our emotions—by our hopes and fears, ambitions and insecurities—and that often we find ourselves seeking for things that our better judgment knows is not in our self-interest. For example, tobacco, alcohol, and junk food are things we commonly seek for our bodies *knowing*, at least partially, that these things are not good for us.

Similarly, we know at least partially, that emotions such as envy, greed, guilt, and worry, together with the desires that generally follow from them, are not good for us and yet we actively pursue them, in some cases devoting our whole lives to them. And when we say "not good for us," we do not mean that such emotions are "bad" or "immoral"; we mean only that such emotions are harmful to the person who suffers from them. Thus in order to better understand why we desire things that are *not* good for us and in order to align our desires with our knowledge of what *is* good for us, we must develop a theory of emotions.

Spinoza's theory of emotions is based directly on his underlying metaphysics. A human being is a part of God, which part we call *the body* when we conceive of God as constituting the physical universe, and *the mind* when we conceive of God as constituting the mental universe. Recalling our concept of holistic embedding and considering for the moment just the body, it is obvious that the body is both embedded within a larger physical system, and is itself a larger whole that contains within itself many other bodies and systems of bodies; and each of these other bodies, such as a cell, is also both embedded in a larger whole—an organ, say—and is itself a larger whole within which other bodies—e.g., molecules—are contained. The human body is thus composite to a high degree. And since for each body there is a mind or idea, it follows also that the human mind—the personality—is composite to a high degree.

Now, the human body is in dynamic equilibrium with its environment. "Dynamic" means that the body continuously interacts with its environment. "Equilibrium" means that throughout these interactions the body seeks to *persevere in its own being,* that is, to maintain its own form. For, if the parts of the body fail to sustain a harmony with one another, or should the body as a whole fail to sustain a harmony with its environment, then the body weakens, sickens, and dies. The body's endeavor to persevere in its own being is therefore simply its ability to maintain its own form while continuously interacting with its environment.

Of the many and diverse interactions between the body and the external world, some of them (1) increase the body's ability to persevere in its own being; others (2) decrease the body's ability to persevere in its own being; and still others (3) neither increase nor decrease the body's ability to persevere in its own being. Some examples might be (1) eating healthy foods, moderate exercise; (2) breathing polluted air, addiction to various drugs; and (3) simple sense perception (with no emotional overtones). We define an *emotion* to be any increase or decrease in the body's ability to persevere in its own being, or power of acting, together with the corresponding idea of that increase. Let us now explicate this definition.

Power of acting
By the phrase, "power of acting," we mean to refer to the body's (or the mind's) ability to maintain its own form, or persevere in its own being, in the midst of continuous interactions with other bodies (or minds). For example, two bodies may be exposed to the same infectious disease, yet one contracts the disease, the other does not. We say that the one who does not contract the disease has a greater ability to maintain its own form—has more strength or power to

resist an external body that seeks to weaken it—than the one who becomes ill. Similarly, two individuals may be criticized in the same way, yet one becomes despondent and the other simply resolves to correct his mistake. Clearly, the latter person has what therapists would call greater ego strength—a greater ability or strength to maintain his sense of self while interacting with others. The reader is cautioned not to associate Spinoza's phrase "power of acting" with the ability to get one's way with others, push people around, or accomplish many worldly things.

Indeed, the terms "act," "action," and "acting" are technical terms in Spinoza's system. An action, whether of the mind or the body, is for Spinoza, *self-motivated* behavior. Very little of human behavior is self-motivated in Spinoza's sense; most behavior (including what we think as well as what our body does) is a passive *re-action* to our perceptions of others, as experienced through a highly distorting filter of internalized emotions, desires, and beliefs. For example, a person who seeks political power to control others is not "powerful" in Spinoza's sense; on the contrary, such a person is generally motivated by various fears and insecurities that were caused by forces external to himself (such as childhood experiences) and of which he is unaware. Although such individuals may make a lot of noise, their behaviors are merely passive reactions, not actions. The highest action, as we shall see, in which the mind can participate, is contemplation of God.

Thus, the phrase "power of action" means something like "the ability for self-motivated behavior." This ability differs from person to person and, within the same person, may fluctuate widely from one time to another.

By the phrase "corresponding idea" we do *not* mean an abstract intellectual construction, or "theory," or "conceptual understanding" that we may form to "explain" our behavior. This would imply that emotions are one thing and their ideas something else. We remind the reader that for Spinoza *ideas* are not something passive, like "dumb pictures on a tablet," which would require a mind to "have" or "think" them. Rather, just as "body" is the generic term used to refer to any mode of Extension, so "idea" and "mind" are generic terms used to refer to any mode of Thought. The human mind is the idea that corresponds to the human body; or, as Spinoza puts it, the human mind and the human body are one and the same mode of God expressed in the Attributes of Thought and Extension, respectively. Now, *within* the human body there are many other bodies (e.g., cells), systems of bodies (e.g., the digestive system), and processes involving dynamic interactions among many bodies (e.g., digestion). Therefore, *within* the idea that is the human mind, there are many other ideas or minds, systems of ideas or minds, and processes involving dynamic interactions among many such ideas or minds. So, if the human body—either as a whole, or some part of it, or some part within it— is strengthened or weakened, then the idea or mind that corresponds to it—or some part within it—will also be strengthened or weakened. Then its power of acting increases or decreases, and this is what constitutes an emotion.

Almost all emotions are inadequate ideas. For example, if our body's power of acting has been increased due to some interaction with the external world, then the cause of that increase must involve the natures both of our own body and the external body. Hence, the idea or mind that corresponds to that increase—which idea or mind *is* the emotion or feeling—is caused by both our own mind and the mind of the external body.

The structure here is the same as in sense perception. For whenever our body, or portion of our body, interacts with an external body, it becomes part of a larger physical system, which system includes all the interacting bodies *and* has holistic properties not reducible to the sum of the bodies that constitute the system. The idea or mind that corresponds to this "larger mental system" contains within itself both our own mind and the mind of the external body. This "larger psychic system" is itself an adequate idea in the Attribute of Thought, and it has holistic properties not reducible to its constituent minds. What we experience as emotions are holistic properties within this larger psychic structure and hence they are inadequate when referred to our mind alone.

We note that because the human body has a very rich internal structure, containing within itself many bodies that are themselves constituted by other bodies, etc., it is quite possible for a given interaction to simultaneously strengthen one part of our body while weakening another part; or it is possible that a given interaction could strengthen a part of the body while weakening the body as a whole. So it is possible for one and the same external body to trigger many conflicting emotions within us. We will elaborate on this later.

At this point we wish to clarify our usage of the term "the human mind." Spinoza himself characterizes the human mind as the idea of the body, which means, as we have often emphasized, not some idea that the body *has,* which would be absurd, but rather that idea in the Attribute of Thought that corresponds with that particular mode in Extension that *is* the human body. But this characterization has led to much confusion about his claim that the mind does not perish with the body; for, if the mind is the idea of the body, why does it not perish when the body dies? Spinoza exacerbates this confusion when, after acknowledging that all memory—and everything that pertains to the Imagination—perishes with the body, he states that, nevertheless, some part of the mind does not perish. So, as many commentators have asked, how can there be a mind, or a portion of a mind, when there is no longer any body, if we conceive the mind to be the idea of the body?

In order to avoid such questions—which really involve the error of thinking that the mind is a temporal object—it seems to me better to conceive the mind as a mode of thought, as an idea within the Mind of God, and as such, eternal. The word "eternal" means simply "not within time"; it does not mean something that lasts forever in time. Now, as a portion of the physical world begins to organize itself into the form of a particular body (human or other), a portion of the mind begins to organize *itself* into a form that is the consciousness associated with that particular body (and vice versa; although language forces us to use temporal terms like "begins," this is ultimately not a temporal process). This consciousness is simply the idea or the mind that correlates with the body's experiences and contains within itself all memories, sense perceptions, and emotions. We have been calling this the Imagination, or the imaginative portion of the mind, or the personality. The Imagination is thus a structure of psychic organization that has its being within a larger psychic structure, which we have been calling "the whole mind," or the "larger mind," or the "higher self."

Earlier, we gave an example from physics to show how the entire temporal order of physical things could be contained within an eternal object. Now, although the Imagination, insofar as it is a mode of thought, does not exist in time, it is nevertheless a structure of psychic organization to which—or to whom—time appears real. But this "appearing real" is itself contained within a pattern of psychic organization, of the whole mind, which experiences itself as eternal. And thus again, the temporal is contained within the eternal.

At any rate, it does not matter for our present purpose whether we interpret the phrase "the human mind" to refer to the whole mind or just to its imaginative portion, because only the imaginative portion is involved in human emotions. For given any decrease or increase in the body's (or any part of the body's) power of action, there is a corresponding idea in the Attribute of Thought, which idea exists within the imaginative portion of the mind. For brevity in our discussion of the emotions, we may drop the qualifying phrase "the imaginative portion."

We may thus use the name of any specific emotion to refer either to the specific state of, or within, the body, *or,* to the associated idea of that state, *or* to both. The term "depression," for example, may be used to refer to the psychological nexus of feelings and moods, or to the physiological state of the body that accompanies the psychological state, or to both. However the words are used, it should be clear that every emotion has both a physical and a mental aspect. The physical aspect is simply the physiological changes within the body that constitute an increase or decrease in the body's power of action; the mental aspect is the idea or mind of that change, which idea or mind constitutes the corresponding increase or decrease in the (imaginative portion of the) mind's power of action.

It will be good, before proceeding further, to gain a more experiential understanding of the term "power of action." Now, there are very obvious examples of increases and decreases in our power of action. For example, our power of action is relatively lowered when we are in pain or are depressed, and it is relatively heightened when our body is alert after moderate exercise, or when we feel especially self-confident. But our power of action fluctuates many times throughout the day, and it is important to begin to cultivate a sensitivity to these more subtle changes. For, although all of these changes are emotions, not all emotions have names, and we wish to bring awareness to these fluctuations themselves, regardless of whether they have names.

EXERCISE 10: At the end of the day, reflect back upon the various interactions you had with other people. You will notice that some of your interactions were more enjoyable than others. The enjoyable interactions were the ones in which you were relatively more expressive of yourself; you felt more free to say what you were thinking and feeling. The more difficult interactions were the ones in which you were relatively less expressive of yourself, or you felt inhibited to say what you were truly thinking. Focus now on one expressive interaction and one inhibited interaction, recalling the details of each one in turn, and feel the difference in your body. For example, the feeling in your body during a relatively inhibited interaction may be a tightness in your chest or throat, a hollow feeling in the pit of your stomach, shallow breathing, etc. This feeling is the decrease in your body's power of action. Later we will learn what we can do toward alleviating such feelings; the first step is to become as conscious as possible of these fluctuations. Eventually, we wish to bring such awareness to our interactions while they are happening, so that in the midst of a given interaction a part of our awareness is focused on the changes, sometimes subtle, sometimes obvious, occurring within our body.

Joy and sorrow, the primary emotions

Spinoza uses the words "joy" and "sorrow" to refer to any increase or decrease, respectively, in our power of action. In Spinoza's words:

> By *joy*, therefore, I shall understand in what follows, that passion [1] by which the mind passes to a greater perfection [2]. And by *sorrow*, that passion by which it passes to a lesser perfection. The emotion of joy which is related to the mind and body at once [3] I call pleasure or cheerfulness, and that of sorrow, pain or melancholy [depression]. But it should be noted that pleasure and pain are ascribed to a man when one part of him is affected more than the rest, whereas cheerfulness and melancholy are ascribed to him when all are equally affected [4].
>
> "I have (previously) explained what desire is, and apart from these three (desire, joy, and sorrow) I do not acknowledge any other primary emotion. For I shall show in what follows that the rest arises from these three [5]." (*Ethics*, pt. 3, prop. 11)

Let us comment:

1. "Passion" is to be contrasted with "action." The term "passion," for Spinoza, does not mean, as it does in ordinary English, an intense emotion; rather, it means something with respect to which we are passive. A passion is an inadequate idea; it is something of which we are a partial cause only, the remainder of the cause being external to ourselves. So, to the extent that the cause of any given emotion is external to ourself, to that extent is the emotion a passion and we are said to suffer from it. And this is so regardless of whether the emotion is a joy or a sorrow; that is, regardless of whether the emotion involves an increase or a decrease in the body's power of acting and/or the mind's power of thinking; so long as that increase or decrease involves an external cause, it is a passion. Since almost every emotion arises through interaction with the external world, it follows that almost every emotion is a passion.

2. Emotions are inherently transitory; they come into being not with the *arrival* at a state of greater or lesser perfection, but with the *passage* to such a state. The phrase "greater perfection" should not be construed in any absolute or moralistic sense. Indeed, the whole phrase "passes to a greater or lesser perfection" is more idiomatically expressed in English as "becomes relatively strengthened or weakened." Thus, for example, a child, hoping to receive a special toy for his birthday, experiences joy if he gets it and sorrow if he doesn't; but, as every parent knows, the joy or sorrow does not last, for the emotion comes into being with the transition from a state of expectation to a state of either getting the toy, in which case joy is experienced, or not getting the toy, in which case sorrow is experienced. Once the child has accommodated to this new state, the joy or sorrow quickly dissipates.

3. Of course, *every* emotion involves both the body and the mind, since for every modification of our body there is an idea in our mind, which is the idea of the given bodily modification (whether or not we are conscious of that idea). And vice versa, for every modification of the imaginative portion of our mind, there is a counterpart in our body. What is meant here is simply that many of the terms we use to talk about our emotions refer to the emotion under one Attribute or the other. If, for example, we say of a man that he is envious, or in love, we usually mean to refer to something in his mind—in his psychological makeup. There is of course something going on in his body that corresponds with the feelings of envy, love, etc.; but the term "envy" refers more to the state of his mind than to the parallel physiological state of his body. On the other hand, terms like "pain," "pleasure," "cheerfulness," and "depression" (the term "melancholy" is hopelessly old-fashioned; I will use "depression" from now on) refer to both the psychological state and its physiological counterpart.

4. The human body (and mind) is composite to a high degree, that is to say, it is constituted by many other bodies (and minds). A given interaction may affect one or more constituent parts of the body (mind), or it may affect the body as a whole. A person with an ulcer, say, experiences pain in his stomach, but a person who is depressed experiences an overall decrease in his body's—and each part of his

body's—power of action. It should be noted that in our culture depression is far more common than cheerfulness, which means that our interpersonal interactions are on the whole far more destructive than conducive to individual physical health and psychological well-being.

5. Spinoza here is making the truly remarkable claim that the full richness and variety of human emotional experience is derivative from—is built up from—the three primary emotions, joy, sorrow, and desire. This claim that "the rest arises from these three" is so important to Spinoza's theory of emotions and its consequent therapy, and so likely to be regarded as implausible by the reader, that it will be good to discuss it at some length.

   (a) First of all, the claim, as Spinoza states it, is not quite correct. More accurately, as we shall see from numerous examples, the rest of the emotions arise from joy, sorrow, and desire only when the latter are conjoined with beliefs about their cause. *Hatred* toward a given person or object, for example, is defined as *sorrow* together with the *belief* that the given person or object is the cause of the sorrow. As everyone knows, beliefs about the causes of things may be very complex. Also, we may not be fully conscious of all of our beliefs. And of course, beliefs do not have to be true in order to play a causal role in generating emotional experience; for everyone experiences the world according to his or her beliefs, regardless of their accuracy.

   (b) The claim follows rigorously from the general metaphysical system we have previously developed. For a human being is a mode of God, which when conceived under the Attribute of Extension is the human body, and when conceived under the Attribute of Thought is the human mind. As such—as a mode of Extension or Thought—it endeavors or strives to persevere in its being, to increase its power of acting or thinking. But this *striving* does not occur in a vacuum. The striving of the body occurs in the context of constant interaction with other bodies; the striving of the mind occurs in the context of constant interaction with other minds. Any given interaction must either increase, decrease, or leave unaffected the body's (mind's) ability to persevere in its own being. The first two we experience subjectively as joy and sorrow, respectively. Thus, the emotions are defined in terms of the metaphysics in a very natural way.

(c) Again, from the metaphysics, we know that the human being, in both mind and body, is a highly complex mode of Substance, consisting of numerous other modes (conceived both as bodies and as minds), which in turn are constituted by still other modes, etc. Now, the *striving* referred to under (b) is a most general feature of every mode of God, in every Attribute whatsoever. The existence of each thing—its coming to exist, its continuing to exist, and its ceasing to exist—follows from the Nature of God. What we have called the *striving* of a given thing is simply—to put it somewhat anthropomorphically—how that thing experiences God's intent that it be. Therefore, considering now the human being, this *striving* pertains not only to the human being as a whole, but also to each part within the human being, to each part of each part, etc., It is thus quite possible for one and the same interaction to increase the power of one part of us while simultaneously decreasing the power of another part; or for a given interaction to increase the power of one part of us while simultaneously decreasing the power of our body (mind) as a whole. When coupled with what we have said about beliefs, this shows the general possibility of a rich complexity of emotions, e.g., that we can love and hate the same person at the same time.

(d) And finally, the *holistic* nature of Spinoza's system must be kept firmly in mind, otherwise one may raise spurious objections, such as "the emotion of love just doesn't *feel* like joy plus a belief about its cause." Of course it doesn't.

Neither does salt taste like a combination of sodium plus chlorine. The whole—whether conceived as physical or as mental—always has properties not reducible to the sum of its constituent parts. Furthermore, properties of the parts need not also be properties of the whole that they constitute. Thus, we are not surprised that salt neither burns at room temperature nor is lethal to humans, even though it is constituted by sodium—which *does* burn at room temperature—and chlorine—which *is* lethal to humans. The same holds for ideas. A given idea, say, a specific feeling of love toward some object, may be constituted by an idea that is a feeling of joy plus another idea that is a belief that the object caused the joy, and yet have holistic properties not reducible to the latter, constituent ideas.

Love and hate

Hopefully enough has been said to explain and make plausible Spinoza's claim that "the rest arises from these three." We now proceed to show *how* the rest arises from these three. Spinoza defines *love* as "joy with the accompanying idea of an external cause" and *hate* as "sorrow accompanied by the idea of an external cause." There is probably no word in the English language about which there is more confusion than the term "love." To remove at least some of the confusion and to better understand Spinoza's usage of the term, we here introduce a philosophical distinction.

Sometimes we use the expression "I love X" to describe a feeling I am now having toward X; we will call this the *occurrent* usage of the expression (because the expression occurs or is used at the same time that the feeling occurs). Other times, we use the expression "I love X" to refer, not to a present feeling of love toward X, but rather to a general tendency, or disposition, to have loving feelings toward X; this is the *dispositional* use of the word "love." Thus, a person may now be experiencing hatred toward another for whom he generally feels love. Consider, for example, a friend who says to you "I love my husband but I can't stand him when he criticizes me so much." Here, the word "love" is being used in its dispositional sense—the friend is saying, "most of the time when I'm around my husband, or think about him, my power of action increases, that is to say, I feel love toward him; but at those times when he criticizes me too much, my power of action decreases, that is to say, I feel hate toward him."

And, to further complicate things, the word "love" is sometimes used in its spiritual sense ("agape" is the Christian word). Used in this sense, it refers to an ability, or power, to feel and extend unconditional caring to all other human beings. We do not have this power except insofar as we become conscious of the union that exists between our own mind and the Mind of God. Much confusion arises when people romanticize their emotions and falsely believe themselves capable of unconditional caring.

There is yet another sense of the word "love," which greatly adds to the confusion between the dispositional sense and the occurrent sense. A person may use the expression "I love you" toward another with whom he has no true feeling of love, either occurrently or dispositionally, but with whom he is in a relationship that society dictates *should be* loving.

For example, two people may be in a relationship—husband-wife, parent-child—which for years has been devoid of any real positive feelings for one another. They may still mechanically say "I love you" to one another, but such expressions in this context refer only to a social role and not to any really occurring positive feelings. People may actually believe they love one another, even though the real feelings may be resentment, bitterness, and anger. We will use the term "nominal" (meaning, "in name only") to characterize the usage of the word "love" in the absence of any real feeling of love, that is to say, in the absence of any increase in one's power of acting.

Spinoza uses the term "love" primarily in its occurrent sense—to describe a feeling that one is *presently* having. Nevertheless, since the nominal sense is very widely used—leading to much self-deception—and since it is used mainly in the context of familial relations, which are in themselves of immense importance, we wish to say a few things about such relations in general.

We have already said that since everything is an expression of God's Nature, it is therefore no accident, no cosmic fluke of fate, that each person has in his or her life the particular individuals who are his or her parents, children, siblings, lovers, etc. And, as we have also already said, if such relationships are no accident, then they are on purpose. This "purpose" is determined, not, of course, by the personality, which is itself a consequence of the purpose, but by the soul in which the personality is embedded. Moreover, what is true for us individually is also true for those with whom we are in close relationship; that is, if the soul that contains the personality named John has chosen the personality named Mary to be his (John's) mother, then the soul that contains the personality named Mary has chosen the personality named John to be her (Mary's) son. Since this mutuality extends to all relations between and among all people, it follows that the degree of cooperation and harmony among souls is such as to far exceed the ability of human imagination to comprehend (although our reason tells us that this must be the case, since it follows from the metaphysics that the souls must collectively constitute the mind of a single individual, which Plato refers to as the "World-Soul").

We *can* speak of a force operating in the Attribute of Thought that attracts various souls together for a common purpose, and this force can be thought of as "spiritual" love. We can thus conclude that any personality with whom we are in close relationship—and this includes adversarial as well as supportive relationships—is in our lives as a consequence of the spiritual love that exists at the soul level. But just as two actors can be good friends and yet play adversarial roles on the stage, so also can souls be good friends, so to speak, and yet play adversarial roles in the theater of life.

We must not deceive ourselves into thinking that, because there is necessarily great love between the souls, or higher selves, of two individuals, that the associated personalities will also experience love. To the contrary, the personalities may very well experience intense hatred. We can acknowledge, therefore, that all familial relations come to be because of love between and among the souls involved and, at the same time, acknowledge that we do not experience this love, or anything like it, insofar as we are associated with our bodies.

Indeed, *love,* as Spinoza defines it, is a temporal term indicating a *passage* to a greater perfection and applies only to the personality. We must agree to use the term "love" (and all other terms signifying emotions) so that it refers to something we experience as real. So long as we are not experientially conscious of our connection with God, we are not able to experience as real the love that exists between souls. To think that we love a parent toward whom we in fact feel enormous amounts of guilt, resentment, etc., is a form of self-deception. We may, in such a case, intellectually acknowledge and even appreciate their role as our parent or assure ourselves of the spiritual love that exists between the souls involved, but this is not what we are in fact feeling at present. The present feelings are (by hypothesis) guilt and resentment, which, insofar as they involve a decrease in our power of action, are forms of hatred. We may *wish* to feel love, but the first step is to acknowledge and experience our true "here and now" feelings. We must, therefore, as much as possible, avoid using the word "love" in its nominal sense. The following exercise will assist the reader in becoming more aware of his or her true feelings.

EXERCISE 11: On a piece of paper, make a list of your immediate familial relations—parents, children, spouse (you may include lovers and close friends). One at a time, visualize or imagine each person on your list; spend at least three or four minutes with each person. As you are visualizing a given person, notice the feelings you are experiencing and write them down. Pay attention to the subtle changes in your body as you experience your feelings. For example, when you imagine your father, does your throat constrict? Does your stomach tighten? Is your breathing more shallow? These are indications of an overall decrease in your body's power of acting. Or, is your breathing freer and more expansive? Do muscles relax in your body? These are indications of an overall increase in your power of acting.

We emphasize the importance of developing a sensitivity to our own body because although it is not uncommon to deceive ourselves intellectually about our true feelings toward those closest to us, our body does not lie. By becoming more sensitive to its responses, it (the body) becomes an indispensable tool in our journey of self-discovery.

Some additional consequences
After defining the emotions of love and hate, Spinoza proceeds to define all the other emotions in terms of these two. Although it is not our intention to replicate all of the definitions here—the interested reader is referred to part 3 of the *Ethics*—we do wish to give some indication of how the definitions work. The emotion of *blame,* for example, may be defined as hatred together with the belief that the object of hatred could have and/or should have behaved otherwise. So *blaming* another person involves (1) a decrease of one's own power of action, (2) the belief that the other is the cause of this decrease, and (3) the belief that the other could have and/or should have behaved differently.

Similarly, the emotion of *guilt* may be defined as blame directed at oneself. When we feel *guilty,* we are experiencing (1) a decrease in our power of action, (2) the belief that something we did is the cause of this decrease, and (3) the belief that we could have and/or should have behaved differently.

Some emotions also involve desire. The emotion of *anger,* for example, may be defined as hatred together with a desire to remove the object of the hatred. When we are feeling anger toward another, we are experiencing (1) a decrease in our power of action, (2) the belief that the other is the cause of this decrease, and (3) the desire to weaken or injure the other. Or in other words, when we are angry at another, we endeavor, either in our behavior or in our imagination, to lower the other's ability to affect us with sorrow.

Let us consider some further applications of these definitions. We generally endeavor to sustain and strengthen those things toward which we feel love. Why? Because the feeling of love toward a given thing or person is a feeling of joy together with the belief that the given thing is the cause of our joy. But the feeling of joy is itself an increase in our power of action. Now, everyone endeavors, as much as is possible, to persevere in his own being, which means that everyone strives to increase his or her power of action. Therefore, if we believe that an increase in our power of action is caused by some external object—that is to say, if we love the object—then we transfer, or project, a portion of our striving onto the external object and seek to strengthen the object so that it will be even more able to affect us with joy.

Hence, if we love another person, we generally strive to make the other person love us. To be specific, let us suppose that John loves Mary. From the definition of "love" it follows that John believes that Mary is the cause of his feeling joy. Part of his endeavor to continue feeling joy will involve maintaining and strengthening Mary's ability to affect him with joy. That is, he will seek to cause an increase in Mary's power of acting; or, in other words, he will seek to affect her with joy, with himself as the cause; that is, he will seek to make her love him. Thus, John's wanting Mary to love him is part of his endeavor to persevere in his own being.

On the other hand, if we hate another person, we generally seek to weaken or destroy that person. To take the above example, if John hates Mary, then from the definition of "hatred" it follows that John is affected with sorrow—that is, his power of action is decreased—and he believes that Mary is the cause of his hatred. As part of his effort to persevere in his own being, John will strive to remove his sorrow; but since he believes that Mary is the cause of his sorrow (i.e., he hates her), his effort to remove his own sorrow takes the form of an effort to remove (or weaken, or destroy) what he believes to be the cause of his sorrow, namely, Mary.

Now let us assume that a third person, Paul, affects Mary with hatred, then John will love Paul. Why? Because if Mary hates Paul, then Mary feels sorrow and believes Paul is the cause. Insofar as Mary feels sorrow, her power of action is decreased, and hence her ability to affect John with sorrow has decreased. But John, believing that the cause of his sorrow has weakened, passes from a relatively greater to a relatively lesser state of sorrow himself, which passage is a joy. If he also believes that the cause of Mary's sorrow is Paul, then he will also believe that Paul is the cause of his own passage to a state of relatively less sorrow. That is to say, he will experience joy together with the belief that Paul is the cause of the joy; in other words, he will love Paul.

We remind the reader that all emotions involve a *passage*—and hence are necessarily transient—to a relatively greater or lesser ability of the body-mind, or any portion thereof, to sustain its own form as the particular mode of Extension and Thought that it is. The emotion ceases as soon as the passage is completed. This is why we generally cease to be emotionally excited about a new situation once we get used to it. For example, most people in our culture have been conditioned to believe that acquiring wealth brings happiness. Because of this programming, the acquisition of a million dollars will indeed be accompanied by a feeling of joy; but the joy ceases as soon as the person has become accommodated to her new wealth. Then it will require the acquisition of still more wealth for her to feel joy again, because the joy arises from the transition, not from the having.

One further point. We have emphasized that the terms "love" and "hate" are to be understood in their occurrent sense. That is, the expression "if John loves Mary" should be read as "if John is *now* feeling joy and believes that Mary is the cause," etc. However, we will at times use these terms in the dispositional sense, as when we speak of a *loving* or a *hateful* individual. A *loving* person is one whose body-mind has been conditioned to produce the emotion of joy is response to a relatively wide range of external events; similarly, a *hateful* person is one who has been conditioned to produce the emotion of sorrow in response to a relatively wide range of external events. There is thus a structural difference between the body-mind of the loving person and that of the hateful person, and this structural difference exists whether or not the respective individuals are feeling love or hatred in the moment.

SELF-KNOWLEDGE AND THE EMOTIONS

Self-knowledge is not easy, and society has erected many barriers against pursuing the Delphic Oracle's injunction to "know thyself." Although self-knowledge ultimately consists in knowing, that is, in experiencing, our connection with God, a necessary step along the way is the knowledge of our emotions: not mere intellectual knowledge such as a *theory* of emotions might provide, but rather the experiential knowledge of how we truly feel on a day-to-day, moment-by-moment basis. The barriers against knowing our true feelings are not so much outside of us as they are a part of us—similar to the way in which Freud's concept of a "superego" is an *internalized* (part of our mind's) representation of social values. We have already given one example of this: the belief that we "should" love our parents, and that it is "wrong" not to love our parents, can be an obstacle to knowing how we truly feel about our parents if our real feelings conflict with how we think we "should" feel.

Some other examples are: (2) a person may come to believe that hatred and envy are "unspiritual" or "lower" emotions, and this belief then functions as a barrier against his coming to know his own feelings of hatred and envy. Or (3) a so-called "macho" man whose identity as a man involves the belief that a man never feels weak, uncertain, or vulnerable will not be able to experience his own feelings of weakness, uncertainty, or vulnerability. Or (4) a person could become so enchanted with various computer models of the mind—so fashionable in psychology today—that he may deny that he has any feelings whatsoever. And even though he may argue his point quite passionately, he remains blind to the obvious incongruity between what he says and how he says it.

These beliefs are all examples of internalized representations of social values. Since (a) these beliefs structure our individual experiences quite deeply, (b) we have all been conditioned by the values of our society, and (c) the values of what is loosely called Western civilization are at present a powerful force against emotional self-knowledge, it will be useful to discuss these issues at some length.

Beliefs and emotions
How is it possible for a belief to affect experience? Recall our earlier discussion of sense experience. In that discussion we argued that there is no "little man" inside our head who passively peers through our eyeballs and registers what is "out there." Rather, what we see when we open our eyes and look is produced by the body in

response to electromagnetic radiation that enters our eyes. *Emotional* experience, like sense experience, is produced by the body in response to some interaction with one or more external bodies (including of course, *human* external bodies). Thus, the nature and state of one's own body is causally involved in the production of emotions. Since Spinoza's psychophysical parallelism tells us that every state of the body has a counterpart in the mind, we could say that the mind is also causally involved in the production of emotions. Or, to put it in more Spinozistic terms, for any given emotion, the body is involved in producing the specific enzymes, electrical impulses, muscular contractions, etc., that constitute the emotion insofar as it is a mode within the Attribute of Extension; whereas, the mind is involved in producing the accompanying feeling that constitutes the emotion insofar as it is a mode within the Attribute of Thought. What we are calling a "belief that structures emotional experience" is simply a portion of the mind, conscious or unconscious, that is causally involved in producing the given emotion.

Consider, for example, two people who are exactly alike in all respects except that one believes that people are basically good and trustworthy, whereas the other believes that people are basically self-centered and untrustworthy. According to Spinoza's psycho-physical parallelism, this difference in belief must be accompanied by a difference in the structure of their bodies. Because of this difference, the respective responses of their bodies to the same external event will be quite different and hence the consciousness that accompanies the bodily response—that is to say, the actual conscious experience of the event, will also be different. Keep in mind that *all* imaginative experience is simply the consciousness, in the Attribute of Thought, that accompanies this or that particular modification of the body.

To continue the above example, let us suppose that two individuals, A and B, differ with respect to some given belief; this difference in psychological, or mental, structure must be correlated with a difference in the physical structure of their bodies. To be specific, we may assume that the body of A (who is generally trusting of others) differs from the body of B (who is generally suspicious of others) at least in the tendency of B's body to produce more adrenaline when in the presence of strangers. The consciousness that accompanies a body with relatively more adrenaline will be different from the consciousness that accompanies a body with relatively less adrenaline. B will feel more anxious, etc., than A. This is what we mean when we say that our beliefs structure our experience. For B's experience of anxiety when faced with an unfamiliar social situation is structured by his deeply rooted belief that people are generally not to be trusted.

The social conditioning of belief

What we are calling a "deeply rooted" belief is one that has been internalized, usually in childhood, through the process of social (including parental) conditioning. Such beliefs generally operate beneath the level of conscious awareness. Indeed—as the process of psychotherapy has demonstrated over and over—we often not only actively resist becoming aware of such beliefs, but also, when confronted with them, will claim that they are not "mere" beliefs but rather truths about the way things really are.

The suspicious man, for example, believes not only that people cannot be trusted, but also that his belief that people cannot be trusted is not just a matter of belief but is a truth about the world. He will judge that those who do not believe as he does are as unrealistic, idealistic, etc. He will think that his belief that people cannot be trusted is objectively derived from his experience, rather than that his experience is, at least partially, subjectively derived from his belief. For the suspicious man approaches every interaction with others with an attitude of distrust and cynicism. This attitude induces in others a certain wariness and caution, which, in turn, seems to justify to himself, and hence perpetuates, his initial belief. This circular pattern cannot be broken until the suspicious man is willing to take responsibility for his experience by examining those beliefs and attitudes that structure his experience. This is the path to self-knowledge; it is extremely difficult.

No one escapes social conditioning. Everyone's mind has been deeply programmed by the beliefs and attitudes prevalent in the culture in which she was raised. Although there is, of course, a wide range of individual variation within any given culture—e.g., the range in personalities between trusting and suspicious, introvert and extrovert, etc., are variations that occur in all cultures—nevertheless, cultural conditioning is usually so thorough and complete that the individual typically believes that what are really the beliefs and values of his culture are objective truths about the way things are, independent of his culture. It is easy to recognize this kind of "projection" when examining other cultures; it is difficult to see this kind of projection operating in ourselves. A few examples will clarify this point.

1. Consider three individuals, X, Y, and Z, about whom the only thing you know is that X was born and raised in Italy, Y was born and raised in Iran, and Z was born and raised in India. This knowledge will generally be sufficient for predicting many things about the beliefs

and attitudes of the given individuals. X most likely will believe in Catholicism, Y in Islam, and Z in Hinduism. These respective belief systems, like their native language, are deeply rooted in the individuals' minds;— that is, they actually constitute a major portion of the individuals' minds— and actively structure their respective experiences and behaviors.

2. A person born and raised in Israel will probably have a negative attitude toward Palestinians; and a person born and raised in a refugee camp in Palestine will most probably have a negative attitude toward Israelis. So given a newborn infant, we can program it to hate Israelis by raising it in Palestine, or we can program it to hate Palestinians by raising it in Israel. This hatred forms part of the content of the individual's mind, structuring both his behavior and his experience of external events. For example, the same external stimulus—say, the Israeli flag— will evoke totally different emotional responses in the Israeli and the Palestinian: pride and comfort in the former; hatred, fear, and rage in the latter. The true cause of the respective emotions is, according to Spinoza, not the external stimulus, but rather the years of psychological conditioning that has programmed their minds to produce the various emotions in response to the given external stimuli. It is easy to see that all forms of ethnic and religious animosity, and the emotions and behaviors that follow from such are caused by social conditioning, with respect to which, I might add, the individual is entirely passive.

These examples illustrate several important aspects of Spinoza's philosophy. From a metaphysical perspective, Spinoza's holism informs us that whenever two or more bodies, human or otherwise, interact, they constitute a whole that is not reducible to the sum of its parts. Similarly, whenever two or more minds interact they form a whole that also is not reducible to its constituent minds. This whole, like any other individual thing, will endeavor to persevere in its own existence. This is why it is quite appropriate to attribute psychological characteristics to cultures as a whole, as anthropologists do all the time when they describe the beliefs and practices of this or that culture.

Now, part of the endeavor that a given culture makes in order to persevere in its own being may involve an aversion or hatred toward other cultures that it regards as threats to itself. Often the mere existence of a different culture is perceived as a threat. A religion, for example, which holds that it alone possesses the truth about God will necessarily perceive the existence of other religions as a threat to itself and will seek to destroy, convert, and subjugate people of other religions, as happened with Christianity.

The relationship between the imaginative portion of the mind of a given individual and the mind of the culture into which she was born and raised is structurally similar to the relationship between a cell within the body and the body as a whole; or, perhaps better, it is like the relationship between an individual bee and the hive to which it belongs. The behavior of the bee, the cell, or the person (insofar as the latter's behavior follows only from the imaginative portion of his mind), is determined by the whole to which it belongs. For, the "whole" of which we speak is an organic individual entity that produces, or grows, the "parts" that constitute its being. These parts—cells, bees, humans—come into being deeply programmed to serve the whole. They have no independent existence, either in mind or in body.

Let us apply this to our earlier examples. If we consider the respective minds of an individual Catholic, Muslim, and Hindu and ask why it is that these particular individuals have the particular beliefs they in fact have—for example, the mind of the Catholic contains the belief that Jesus is the Son of God, the mind of the Muslim contains the belief that Mohammed is the greatest of the prophets, and that of the Hindu contains the belief in the doctrine of reincarnation—the answer will be that these beliefs were programmed into the respective individuals. These beliefs were produced (or generated, or grown) in the minds of these individuals by the culture, or the religious aspect of the culture, into which they were born; indeed, such deeply rooted beliefs are *cultured into* the minds of the individuals, and this whole process—which we are calling "conditioning," "programming," or "culturing"—may be regarded as part of the endeavor that the culture *as a whole* makes in *its* effort to persevere in *its* being. In each case, the individual is totally passive with respect to what he believes. The beliefs are programmed into him, and the experiences and behaviors which these beliefs structure are but mechanical executions of the program.

Or, considering again the example of the Palestinian and the Israeli, their emotional responses to the same stimuli—the Star of David, the Palestinian flag, etc.—will be quite different. If we ask what is the cause of the emotion of, say, anger, that the Palestinian feels in the presence of an Israeli symbol—or, what is the cause of the emotion of, say, pride, that the Israeli feels in the presence of the same symbol—the answer in both cases is social or cultural conditioning. The respective emotions of anger and pride are conditioned responses with respect to which the individuals are passive. The individuals may believe that the cause of their emotions is the external stimulus; but in fact the external stimulus functions mainly as a catalyst that triggers the specific emotional responses that have been deeply programmed into the individual; and hence, the true cause of the emotions, therefore, is the process of programming itself.

The matter is the same here as in the well-known phenomenon of post-hypnotic suggestion. While under hypnosis, the subject is given the instruction (I) to execute a certain response (R) when presented with a certain stimulus (S). The stimulus can be anything whatsoever: the hypnotist snapping her finger, the sight of another person, the time of day, etc. The response can be emotional, or behavioral, or both. For example, the instruction could be "feel hot and open the window at 2 o'clock" or "jump up and down when I snap my fingers." The instructions all have the form: I = given S, execute R. The cause of any response is, not S, but rather, I. The subject into whose mind is programmed a given instruction executes R mechanically and passively when presented with S. The subject is also unaware of I, and when asked why he felt or performed R, will generally refer to the stimulus S, or (since he may not be conscious of S or its connection in his mind with R) will attribute R to his own "free-will."

Even though social conditioning is a much more involved, complex, and thorough process than simple post-hypnotic suggestion, it is nevertheless the same kind of process. For, if we let "S" stand for a symbol of Israel, "R" stand for feeling proud, and "R*" stand for feeling angry, then the mind of the Israeli contains the instruction: I = given S, execute R; whereas the mind of the Palestinian contains the instruction I* = given S, execute R*. The commands, or instructions I and I* are modes of thought existing in the respective minds of the given individuals; . although Although the individuals may not be conscious of I and I*—and may even deny that he has been thus programmed, which denial is itself a part of the programming—these ideas, I and I*, are causally active, since in their absence, the responses R and R* could not occur.

This example makes very clear why the emotional responses R and R* are inadequate, or passive, modes of Thought. They are *inadequate* because, even though their respective causes, I and I*, are internal to the minds of the individuals, they (I and I*) originate in the social and cultural conditions in which the individuals are raised—that is, they are internalized representations of those cultural conditions—and hence, are caused by a process that is external to the minds of the individuals. The occurrence of those specific emotions in the minds of those specific individuals therefore can be understood only in terms of those specific cultural conditions. The individuals are *passive* with respect to the emotions R and R* because these emotional responses are automatically determined, or produced, by I and I*, respectively. R and R* are, in a way, mental reflexes. Just as, say, the muscles in the leg have no choice but to contract when the appropriate stimulus is applied at the knee, so also the respective minds of the two individuals have no choice but to produce the emotions R and R* when the stimulus S is applied. The individuals may believe they are free, but this belief arises, as Spinoza repeatedly tells us, because people are generally conscious of their emotions (R and R*) and of the desires that follow from their emotions, but not of the causes (I and I*) of their emotions and desires.

The belief in free will is, in this context, a form of what therapists call "denial." A person who believes that his emotional responses and their consequent desires result from free will is *denying* that they are causally linked with anything of which she is not aware. She will then be unwilling to examine the true causes of her own feelings and desires. This resistance to self-examination is, of course, also the result of social conditioning. For the hypnotist who programs a subject with the post-hypnotic suggestion, I = given S, execute R, *also* programs the subject to not remember that he was thus programmed. The subject, when out of trance, has no conscious awareness of the program, I, and will generally deny that his response R was caused by I.

So, the person who believes in Catholicism, Islam, or Hinduism will usually also believes that the reason she believes in her religion is because it is the "true" or the "best" religion. That is, she will *deny* that her belief is the result of social conditioning. But this "second-order" belief—this "denial"—is programmed into the individual's mind by the same social process that programmed the belief in Catholicism, etc., in the first place. It is as if the program says, "believe in X *and also* believe that the reason you believe in X is because of the intrinsic merits of X over any other belief system." Or, "given S, execute R *and also* believe that the reason you are experiencing R is because of the nature of S, or because of your own free will." These second-order beliefs are major impediments to self-knowledge; they keep us in bondage to mechanical and repetitive behaviors, emotional responses, and desires; they are very powerful.

The programming of the mind by Western society—
A major impediment to self-knowledge
The reader may have gotten the impression that this analysis holds only for

people who have been indoctrinated into a particular religion or ethnic group. Nothing could be further from the truth. The examples above were chosen because of their simplicity; it is much easier to see the causal structure of emotions in examples of homogeneous conditioning. As we shall see shortly, it is a gross self-deception for the so-called educated Western mind to believe that only those who narrowly identify with the religion or ethnicity of their birth are products of social conditioning.

This belief—that only those who narrowly identify, etc.—is actually what we have called a "second-order" belief. It attempts to deny that the beliefs and emotional responses of, say, a university-educated man or woman who typically is neither religious nor ethnically bound, are produced and determined in just the same way as those of the religious or ethnic fanatic. The only difference, however, lies in the complexity of the causal structure. For unlike the homogeneously conditioned individual who has internalized a fairly coherent set of instructions for generating specific emotional and behavioral responses to specific external circumstances or stimuli, the heterogeneously conditioned Western person has internalized numerous and diverse instructions that do not form a coherent set. In a way, it is because modern man has been programmed with inconsistent instructions that compete among themselves for control of his mind that he is culturally more alienated from himself than in any culture in history.

It is important to acknowledge that every human being, without exception, is born into a social context—a culture with specific beliefs and values. These beliefs and values are acquired by the child in the same automatic way that she acquires her native language. What we call "education," from grade school through college and beyond, is part of the process of conditioning whereby the beliefs and values of our culture are internalized in the mind of the individual. Education is, therefore, the means by which our culture perpetuates itself—by programming the minds of its constituent members.

There are doubtless many ways to delineate the beliefs and values of a given culture, including our own, but I think as good a way as any is to ask the question: What does the culture take to be the measure of a worthwhile and successful life? And related to this is the question: What are the psychological qualities that an individual must possess or acquire if she is to be successful in that culture? It is probably fair to say that the overall measure of success in our culture is external achievement. The individual is programmed to believe that her worth and value as a human being depends upon her quantifiable achievements, usually measured in terms of wealth, status, or fame. Of course, there is nothing wrong with worldly achievement, but consider some of the consequences when outer achievement is taken to be the measure of self-worth. The main consequence is that when only outer achievement contributes to self-worth, then inner experience becomes unimportant. The individual comes to believe that only what she *does* has value, not how she *feels*. We thus live in a society that systematically denies the importance of the quality of inner life, and quite often, as therapists will attest, those who are most successful by society's standards (e.g., corporate presidents, politicians, etc.) are least in touch with their own feelings.

Our society conditions its members, especially men, to inhibit the expression of most feelings. But just as a muscle that is never used will atrophy, so also, the ability to be aware of one's own feelings, if never used, will whither away. If it is true that the "kingdom of heaven lies within," then modern man will never find it, because he has been taught, from kindergarten through university, to focus only on outer things and hence to ignore what lies within. If we are, as Spinoza says, connected with a higher consciousness, with a soul, with God, and if the awareness of this connection lies within our own mind, then modern man will have much difficulty experiencing this connection because he has been programmed to focus his awareness only on outer events and to deny the importance, even the existence, of inner experience.

Even the concept of God prevalent in our present culture supports the alienation of human beings from their inner life. For, as we have already discussed, God is conceived as a being external to individual human beings, thus motivating us to look outside of ourselves for comfort and salvation. Furthermore, God is conceived as valuing and rewarding us in accordance with what we do and, consequently, the organized religions of our culture teach us to look to some external authority—a book, a priest, a moral code, etc.—to tell us whether we are "doing it right."

And, we hasten to add, the so-called nonreligious man has *also* been taught to look to some external authority—his boss, his wealth, his status, the opinions of others, etc.—to measure his self-worth. Contrast this with Spinoza's views: because *only* God exists, the world and everything in it, including ourselves, is a part of the Divine Being. Therefore, the value and worth of any given thing, such as a particular human being, lies in the fact that it exists. Our self-worth is intrinsically given in our very existence; it is not extrinsic in what we do.

There are thus very powerful forces in our culture that mitigate against self-knowledge. These forces are, of course, not simply "out there," but have been deeply internalized by every individual. For example, we feel good when praised and bad when criticized, and we falsely believe that the cause of such feelings lies in the external praise or blame. But these feelings arise only because we have been programmed to believe that our self-worth requires external validation; and hence, *because of this programming,* our sense of self-worth increases when praised and decreases when criticized, resulting in the respective feelings of joy and sorrow. That is, the feelings of joy or sorrow that we experience when praised or criticized are conditioned responses to an internalized program that conditions us to produce those emotions given those stimuli. Hence, our emotional responses and consequent behaviors are programmed into us in just the same way as we discussed in the previous examples of those whose minds have been programmed into narrow religious or ethnic beliefs.

Now, although the most general feature of the conditioning of the Western mind is the instruction to make one's sense of self-worth depend upon external validation, the particularities vary widely from one individual to the next. For each individual internalizes not only the overall beliefs and values of her culture in general, but also the particular beliefs and values that pertain to the particular circumstances of her education and childhood experiences, such as economic class, religion, race, and, most important, the psychological environment provided by her parents.

A given individual, therefore, has internalized many instructions from many sources, which we hasten to remark are not infrequently incompatible with one another. For example, a business person who believes that her self-worth depends upon how much profit she makes may resort to unethical behavior in order to get ahead; but that same business person may have been raised by parents who taught that a good person should always be honest and fair. These two instructions will often compete for control of the individual's emotions and behavior. If she is, say, presented with an opportunity to make a big profit by being less than honest in her business dealings, she will necessarily experience conflict, or what Spinoza calls "vacillation of mind," because it is impossible to execute both programs simultaneously. The former instruction tells her that her self-worth depends upon monetary gain; the latter instruction tells her it depends on being fair and honest. Whichever program is in fact executed, the individual will not feel at peace within herself.

To summarize, almost all of our emotions and behaviors are responses to outer events, responses that are caused, not by the outer events, although that is what we have been conditioned to believe, but by an instruction or set of instructions that we have internalized during the long process of conditioning that began in earliest childhood. Our emotions and behaviors are thus determined by, or structured by, these instructions which, once internalized, become our deeply rooted beliefs and values, and to which we are in bondage. Since all such instructions originate outside of oneself, they are, once internalized, inadequate ideas, and thus the emotions that follow from them are also inadequate ideas in us, and we are passive with respect to them. Spinoza's path to freedom lies in (1) becoming aware of our real emotions; (2) connecting our emotional responses not with the external events that appear to cause them, but rather, with our internalized beliefs and values, thus extending the range of our awareness to these deeply rooted beliefs and values; and (3) gradually replacing these beliefs and values with one's own metaphysical understanding of one's self as a portion of the Divine Being.

Social schizophrenia, the split between feeling and behavior
The very important first step, then, is to become fully aware of our real feelings. This is not easy to do in a society that teaches that feelings are not important; we do not know how to look within because we have been taught to ignore, suspect, deny, and repress our emotions. Furthermore, our society has conditioned us to behave according to how we think we "should" feel, not according to how we truly feel. For example, a person interviewing for a job will hide her nervousness because she thinks she should project self-confidence; a man on a date with a woman he wishes to impress will attempt to conceal feelings of awkwardness or anxiety; a person who hates his boss will attempt to conceal such feelings in his boss's presence; a person who is bored at family gatherings will pretend to be interested, etc. Thus, in growing up, we learn to mechanically execute various behaviors under various external circumstances, behaviors that are often incongruent with how we truly feel under those circumstances. This "social obligation"—which is, of course, an internalized instruction—to make behavior depend on social context rather than on how we feel, splits us off very deeply from our inner life. It is no wonder that so many people become dull and depressed after years of merely "going through the motions."

This split or incongruity between inner feelings and outer behavior is especially severe for men in our culture, who are taught from earliest childhood never to show any feelings of vulnerability, insecurity, and uncertainty and to always behave with self-confidence and assuredness. In adulthood, this takes the form of a split between a man's "personal" life and his "professional" life. This split is actually a form of schizophrenia, both in the individual and in society as a whole, and would easily be recognized as such were it not for the fact that everyone, including psychotherapists, has been programmed in this way. *And*, I might add, we have also been programmed to believe that such schizophrenia is necessary and normal, and that a person who has not succeeded in separating his "personal" life from his "professional" life is in some sense immature. But this separation places an unbearable burden on the individual, resulting (aside from various forms of physical dis-ease) in a gradual atrophying of the awareness of inner life.

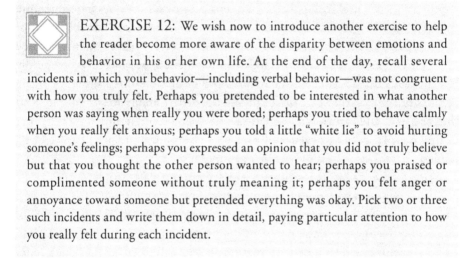

EXERCISE 12: We wish now to introduce another exercise to help the reader become more aware of the disparity between emotions and behavior in his or her own life. At the end of the day, recall several incidents in which your behavior—including verbal behavior—was not congruent with how you truly felt. Perhaps you pretended to be interested in what another person was saying when really you were bored; perhaps you tried to behave calmly when you really felt anxious; perhaps you told a little "white lie" to avoid hurting someone's feelings; perhaps you expressed an opinion that you did not truly believe but that you thought the other person wanted to hear; perhaps you praised or complimented someone without truly meaning it; perhaps you felt anger or annoyance toward someone but pretended everything was okay. Pick two or three such incidents and write them down in detail, paying particular attention to how you really felt during each incident.

The reader is urged, once again, to do this exercise—and indeed, all the exercises in this book—in a spirit of nonjudgmental self-acceptance. There may be a tendency to feel bad about oneself, or guilty, when one begins to realize the pervasive extent of the lack of congruence between inner feelings and outward behavior. But this is not a matter of right or wrong. The purpose of this exercise is neither to feel guilty about nor to try to change our behavior, but simply to bring more awareness to our inner life so that our true feelings are more and more known to us. If one is judgmental about oneself and believes, say, that anger is not good, then that belief will function as a shield to inhibit the awareness of one's own anger. But, as is well known, anger that is repressed does not simply go away; repressed emotions may, over time, generate in the psyche cynicism, depression, and a reduced capacity for enjoying life. And in the body, repressed emotions may lead to an overall decrease in the functioning of the immune system. Therefore, it is important to relinquish our self-judgments—our beliefs that some feelings are "good" and others are "bad"—in order to truly experience our inner life. The reader should remind herself over and over again that all things follow from the Nature of the Divine Being and that her inner life, including those feelings and behaviors of which she disapproves, are in no way exceptions to the "all things" that follow from the Nature of God.

If it be objected that society requires this split between inner feeling and outward behavior and that we must, after all, adapt our behavior to the requirements of social reality, I reply that our present society does indeed require this split, but I urge that our present society is not the only possible form of social organization. A society that requires and conditions its members to be schizophrenic cannot, by any stretch of the imagination, be called psychologically healthy. This dissociation from our inner life has resulted in a situation where we are presently on the verge of destroying the earth's ability to sustain life. And this, as I have said earlier, is a dramatic act of ultimate and terminal insanity. Let us heal our planet as we heal ourselves, and we begin to heal our self as we bring nonjudgmental awareness to bear on our inner life.

One further point: It is neither necessary nor advisable to *try* to make one's behavior congruent with one's feelings. Indeed, any such effort will take awareness away from the feelings themselves. Rather, as one becomes increasingly aware of one's inner feelings—as one practices nonjudgmental awareness of the lack of congruence in specific, concrete situations—one will discover that one's outer behavior gradually and effortlessly aligns itself with the inner feelings. The reader is urged to practice the above exercise repeatedly until it becomes second nature.

A reminder
Let us once again remind ourselves of Spinoza's general metaphysical framework within which we are endeavoring to understand our own emotions. The human body, like all other bodies, is a particular form of organization within the physical world, the Attribute of Extension; the human mind, like all other minds or ideas, is a particular form of organization within the spiritual world, the Attribute of Thought. What we have been referring to as the imagination, or as the imaginative portion of the human mind, is that portion of psychic organization within the human mind that constitutes the awareness, in the Attribute of Thought, that correlates with the body. The human body is in continuous interaction with other bodies; some of these interactions affect or modify the human body in such a way as to relatively raise or lower the body's

ability to maintain its own structure (which structure includes, of course, the effects of social conditioning). These modifications of the body, together with their correlative ideas, constitute the emotions.

Recall that any given body, and every modification of that body, is but a mode of Substance, or God, manifested in the Attribute of Extension; the idea, or mind, or awareness of that body is that same mode of Substance expressed, or manifested, in the Attribute of Thought. The idea that expresses in Thought the same mode of Substance, which in Extension is a relative increase or decrease in our body's power of action, is a modification of the imaginative portion of our mind, which modification is nothing other than the feeling itself of joy or sorrow. Love (or hatred) toward a given object is simply a feeling of joy (or sorrow) together with the belief that the given object is the cause of the joy (or sorrow). Of course, *whether or not* a given person is affected with love or hatred or indifference toward any given thing depends mostly on that person's prior conditioning, which we regard as the true cause of the love or hatred. Thus, as we have seen, a particular religious symbol may affect one man with love, another with hatred, and yet another with indifference. We note that the prior conditioning that determines the emotion each man experiences is rooted not only in his mind, but also in his body. For, physiologically speaking, the same pattern of reflected light—reflected, say, from a given religious symbol—enters the bodies through the eyes of the three men. The similar retinal patterns then affect the respective brains of the three individuals, and because the effects themselves—love, hate, and indifference—are so markedly different, it follows that the brains that produce these effects must also be quite different. For each brain has been programmed to produce its own specific emotional responses to the same electromagnetic stimuli.

As we continue to develop Spinoza's theory of emotions, it is important that the reader *apply* the theory to herself; otherwise, there can be no real understanding. For Spinoza, a real understanding of emotions involves making a *personal*—as opposed to a merely conceptual or academic—connection with the theory. This is not easy and will require sustained awareness. For, after years of "education" that teaches us not to value our inner life, we easily lose the ability to know what it is. Our universities play a major role in this conditioning process, for they teach only how to analyze, which requires no feeling, but not how to appreciate, which begins with feeling. But analysis in the absence of appreciation is absurd. What is the point of analyzing a Beethoven quartet, a Whitman poem, or a Platonic dialogue if one has not been *moved* by it—that is to say, if one has not experienced some connection between the object of analysis and one's personal life? The triviality of most academic research lies in just this point; the kind of analysis given by people who are not personally connected with what they are analyzing—and academics are especially trained to be this way—is necessarily shallow and will at best belong to what we have previously called the "true but useless" category.

Even psychiatrists and psychotherapists, who are supposedly trained to guide others through the maze of inner feelings, are themselves often deeply unaware of their own feelings, because their own training teaches them various theories, concepts, and methods of objective analysis, but it does not teach them how to become more aware—how to experience deeply—their own inner life. Whether it be of people or poetry, of music or nature, analysis without feeling is blind. It is worse than blind. Analysis that is separated from inner life is *precisely* the schizophrenic split that is the root cause of humanity's collective death wish. What is the point, after all, of being alive if losing touch with one's inner life is the requirement for belonging to society? The unexamined life is indeed not worth living, and the same social and psychic barriers humanity has developed to "protect" itself from an awareness of inner life are presently destroying the planet's ability to sustain life altogether. Collectively, we have no choice: either we must examine our lives—which means, of course, our inner lives—or perish. Individually, we can use such considerations to strengthen our resolve to give primary attention to our own inner life. We can resolve to relinquish socially acquired outer-directed goals, such as for more money, more status, more material things, etc., and begin to replace them with inner-directed goals, such as forgiving those we believe have wronged us.

Knowing our emotions

Spinoza's theory of emotions automatically leads to the formation of new goals and provides a joyful and refreshing sense of direction. For the *understanding* of Spinoza's theory is itself a new element in our psychic structure that *can* lead to a transformation within that structure. For when we understand something, the understanding is itself a real mode of thought with real causal properties—the act of understanding something within our mind is itself a new element within our mind that affects, alters, and transforms the mind itself. To paraphrase Spinoza, the more we understand in this way, the more our *ability* to understand increases. But this dialectical process cannot get off the ground until one has learned to experience one's feelings simply and directly and without judgment.

How is one to do this? Spinoza's technique is deceptively simple, and we have already hinted at it in a previous exercise. Consider for the moment how you might respond to the question, what does anger *feel* like? Or, what does fear *feel* like? Or what does jealousy *feel* like? Or what does pride *feel* like? I think that a sustained effort to give verbal answers to these questions can lead to two insights: first, it is really not possible to give an adequate verbal description of what any emotion *feels* like. This is because our feelings occur at a deeper level of our being than the level of discursive thinking, which is ruled by language. We can experience our emotions, but we cannot adequately describe them verbally. Second, if we are nevertheless pushed to describe them as best we can, we would, I think, describe them in terms of kinesthetic sensations in our bodies. In physical terms, we feel anger as, say, tightening of muscles, increase in heart rate, etc. Indeed, such bodily symptoms *are* the emotions insofar as the emotion is manifested under the Attribute of Extension. Therefore, the way to experience our feelings directly is to be aware of them as kinesthetic sensations within our own body.

This requires attention. For generally, when under the influence of a strong emotion, our awareness is directed toward the external object or event that triggers the emotion, rather than to the emotion itself. When we become angry in response to someone else's behavior, our awareness is focused on the other person's behavior or to associated thoughts concerning the other person, rather than to the actual feelings occurring within our own body. Our subsequent response to the other person inevitably will be a passive reaction to our own emotions, which are themselves passive, that is, programmed, responses to the other's behavior.

Of course, when we are angry we often know that we are angry; but knowing that we are angry is not the same thing as *feeling* our anger. When I say that we are not usually aware of the feeling of anger, I mean simply that our mind, or consciousness, is focused primarily on the external situation that we (falsely) believe caused the anger. Our mind is not focused on the feeling of anger itself, within our own body. And this is what Spinoza urges us to learn how to do.

The situation in this case is similar to that which we discussed earlier pertaining to sense experience. When we are said to see a tree, the physical correlate of the mental experience of seeing a tree is not the tree as it appears in our visual experience, but rather the physiological state of our body. Similarly, when we are said to be angry at a given person, the physical correlate of that mental state is not the other person, but rather the state of our own body. The "illusion" of those ideas we call sense experience is that we confuse the content of the idea with the cause of the idea, believing the former to be the latter. And similarly, the "illusion" of those ideas that are emotions is that we believe the content, or a part of the content of the idea (say, anger toward John), is caused by a part of the content (John) itself. But just as the mode of Extension that correlates with the visual perception of a tree is the state of our own body—not the tree as it appears in our perception—so also the mode of Extension that correlates with the emotion of hatred toward John is not John, but rather the state of one's own body. As long as we believe that our emotions are caused by external events, we relinquish our power-of-action to those events.

Emotions and sense experience differ, however, in that the former can, with practice, be experienced directly as modifications within our own body—which is what they really are. Joy and sorrow, and all the emotions that are based on joy and sorrow, can be felt as physical processes within the body. This is what we mean when we use phrases such as "feeling our emotions," "experiencing our feelings," or "emotional self-knowledge." To "feel an emotion" is to feel what is going on within our body during the emotion; it is to withdraw attention from the external trigger event and place it on the body, so that the content of awareness becomes one's own body, rather than some external body or event. To do this is to begin to take back one's power from the external event; it is the beginning of freedom.

> EXERCISE 13: Recall a recent event that triggered an emotional response in you. Let your mind dwell on the details of the external event for a few minutes. Now begin to shift your awareness away from the external event and toward the sensations occurring in your body as you think of the external event. For example, does your breathing become deeper or more shallow, faster or slower? Do the muscles around your stomach contract or relax, etc.? Take the time to slowly scan your whole body. You might ask yourself, what am I feeling in my jaw? In my throat? In my neck? Around my heart? This is a good exercise to do while at the cinema, since a good movie engages us emotionally, and also the fictitious nature of movies should make it easier to move our awareness back and forth from the external events on the screen to the feelings in our body. As much as possible, try to locate the feeling within your body. A good rule of thumb, used by many therapists, is: you have not fully experienced an emotion until you can locate it within your body.

This exercise should be practiced over and over. It might be easier to begin with events that are at the periphery of one's life—such as a stranger wishing us a good day, a salesperson being less that polite to us, etc., rather than with events that are more emotionally charged. Our goal in practicing this exercise is to develop the ability to automatically shift our awareness from the thought of some external event to the kinesthetic sensations within our body, so that instead of giving up our power to the external event (e.g., "what you did made me angry"), we take back our power and "own" our feelings (e.g., "when you did that I felt anger in my body" or "when you did that I felt a constriction around my throat and a hollowness in the pit of my stomach").

The importance of this exercise—of feeling our emotions within our body—cannot be overemphasized. For, until we bring awareness to our emotions, we only passively act, or rather, react, out of our emotions and are controlled by them. Our emotions may then be said to "have us" rather than vice versa. Since emotions are themselves conditioned responses to external events, the person who does not bring awareness to his emotions is in a kind of double bondage: first to the internal programming itself, which determines which emotion shall be produced in the individual in response to some given external event; and second, to the emotion itself, which determines and structures our subsequent thoughts and behaviors. Insofar as we are unable or unwilling to direct our awareness away from the external event that we falsely believe caused the emotion, we are in the grip of the emotion and are controlled by it; insofar as we are willing and able to direct our awareness to the feeling of the emotion within our body, we gain some autonomy.

Without this awareness, therapy—or at least Spinoza's therapy—is not possible. For Spinoza's therapy involves uprooting the whole system of culturally conditioned emotional responses, which requires the ability to be aware of what those responses are. And we emphasize that we do not mean mere intellectual awareness, for that is trivial. It is easy, for example, to be intellectually aware of the fact that one is angry while in the midst of a temper tantrum. But the temper tantrum is a passive behavioral response to the anger and ceases as soon as we bring awareness to the feelings within the body. So perhaps we should distinguish between a *feeling* awareness—an awareness *of* a sensation within our body—and an *intellectual* awareness, an awareness *that* something or other is the case.

The above considerations reinforce our earlier insistence to use words that refer to emotions in their occurrent sense as much as possible and never in their nominal sense. For, it is tautological to say that we can feel an emotion in our body only while the emotion is actually occurring in our body. But it is a form of self-deception to think that we love someone—that we *feel* love for someone—merely because we are in a relationship (child, parent, lover, etc.) with that person which society has conditioned us to believe must be loving. Suppose, for example, a mother beats her child who has misbehaved in a public place, embarrassing the mother. (We hasten to note that the child's behavior is not the true cause of the mother's embarrassment; the latter is caused by internalized social rules that dictate to the mother not only which of her child's behaviors are inappropriate in public, but also what should be her emotional response to her child's so-called inappropriate behavior.) The mother may think to herself that she is beating her child to "teach him a lesson" because she cares for, or loves, him. But actually, the emotion of embarrassment involves a lowering of her own self-esteem, and accordingly a relative decrease in her power of action, together with the belief that the child's behavior caused the emotion; thus, she is, at that moment, hating the child. If she says to the child, while beating him, "I'm only doing this because I love you; it's for your own good," the child learns to associate the words "love" and "good" with acts of violence. If, on the other hand, the mother were able to focus her awareness on the feelings within her body, rather than on the child's behavior, then her violence toward her child would abate.

Or consider a man who murders his lover "because" she had threatened to leave him. He says afterward that he killed her because he "loved" her too much to let her go. But had he been able to experience his true feelings, he would have found that the contemplated rejection triggered in him a lowering of self-esteem that, together with the belief that his lover caused the lowering of self-esteem, produced the emotion of hatred toward his lover; and his act of murder was, therefore, an attempt to regain his self-esteem by destroying the object of his hatred. Violence is always motivated by hatred, never by love. Much confusion will be avoided by using the terms "love" and "hate" in their occurrent sense as much as possible.

The socially programmed mind is a great deceiver. It can make us think that what we feel is the opposite of what we really feel. It can make us think that hatred and indifference are love. It can make us think that we are not having feelings when we are, as with the so-called macho man whose whole body is contorted with the effort to deny his real feelings. But our mind can deceive only as long as our awareness is riveted to outer events. As soon as we withdraw awareness from outer events and place it on the feelings within our body, we can, with practice, come to know our true feelings. The body does not lie.

4 FREEDOM FROM BONDAGE

EMOTIONS AND THE PROCESS OF IMAGING

Although we have said that emotions are conditioned responses to external events, we all know from our own experience that emotions may arise in response to our own thinking, even in the absence of any external event. Simply *thinking about* or *imagining* a person whom we like or dislike dispositionally may produce in us the emotions of love or hatred, respectively. Often, in fact, the emotions we experience through our imaginative fantasies are even stronger than those that arise in response to external events. This is an expected consequence of Spinoza's system.

Recall, from our discussion of sense experience, that there is no essential difference between a veridical sense perception and a hallucination. In either case, the idea that is the sense perception or the hallucination is a mode of Thought that corresponds to a particular modification of the body. It does not matter, as far as the idea or mental experience is concerned, *how* the body got to be modified in that particular way—whether through interaction with external bodies, as in veridical sense perception, or through the electro-chemical activity of the body in itself, as in hallucinations.

There is, of course, a distinction to be made between (1) seeing something that is there (veridical sense perception), (2) seeing something that is not there (hallucination), and (3) thinking about something that we know is not present (imagining). We have already discussed (1) and (2) and noted that the body could be in the same state, and so the corresponding idea would be the same, regardless of whether (1) or (2) is the case. In any event, the content of the idea—what we see—is not the same as what is or is not present.

The third case seems different from the first two, because there we do not experience the content of our thinking to be external to ourselves. If we think about a friend who is not present, we do not therefore "see" or experience the friend as present. The reason for this, Spinoza tells us, is *not* because there is some qualitative difference between the idea we have when we see our friend as present and the idea we have when we think about our friend whom we know to be absent.

Rather, in the second case we have, in addition to the idea of our friend, other ideas—such as the knowledge that our friend is not present—which exclude the content of the former idea. The difference between a person who hallucinates a tree and a person who thinks about a tree that is not present is that the latter has in his mind, simultaneous with the idea of a tree, other ideas that prevent the thought about the tree from becoming so forceful that its content—the tree—is experienced as external to the person.

Spinoza, as we have said, uses the term "Imagination" to refer to all modes of thinking that involve images, regardless of whether or not a given such image is believed to be, or experienced as, actually present. Nevertheless, for our present purposes we wish to distinguish that portion of our imaginative thinking that involves images of things believed to be present (1 and 2 above) from that portion that involves images of things believed not to be present (3 above). With some understandable reluctance, I will use the term "imagine" in its ordinary sense to refer to that power of the mind by which it produces images of things believed to be not present. We *imagine,* for example, whenever we think about the past or the future, as well as when we fantasize our present situation being other than what it is. Because our culture has conditioned us to attend far more to outer events than to inner events—i.e., to that portion of our Imagination that, in Spinoza's terms, represents external objects as present—we tend to ignore, underestimate, and undervalue the activity of imagining. In particular, we do not appreciate the role imagining plays in producing and structuring our emotions.

The nature of our "inner dialogue"

We wish to stress the reality of the process of imagining. Suppose a person remembers some past event or, to put it in other words, she forms an image of the event in her mind, or, she imagines it. Of course, *what* she imagines, the *content* of her idea, no longer exists, but the idea itself—the process of imagining—does exist. It is a mode of Thought, and the mode of Extension to which it is correlated is the person's body.

Because our ideas are correlated not with their content, but rather, with our bodies, the reality and power of an idea does not depend on whether its content exists. So even when we are imagining something altogether fictitious, say, a flying elephant, we are doing something real. The idea is real even though its content, the flying elephant, is not. And because the idea is real, as is the bodily state to which it is correlated, it will have real consequences. Let us consider this further in an exercise.

EXERCISE 14: (a) With eyes closed, imagine yourself in pleasant surroundings, e.g., walking along a beach on a beautiful day, in the mountains, conversing with good friends, etc. Make the scene as vivid as you can and spend four or five minutes immersed in the content of your imagining. Then (b) repeat, but this time imagine yourself in unpleasant surroundings, e.g., stuck in traffic, caught in the rain, having to talk to people you do not like, etc. Be aware of the sensations in your body that accompany the images in (a) and (b), respectively. The images in (a) generate feelings of well-being, peace, and joy; they increase our power of acting. The images in (b) generate feelings of discomfort, frustration, and annoyance; they decrease our power of acting. The reader should experiment with this exercise, observing the effect on the emotions of imagining himself in various circumstances and situations until he becomes convinced of the reality of the process of imagining.

The next thing to notice is that this process of imagining—of thinking about things that we know to be fictitious or related to the past or future—goes on almost *all the time*. It is what has been called the "inner dialogue," or "stream of consciousness." We note several properties of this inner dialogue.

1. It is automatic. The various images flow through our mind in the same way that blood flows through our veins. It temporarily ceases, or becomes significantly less intense, only during so-called peak experiences, e.g., sexual ecstasy, or strong aesthetic experiences. We have already discussed this point at some length when we talked about free will. For the most part, our thinking is automatic and involuntary. As we previously noted, even when we consciously direct our attention to some specific thing, the thought that tells us where to direct our attention itself comes involuntarily. And even when our attention is directed to something specific, the inner dialogue still continues, as we shall see below.

2. The content of the thoughts that constitute our inner dialogue either refer to the past or future, or they are altogether fictitious. Let us experience (1) and (2) through the following exercise:

> **EXERCISE 15:** [a] In a context where your attention is relatively undirected, such as walking, driving your car, sitting alone, etc., observe (1) *that* you are thinking and (2) *what* you are thinking about. This is your inner dialogue. Then [b] in a context where your attention is directed, such as reading, talking with a friend, etc., observe that the inner dialogue is still going on. That is, even while conversing with a friend, only a portion of our attention is directed toward the conversation; another portion is constituted by our inner dialogue—thoughts about the past or future. Indeed, under some circumstances, worrying about some future event for example, our mind may be so filled with thoughts about that future event that we are only marginally aware of the conversation in which we are presently engaged. We will return to this point again in the next exercise.

3. A third property of our inner dialogue, which we have already noted, is that it is causally efficacious in the production of emotions. We saw in a previous exercise that just thinking about, or imagining, being in comfortable surroundings produces feelings of comfort, and imagining ourselves in uncomfortable surroundings produces feelings of discomfort. If the reader is still not convinced of the causal power of imagining, simply repeat that exercise using more forceful examples. Imagine yourself in a situation in which you are terribly embarrassed; imagine that someone you love has a fatal illness, or imagine yourself accomplishing something for which others praise you. You will see that imagining something of which you are embarrassed, fearful, or proud engenders those very feelings. Similarly, imagining something that pertains to the past, that is, remembering some past event, will recreate in the mind emotions similar to those that were experienced when the event actually happened. Indeed, many people, when talking about a past event that upset them, become just as upset as when the event occurred. It is clear, in examples such as this, that the individual's present upsetness is produced by his own thinking, since the event in question no longer exists.

This last example is very instructive, for it demonstrates quite clearly that our emotions *do* come into play in response to our own thinking and in the absence of any present external event. This is because our thinking, our process of imagining, our inner dialogue, are real modes within the Attribute of Thought, in and of themselves, and hence have real consequences. They are correlated, in the Attribute of Extension, with definite states of our body, which in turn lead to other states of the body, etc. Thus, the thought of something past (or future, or fictitious) is itself something real and is correlated with a definite state of the body or brain, e.g., specific neurons firing in specific ways. But in any individual these specific neurons are connected, through prior conditioning, with other neurons, which are in turn connected with still others, etc., so as to constitute a causal chain that ultimately controls the various glands and other systems that produce the emotions in the body.

The reason why emotions produced in response to our inner dialogue are generally, but not always, less intense than those that arise in response to a present external event is that in the former case there is in the mind, simultaneous with the memory of a past event, the thought that the event is in fact past. This "thought that the event is in fact past" is itself correlated with a specific pattern of neuronal firing, and this pattern acts to inhibit, at least somewhat, the causal chain that flows from the physiology of the memory of the event that leads to the production of the emotion.

But now a very interesting question arises. We like to believe that our emotional responses to outer events are "caused" by the events themselves. Even our language deeply reflects this belief. For example, we commonly say such things as "my feelings are hurt *because* you ignored me," "I'm angry *because* of what you did," "I feel anxious *because* I'm going to speak in front of a group," or "I'm despondent *because* my teacher criticized me." But if it is the case, as we have seen, that emotions can be produced by our inner dialogue alone in the absence of any external event, and if it is also the case that our inner dialogue is always going on, even in the presence of some external event, then it follows that our inner dialogue is causally involved in the production of emotions even in the presence of external events.

The question is, when we are experiencing an emotional response to an outer event, to what extent is the emotion caused, not by the event, but by the inner dialogue? The central point of Spinoza's system of therapy lies in the recognition that virtually all human emotions have their origin in our inner dialogue, not in external events. "If," says Spinoza, "we separate emotions from the thought of an external cause and join them to other thoughts, then the love or hate toward the external cause is destroyed" (*Ethics,* pt. 5, prop. 2). The "other thoughts" referred to here is our inner dialogue, or those aspects of our inner dialogue that are causally involved in producing the given emotion.

One thing should be very obvious: to the extent that we believe that our emotions are caused by outer events, to that extent we have relinquished our power of action to those events. Having given up our power over our happiness, peace of mind, and well being to external events and people, we try to get it back by manipulating and controlling those events and people, to the extent we are able.

But if, instead, we believe that our emotions are caused by our inner dialogue, then there arises the possibility of restructuring our inner dialogue so as to produce increasingly happy emotions. We become fully responsible human beings when we realize that it is *we*—not external events—who produce our emotions. The same mental energy that is used to control and manipulate outer events in the belief that doing so will safeguard our emotional well-being, can now be used (1) to become fully aware of the dominant role of the inner dialogue in the production of our emotional responses and (2) to reprogram the inner dialogue itself. Much of so-called new age philosophy involves various efforts to reprogram the imaginative portion of the mind through creative visualizations and other techniques. Such techniques have a sound foundation in Spinoza's metaphysical system, and we will explore them later. At present, we wish the reader to become more solidly convinced of (1).

We have already observed, in a previous exercise, that our ongoing process of imagining—our inner dialogue—together with its physical counterpart (the specific bodily physiology that runs parallel to the inner dialogue) can by itself produce emotions. We now wish to observe (a) that the inner dialogue is in fact present even when we are interacting with others, and (b) that the inner dialogue in fact plays a strong causal role in producing and structuring our emotional responses to others.

EXERCISE 16: (a) Choose a time when you are conversing with another person and notice roughly how much of your attention is directed toward what the other person is saying (the external event) and how much is directed toward other things (the automatic inner dialogue). This may not be easy to do, partly because we have to "remember" to do it while the conversation is going on (and we cannot control whether we remember to do something), but mostly because our inner dialogue, like a constant background noise, generally escapes our notice. Part of the content of your inner dialogue when doing this exercise, however, may involve the following: (1) The other person has said something that reminds you of past experiences; your awareness then is focused in part on those past experiences (which in turn may structure your emotional responses to that person). (2) The other person has said something that has triggered in you a chain of associations and conceptualizations: a part of your attention, then, is focused on those concepts. (3) Perhaps, as is often the case, you wish to impress the other person, and so you rehearse in your mind what you are going to say when it becomes your turn to talk: in this case your attention is directed toward the future. The reader is urged to do this exercise as often as possible and in a spirit of nonjudgmental awareness. The point is simply to observe the automatic and all-pervasive nature of our process of imagining.

(b) is more difficult to demonstrate directly, for to do so would involve the ability to observe our emotions in the process of being produced, an ability which we do not as yet have. So we shall demonstrate it indirectly through the use of examples and thought experiments.

The causal role of the inner dialogue in producing our emotions
(1) Suppose that you are going to have a business lunch with someone you do not know. Suppose also that a friend has told you to be careful, that the person you are going to meet is not trustworthy. When you actually meet the person, your friend's warning to be careful will form part of your inner dialogue in terms of which everything the person says and every gesture he makes will be interpreted, and this will be so even if you are not consciously thinking "be careful." Now, suppose instead that your friend had told you the person you are going to meet is honest and trustworthy. Your inner dialogue now contains the thought that he can be trusted and hence your experience of the person will be quite different. The difference in your experience of the person is due to your own process of imagining, which contains the memory of what your friend said.

This example can be extended quite generally. A suspicious person and a trusting person will have quite different emotional responses to the same third person. From a psychological perspective, the difference in emotional responses is due entirely to the differences in their respective processes of imagining. For the inner dialogue of the trusting (suspicious) person contains many thoughts to the effect that people can(not) be trusted, and it is through this inner dialogue—which is ongoing—that other people are experienced.

When we consider things from a physical perspective, we attribute the difference in emotional responses to differences in our bodies, which differences come about both genetically and through past experiences and learning. Indeed, the on-going process of imagining, the inner dialogue, is part of that mode in the Attribute of Thought that correlates with the particular mode of Extension, which is our body. Or more simply, the inner dialogue is the idea of the body insofar as we are conscious of it.

2. If it were the case that our emotions were caused by external events, then we might expect that similar external events would "cause" similar emotional responses. But common experience shows this to be untrue. A kind of event that disturbs us at one time, such as criticism from another, may not affect us at another time. A piece of music that moves us on one occasion may have no effect on another. Anyone who has been with children knows that our emotional responses to children are far from consistent; behavior that amuses us on one day may irritate us on another day. Let us make of this an exercise.

EXERCISE 17: Think of a number of specific instances in which your emotional responses to similar events varied to a degree considerably larger than could be explained in terms of differences among the events. In such cases, the differences in our emotional responses can be explained only in terms of differences within ourselves.

We often use the term "mood" to explain these differences. We say such things as "I was in a bad mood, so the children's behavior upset me," or "I was in a good mood, so my mother's criticisms didn't bother me." But the difference between what we call a "good" mood and a "bad" mood lies in the content of our inner dialogue. When we are in a bad mood, our inner dialogue contains many thoughts that involve, say, suspicion and cynicism toward other people, self-doubt, guilt about the past, anxiety toward the future, etc. It is the background flow of thoughts such as these that can produce in the body-mind emotional responses that are way out of proportion to the external events that appear to cause them.

3. Within any given culture, there are many patterns of emotional responses to outer events that are so deeply programmed into the individuals of that culture that any other emotional response is regarded as abnormal or perverse. Earlier, we gave examples to show how a wide range of conditioned emotional responses—from devotion to violent hatred—can be evoked by religious and patriotic symbols and that these responses are regarded, by the people who suffer from them, as perfectly

normal. While it is unlikely that the reader of this book suffers from either religious or patriotic fanaticism, at least not in their extreme forms, nevertheless we *do* suffer from many kinds of culturally conditioned responses that are just as debilitating as the religious or patriotic ones. One example, which we shall explore later, is that feelings of possessiveness and jealousy are widely regarded as normal components of romantic relationships—so much so that the absence of such feelings with regard to a lover is taken to mean a lack of genuine caring. Another example, which we explore below, is that feelings of hurt and/or anger are considered to be normal responses to criticism, especially harsh criticism, from others.

For the purpose of this example, we will distinguish between constructive criticism where the intention of the other is to help us, and destructive criticism where the intention of the other is to harm us. Although we may feel hurt and angry in response to any kind of criticism—constructive, destructive, or mixed—it is with regard to destructive criticism that such feelings are regarded as most appropriate, if not inevitable. We wish to show that this is not the case.

Suppose you have just been the recipient of some destructive criticism, an insult, a "put-down," etc., and you are now feeling hurt and/or angry. What is the cause of these present feelings? The common belief is that these feelings are caused by the other person's behavior—the insult, or put-down. Spinoza's philosophy, on the other hand, teaches that the feelings of hurt and anger are passive responses generated by our own inner dialogue. That is to say, our minds have been conditioned to produce specific emotional responses in the presence of specific external stimuli, and to believe that the cause of the given emotional response *is* the stimuli. We shall give a few counter-examples to this belief, which will show that by altering an individual's internal dialogue, the same external stimulus can evoke markedly different emotional responses.

Suppose you are told that a certain person has a habit of insulting or "putting down" other people, but that this behavior is caused by an affliction to the speech center of the brain. Then, when you are in the presence of this person, you will not be offended or hurt by anything he says, because this information—that his behavior is caused by an affliction to his brain—now constitutes a part of your inner dialogue. So as he is saying derogatory things to you, your inner dialogue contains thoughts such as "he can't help it," "he has something wrong with his brain," "he's not responsible for what he does," etc., and *these* thoughts are more likely to generate feelings of pity than feelings of anger.

To consider another example, suppose you had been raised in a culture that believed that the cause of psychological abuse is extremely low self-esteem on the part of the abuser and that such abusers feel so badly about themselves that they try to hurt others in a desperate attempt to relieve their own misery. Imagine growing up in a society in which children are taught that they have intrinsic self-worth, rather than being taught that their worth depends on being "better" than somebody else (the latter is the teaching that leads to psychological abuse!). If these two beliefs—(1) everyone has intrinsic self-worth and (2) psychological abuse is caused by low self-esteem—become internalized in the mind of the individual, then psychological abuse, whether in the form of a put-down, an insult, destructive criticism, fault finding, etc., would have no more effect on us than the ravings of a madman and would evoke in us emotions of pity and compassion. In our culture, psychological abuse exists and is so widespread because neither the abuser nor the abused believes in the truth of (1) and (2) above.

These examples illustrate the point that the emotions we experience are caused by our own inner dialogue, which contains the deeply internalized beliefs and values of our culture, and not by the external stimuli. These examples also illustrate a very important aspect of Spinoza's therapy. Insofar as we believe that human behavior is *caused* and *determined,* we suffer less from it than if we believe it to be *uncaused* and *free*. For, in the first example we imagined the abusive behavior to be caused physically, by brain damage, and in the second example we imagined it caused by psychologically by, say, insufficient childhood nurturing leading to low self-esteem.

Notice that the specific beliefs about *what* causes abusive behavior are not as important as the overall belief that such behavior is caused. For whether we conceive that such behavior is caused physically by brain damage, muscle spasm, or viral infection, or is caused psychologically by childhood trauma, unresolved Oedipal complex, or the inability to overcome infantile narcism, so long as we believe that it is caused we suffer less from it. We suffer most from another's behavior when we believe it has no cause, or, which is the same thing, when we believe it is "caused" by the other person's "free will."

But, in fact, all behavior *is* caused. To consider the example of verbally abusive behavior, the sounds that emanate from the person's mouth are produced by the vocal chords in the person's throat. The motion of the vocal chords is caused by contractions of the various muscles that control them, and the contractions of these muscles is caused by the action of nerve cells that in turn is caused, ultimately, by the electro-chemical activity of the brain. If it is now asked, why does the brain of that individual generate the electro-chemical activity that causes the firing of particular nerve cells, etc., leading to the production of the particular abusive words, the answer would involve a lengthy analysis of the causal history of that particular brain, from the embryo to the present. Given that history, the brain has no "choice" but to generate the sequence of events leading to the production of the specific abusive words and tone of voice.

It is an important part of Spinoza's therapy that we align our process of imagining with what we know to be metaphysically true. It is easy to see that our emotional responses to external events would be quite different if our inner dialogue contained the knowledge that all events, including human behavior, are caused. The following exercise is designed to "enliven" this knowledge in our imagination.

> EXERCISE 18: Recall to your mind a recent past event in which your feelings were hurt by something another person said. Perhaps you were criticized by a parent, boss, lover, friend, or co-worker. As you recall the event, pay attention to the feelings in your body. Now visualize the causal process outlined above, leading from the firing of specific neurons in the person's brain to the vibrations of the larynx that produces the sound waves that in turn cause the membranes in your ear to vibrate. Consult, if you wish, pictures in an anatomy text to help you visualize this process more concretely. Hold this anatomical picture in your mind as you recall his words and tell yourself that these words are the outcome of a causal process that could not have been other than what it in fact was. Notice any changes in the feelings in your body as you do this.

As a last example to illustrate the role of the inner dialogue in the production of emotions, we consider the remarkable phenomenon of spectator sports. Devotees, or fans, of spectator sports experience a wide range of intense emotions, leading occasionally to violence, injury, and even death. The fan is a very clear example of a person who, temporarily at least, has given up his own power of action to external events over which he has no control.

We ask, what is the cause of the emotions that a sports fan experiences? If we pose this question to a fan, he will attribute his emotional responses while watching a game to the performance, or lack of performance, of the team he wants to win. He will claim that his happiness or sadness is caused by his team's winning or losing. We will show that this is not the case—that his happiness or sadness really has nothing to do with his team's performance, but rather is produced by his own process of imagining.

So let us consider a sports event between two teams, X and Y, which is being observed by four people who have different inner dialogues with respect to the game. Person A is from the same city as team X and wants X to win. Person B is from the same city as team Y and wants Y to win. Person C is from another city, is not a fan of either team, and has no preference about who wins. Person D is from a foreign country where this particular game is not played and has no knowledge of the rules of the game. Now, as the game progresses, the emotions of A and B will fluctuate, but always in opposition, so that whenever A experiences joy, B experiences sorrow, and vice versa. C, who does not care which team wins, will nevertheless appreciate the aesthetic component of the game. And D, who has no idea what is going on, will experience, if anything, a little confusion as he attempts to figure out what the point of the game is. The difference between C and D is that C has internalized the rules of the game and, because the relevant concepts and rules constitute part of his inner dialogue as he watches the game, he is able to appreciate it. The excitement that C feels, but D does not, during a particularly good play, must be caused by something which is in C's mind but not in D's. And this "something" can only be the difference in their respective processes of imagining, which difference is due to the fact that C's mind, but not D's, contains the knowledge of the rules of the game.

A and B, however, unlike C or D, are emotionally invested in the outcome of the game. Every time team X scores or makes a good play, A will feel joy, B will feel sorrow, and vice versa. Suppose that team X wins. What then is the cause of the emotions, often extreme, that A and B feel? If we put this question to A (B), he will reply that his joy (sadness) is caused by the fact that his team won (lost) the game. But clearly the external event—team X winning—cannot be the cause of the emotions that A and B feel. For, if that were the case, how could we explain the fact that A and B experience *opposite* emotions in response to the *same* external event? Clearly, the emotional responses of A and B are caused by their desire for a specific outcome, and that this desire—which itself is caused by years of identification with their particular team—forms a part of their inner dialogue while watching the game. A and B have been programmed to respond emotionally in the way that they do, and this programming is the true cause of their emotional response, not the outer event, which merely activates the program in their brains

Note that when we say that the individual "gives up his power to an external event," we do not mean that he consciously decides to do this. Rather, because he has deeply identified with the team internally, he automatically experiences his team's ups and downs as his own. For whether A experiences joy (a relative increase in his power of action) or sorrow (a relative decrease in his power of action) now depends on an external event over which he has no control. Thus, he is totally passive with respect to the emotions he experiences.

Let us now begin to identify some of the public contexts in which we regularly allow our emotions to be determined by external events over which we clearly have no control. Spectator sports is one such example. Movies are another; we clearly have no control over the images that appear on the screen; yet, we relinquish power over our emotions to those images, allowing the former to be determined by the latter. Driving a vehicle is another context in which most people give up some power over their emotions; for, clearly, we cannot control how another drives his car, or the flow of traffic, and yet we regularly allow ourselves to feel frustration and anger when we encounter a lot of traffic, or bad and inconsiderate drivers.

EXERCISE 19: List several such contexts now and add to the list later as you become aware of more. Do not try to alter your emotional responses; the purpose her is simply *to become aware* of the extent to which we allow our emotions to be determined by events over which we have no control. While watching a movie, say to yourself "Here I am, allowing these images to 'make me' feel happy, sad, afraid, vengeful, and so on." Or, while driving your car, say "Here I am, allowing this other driver to 'make me' feel angry." See if you can, at least for a moment, withdraw your attention from the external event and apply it to your own emotions. Notice what happens when you do.

Summary, and more examples

We began this section by discussing the inner dialogue—the process of imagining—the "stream of consciousness"—or simply, what we are thinking about on a moment-to-moment basis. We showed, through a number of examples (1) how the inner dialogue is causally active in producing the emotional responses catalyzed by external events. We also noted (2) that the content of the inner dialogue is almost always concerned with things that are not real in the present moment: the past, the future, and/or contrary-to-fact imaginings. And finally, (3) we emphasized the automatic, or mechanical, nature of this process of imagining—that is, we are no more able to stop the flow of thoughts than we can stop the flow of our blood. We conclude by giving a few more examples that simply and directly illustrate these points.

Suppose you are feeling guilty about something. This something will, of course, be a *past* behavior, and hence your inner dialogue, when you are having this feeling, involves thoughts about the past, illustrating (2) above. Moreover, you cannot feel guilty about something *unless* you first remember the thing, which illustrates (1) the causal role played by memories—which are thoughts about the past—in producing our emotions. Similarly, the emotion of anxiety involves the thought of a *future* event, the outcome of which we do not know and perhaps fear. The thought (of the future event) is *causally active* in producing the anxiety, since without that thought there could be no anxiety. And finally, suppose you are now feeling hurt or angry or upset about something someone is doing or saying in the present. A little reflection will show that you are not just observing the other person's behavior, but that you are also *thinking*, e.g., that this person should have done or said something different. Such thinking is altogether fictitious, since it involves the metaphysical impossibility that something should be other than it in fact is. Yet, such thinking is causally involved in producing the emotions of hurt, anger, etc.

With regard to (3), I believe that the mechanical nature of the inner dialogue has been amply illustrated. It may be objected that if the process of imagining is mechanical, then there is nothing we can do about it. This objection is entirely correct; there *is* nothing we can do about it, except become aware of it. This "second-order awareness"—what Spinoza calls the "idea of an idea"—is the key to Spinoza's system of therapy. We have, as a matter of fact, used the concept of an idea of an idea in many of the preceding exercises. We now proceed to a more systematic explication.

SECOND ORDER AWARENESS

Metaphysically speaking, the concept of an idea of an idea is a consequence of holism applied within the Attribute of Thought. For any given idea must be contained within a larger idea, which is itself contained within a still larger idea, etc., and this process of holistic embedding continues until one arrives at the system of ideas as a whole, or the Mind of God. The soul, for example, is an idea—that is, a mind, an awareness, a mode within the Attribute of Thought—which has, as part of its content, the human mind as a whole; hence, the soul is an idea that has another idea as part of its content. The human mind, however, is itself constituted by very many ideas—emotions, sense impressions, and the flow of thoughts that constitute the inner dialogue; for each of these ideas there must exist a second order idea which has that idea as its content.

While watching a movie

At this point, we wish to present a few exercises to give the reader an experiential feeling for this concept—it is not as abstract as it may appear.

 EXERCISE 20: While watching a movie, become aware that you are in fact watching a movie. For this and the following exercise it will be helpful to have a watch with a beeper simply to "remind" you to shift your awareness from (1) the action on the screen to (2) the fact that you are sitting down watching a movie. The first order idea (1) is an awareness that has as *its* content the action on the screen. You are absorbed in that action and your emotions are determined accordingly. The second order idea (2) is an awareness that has the first order awareness—the fact that you are aware of the action on the screen—as its content. The second order awareness will contain many thoughts that are not present in the first order awareness, such as "I am now watching a movie," "the acting is very good," "the chair on which I'm sitting is uncomfortable," etc.

Notice that the shift from first to second order awareness—from the idea to the idea of the idea—does not change the content of first order awareness. The action on the screen remains the same as we shift our awareness from (1) to (2). What does change, and changes dramatically, is our emotional response. For if, say, we are watching a horror movie, we suffer from fear only insofar as our awareness is restricted to (1). But as soon as we shift our awareness to (2), the fear begins to dissipate. The action on the screen is the same, but now our mind contains thoughts in addition to what happens on the screen—thoughts such as "it's only a movie," "they probably had a lot of fun making this movie," etc.—and *these* thoughts remove the fear.

Thus, what we are calling "first order awareness" (or "first order thinking" or "first order ideas") has as its content events in the external world. In the preceding example, as we sit absorbed in the action on the screen, our body is being modified by light reflected from the screen and entering our eyes. The idea in the Attribute of Thought that runs parallel to this modification of our body has, as its content, the images on the screen that appear to be external to ourselves. This idea involves not only the images on the screen, but also the thoughts and emotions, which, in a given individual, are associated with those images through prior conditioning. But this first order idea must be contained within another, second order, idea, of which it is the content. This second order idea involves, not the action on the screen, except secondarily, but rather our awareness of that action; and the associated thoughts and emotions that accompany this second order awareness are, as we have seen, quite different.

This example is quite rich—the reader may have noticed the similarities to Plato's allegory of the cave—and we will extract a few more insights from it before applying the distinction between first and second order awareness to real life situations. First, we note again that insofar as we remain within first order awareness, totally absorbed by the events on the screen, we have given up our power of action to those external events over which we have no control. For whether we feel joy or sorrow, love or hate, hope or fear, etc., now depends on what happens on the screen. Regaining our power of action, regaining control over our emotions, lies not in trying to control the events on the screen, which is impossible, but in making the shift to second order awareness. The second order thought "here I am, allowing this movie make me feel afraid" goes a long way toward dissipating the fear.

Secondly, we note that whereas the content of first order awareness, while watching a movie, is fictitious, the content of second order awareness is real and present. Insofar as our mind is absorbed in the action on the screen, the content of our consciousness is fictitious; but insofar as we are able to shift our awareness from the action on the screen to the fact that we are watching a movie, the content of our consciousness is real and present. For then the content of our consciousness is not primarily the action on the screen, but rather the awareness itself of that action, which awareness is necessarily in the present.

Generally then, whatever may be the content of our first order thinking—whether of sensations of the past, the future, or of contrary-to-fact imaginings—the awareness itself of that content is necessarily real and present. For, whatever it is about which we are thinking, the thinking itself is real and present. And when we become aware of that thinking, so that our thinking itself is now the content of our awareness, then both the content of our awareness and our awareness of that content are real and present.

Shifting from the "there and then" to the "here and now"
I do not wish to belabor the obvious, but we are usually so lost in the content of our own thinking that the obviousness of this distinction, between first and second order awareness, is hidden. Consider: suppose you are thinking about, or remembering, some past event. The content of your consciousness—the past

event—is in the past; but your act of thinking about it is in the present. Or, suppose you are thinking about, or planning for, the future. Then the content of your thinking lies in the future, but your thinking and planning are occurring now. Or, suppose you are thinking about something altogether fictitious; then the content of your consciousness is not real, but your thinking about that content is. The shift from first to second order thinking involves making a shift from what you are thinking about to the process of thinking itself. Thus, although the content of the inner dialogue is related to the past, to the future, or to contrary-to-fact imaginings, the inner dialogue itself is occurring in the present. And insofar as we are able to shift our awareness from the content of our inner dialogue to the inner dialogue itself, we gain a certain freedom from the tyranny of our own thinking.

The following exercises will develop a more experiential understanding of the distinction between first and second order awareness:

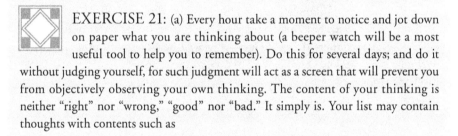

EXERCISE 21: (a) Every hour take a moment to notice and jot down on paper what you are thinking about (a beeper watch will be a most useful tool to help you to remember). Do this for several days; and do it without judging yourself, for such judgment will act as a screen that will prevent you from objectively observing your own thinking. The content of your thinking is neither "right" nor "wrong," "good" nor "bad." It simply is. Your list may contain thoughts with contents such as

1. what you will have for dinner tonight;
2. what you "should have" said to someone;
3. what it might be like to have sex with someone;
4. what you have to do tomorrow;
5. how someone else "should have" behaved toward you, etc.

When you have written down forty or fifty such thoughts, write an "f" beside each one that involves the future, a "p" beside each one that involves the past, and an "h" beside each one that involves a hypothetical, or fictitious, situation. In the above, (1) and (4) involve the future, (2) and (5) involve both the past and a hypothetical, and (3) involves a hypothetical. Notice also any emotions that may accompany these thoughts. For example, (2) may involve guilt, (5) may involve blame, etc.

(b) We now repeat the above exercise, but this time our focus is different. For instead of using the beeper watch to become aware of the content of our thinking, we will use the beeper watch to become aware of the effect that becoming aware of the content of our thinking has on our thinking itself. The moment the beeper sounds we automatically shift into second order awareness. No matter how long or short is the duration of this second order awareness—whether it is sustained for several minutes or whether we immediately get lost again in the content of our inner dialogue—nevertheless, the moment the beeper sounds we are in second order awareness, for at that moment we become aware of the thoughts we are now thinking. As Spinoza puts it, describing his own experience, "although these intervals (of second order awareness) were at first rare, and of very short duration, yet afterwards, as the true good became more and more discernable to me, they became more frequent and more lasting."

Notice also the change in associated thoughts and feelings as you shift your attention from first to second order thinking. If, for example, you find yourself thinking about some past behavior of yours, then the associated thoughts and emotions will pertain to that past behavior. You may find yourself imagining how you "could have" or "should have" behaved; you may find yourself feeling guilty, or proud, or anxious. As you make the shift to second order awareness and become aware that you are thinking about the past, you may find yourself feeling amused or disturbed to notice how your mind relishes living in the past and replaying old tapes. You may connect the thought of your past behavior with other instances of similar behavior and thus come to understand that behavior as part of a larger psychodynamic pattern.

This is the heart of Spinoza's therapy. In order to make these ideas as concrete as possible, we will consider a typical example, cite a few passages from Spinoza, and then apply the latter to the former. So, consider, if you will, some past event in which you were criticized by another. Your feelings were hurt—and indeed, the same hurt feelings may very well resurface as you remember the event—and, depending on the nature of your personality, you will either (1) believe the other is the cause of your hurt feelings, in which case you will project them outward as some form of hatred (e.g., blame, anger, vengeance, etc.) or (2) you will believe that you are the cause of your hurt feelings, in which case you will project them inward as some form of self-hatred (e.g., guilt, depression, etc.) *or* you will believe some combination of (1) and (2).

In the former case, (1), the memory of the past event will be associated with thoughts such as "how dare he criticize me," "I'm right, he's wrong," "he's a jerk," "I'll show him," "I hate him," etc. In the latter case, (2), the memory of the past event will be associated with thoughts such as "I can never do anything right," "I'm not good enough," "I've failed," "I'm inadequate," etc. These related thoughts and feelings will in turn generate desires, which in their turn will lead to behaviors and other feelings. So notice in yourself what thoughts and emotions and impulses to action arise from the memory of that single event.

In a passage already cited, Spinoza says, "if we detach [a] a perturbation of the mind or an emotion from [b] the thought of an external cause and [c] connect it with other thoughts, then [d] the love or hatred towards the external cause and [e] the fluctuations of the mind which arise from these emotions will be destroyed." A little later he says "[f] in proportion then, as we [g] know an emotion better is it more within our control, and [h] the less does the mind suffer from it." And, "everyone has the power, [f] partly at least, if not absolutely, of [g] understanding clearly and distinctly himself and his emotions, and consequently of bringing it to pass that he [h] suffers less from them. We have therefore mainly to strive to acquire [g] a clear and distinct knowledge as far as possible of each emotion, so that the mind may be led [c and h] to pass from the emotion to think those things which it perceives clearly and distinctly and with which it is entirely satisfied, and to strive also that [a] the emotion may be separated from [b] the thought of an external cause and [c] connected with true thoughts" (*Ethics,* pt. 5, prop. 4, note).

So, to apply this to our example, the initial emotion, or "perturbation of the mind" is [a] the feeling of being hurt. If this emotion be projected outward, as in (1) above, it will involve [b] the thought that someone has criticized you, the thought that someone has hurt your feelings. [a] and [b] together—your lowered power of action, coupled with the thought that the other is the cause—constitute [d] hatred of the other, which in turn leads to [e] further dysfunctional emotions or "fluctuations of the mind," such as blaming, thoughts of vengeance, etc. If, on the other hand, the initial feeling of hurt is projected inward, it will involve the belief that the specific behavior for which you are being criticized is the cause of your hurt. In this case, your behavior plays the role of external cause; after all, your behavior—that is, the behavior of your body—is external to your mind. These two together, your hurt feelings or lowered power of action, coupled with your belief that your behavior is the cause, constitute [d] self-hatred, which in turn leads to [e] further dysfunctional emotions such as depression, self-pity, etc.

However, all this is short-circuited as soon as we make the shift to second order awareness. Insofar as we remain trapped in first order thinking, our mind is constrained to thoughts such as "how dare he criticize me" or "I'm a failure," etc., which thoughts are about what is believed to be the external cause. But as soon as we form [g] an idea that has as its content, not some external cause for our hurt, but rather the hurt itself and the fact that we are now thinking about some external cause, then we begin [h] to suffer less. For [f] insofar as we are able to [g] form second order ideas our mind will automatically begin to [c] connect the initial emotion with other thoughts.

What are these "other thoughts," these "true thoughts," which alone promise relief from the bondage of first order thinking? The answer to this question is perhaps obvious by now. Recall once again the play of emotions while watching a movie. If, say, you are feeling afraid during the movie, there is no possibility of release from that fear as long as your awareness is fixed on the action on the screen. To remove or lessen the fear, you must first form a second order idea, e.g., "here I am, watching a movie and feeling afraid." This second order idea will automatically connect to other thoughts at the same (second order) level, such as, "I am allowing the actors and directors to manipulate my emotions," or "why do I watch movies that frighten me," or "it's only a movie" or "this movie is better than most horror movies," etc.

The action on the screen of so-called real life is as determined as the action on the screen of the theater, and we have no more chance of alleviating our suffering through manipulating external events than we do by trying, at the movies, to influence the action on the screen. We cannot even, as we have seen, stop or control the thoughts, memories, and emotions that dance upon the fabric of our consciousness.

But what we *can* do is deepen our awareness of what is—of our feelings and thoughts in the moment—and penetrate the illusion that our emotions are caused by anything external to the imaginative portion of our own mind. And as we shift toward a deepened awareness, toward what I have called second order awareness, the related thoughts and feelings also begin to shift, away from the action *in* the theater of life and toward that which pertains to a clear witnessing of that action. In terms of our example above, the process might look like the following:

Stage 1: First order thinking: "he always finds fault with me," "he has no right to say that to me," "I'll show him," "I can never do anything right" etc.—and the "etcetera" includes the endless rehearsing of future conversations with the other person.

Stage 2: The shift to second order awareness: "here I am again, feeling hurt and blaming someone else," or "here I am, feeling angry and defensive," or "here I am, feeling sorry for myself," or "here I am, rehearsing future conversations wherein I try to get back at him."

Stage 3: Forming a "clear and distinct" idea of the emotion, or knowing the emotion [g]: "this hurt which I am now feeling is simply a temporary decrease in my power of action." "My negative thoughts toward the other is simply an effort of my imagination to weaken what I falsely believe to be the cause of my hurt, thereby lessening (in my imagination) his ability to harm me." "My feelings of self-pity are themselves produced by the imaginative part of my mind while in this temporary state of lowered power of action."

Stage 4: Connecting with other thoughts and larger psychological patterns [c and h]: "My mind has been programmed to produce hurt feelings whenever I am criticized." "I have been conditioned to attempt to protect myself from feeling hurt by blaming others." "This is similar to how I used to feel when, as a child, my parents scolded me." "There is no necessary connection, except in my imagination, between my feelings and another's behavior." "He is criticizing me in an effort to feel better about himself. Perhaps I could feel compassion instead of hurt."

In many of the previous exercises, the reader was asked to recall some past event and then work with the emotional residue from that event. By "emotional residue" I mean the emotions that you *now* experience as you recall the *past* event. For some people, this residue is as strong as were the emotions incurred when the event happened—and when they narrate such past events to others, they do so with the same feelings of hurt, anger, pride, envy, etc., that they felt when the event happened—all of which shows the extent to which they have given up their power of action to the past.

Nevertheless, emotional residues do not have as strong a hold on us as do our emotional responses to present events, and hence, it is easier to practice these techniques on the former. Our goal is eventually to be able to apply these techniques in the present moment, even without a beeper watch. But these techniques can be applied in the present moment, to real life situations as they occur, only insofar as we "remember" to shift into second order awareness, for otherwise our awareness will be controlled by the emotion itself. Therefore, we must train, or condition, our mind to associate second order awareness with the present occurrence of the emotion itself. For just as years of social conditioning have programmed the mind to produce the emotions of hurt, pride, guilt, anger, self-pity, jealousy, etc., in response to another's, or one's own, behavior, so also is it possible to reprogram our own mind to produce second order awareness in response to these various emotions; in this way, the emotions themselves become the catalyst for second order awareness. Working with the emotional residues from past events, as well as with emotions that are produced as we imagine hypothetical or future events, constitutes first steps toward training the mind in this way.

By now, however, the reader must surely have noticed some resistance to doing these exercises—which really is a resistance to shifting into second order awareness. This resistance is not "bad" or "wrong," as we shall explain shortly, but is simply a part of this "human condition" of ours, which appears to consist of an ignorance of who we really are, an ignorance of the "union which exist between our mind and the whole of Nature." This ignorance, whatever may be its ultimate cause, is *actively* maintained by psychological forces present within our own mind.

Mystics everywhere tell us that enlightenment—a state of conscious union with a spiritual or divine Reality—is natural and that our present human condition in which we experience ourselves as separate from others, from the soul of which we are a part, and from the Divine Being, is a sort of illusion. But this illusion, we are saying, is sustained, not by magic, or as "punishment" from God, but rather by psychological forces, the beliefs, fears, habits, conscious and unconscious patterns of conditioning, etc., that operate within our own mind. The road to self-knowledge, or "blessedness," as Spinoza terms it, lies through these inner forces that constitute our resistance to becoming aware. We wish, therefore to say something about the nature of resistance, but first we will make some general remarks about what is called "good" and "bad," "right" and "wrong," etc., since of the many dysfunctional beliefs prevalent in our culture today, none are more debilitating than these.

RESISTING OUR OWN HAPPINESS

The metaphysical impossibility of "good" and "bad"
From the perspective of our metaphysics—in terms of which we understand that, like ripples on the surface of the ocean, the world and everything in it are modifications of a single Divine Being—it is clear that there can be no such thing as good and bad, or right and wrong. For such judgments imply that God could make a mistake, that she could have or should have manifested herself differently, which is nonsense as we have explained earlier. And if it be objected that although God can do no wrong, nevertheless humans can, we remind the reader that the existence of every human being—including those you do not like—and of every human thought, feeling, and behavior—including those you judge to be wrong or bad—follows from the Nature of God in the same way that it follows, as Spinoza is wont to say, from the nature of a triangle that the sum of its angles equals 180 degrees.

Indeed, the belief that some things are "wrong" or "bad" or "evil" in themselves, rather than relative to our own likes and dislikes, rests upon the belief that these things are cosmic errors which could have or should have been otherwise. For to believe that a given action, emotion, or person is "wrong" or "bad" is also to believe that that action, emotion, or person could have or should have been "right" or "good." But once we see that everything whatsoever, without exception, follows from, and is an expression of, the Nature of the Divine Being and that nothing could be different from what it in fact is without that Nature being different—which is absurd—then our judgments about what is right and what is wrong, and who is good and who is bad, must begin to mellow and soften.

Moreover, to judge that something is in itself right or wrong, good or bad, presupposes that we can stand outside the natural order of things and from this platform pass objective judgment on the pageant of Creation. But clearly, there can be no such platform. We do not exist outside the natural order of things but rather, we have been produced by that order. For the same physical and psychical forces that produced our body and our mind also produced the bodies and minds of our planet, of every species and every individual member of every species, and of every other human being—including those who in this life are our adversaries. The human body grows on the surface of the earth in the same way the bodies of other things—plants animals, rocks, etc.—come to exist.

As Spinoza says, "Nature...is always the same and everywhere one...her power of acting, that is to say, her laws and rules, according to which all things are and are changed from form to form, are everywhere and always one and the same, so that there must also be one and the same method of understanding the nature of all things whatsoever, that is to say, by the universal laws and rules of Nature." (*Ethics,* pt. 3, intro). Thus, our body, like all other bodies, is formed according to natural law out of materials existing on the earth, it is sustained in human form through its interactions, also according to natural law, with other bodies also existing on the earth, and eventually perishes according to natural law, its parts returning to the earth.

Indeed, conceiving the matter in this way causes us to realize that any judgment against another must ultimately be a judgment against ourselves. Consider for a moment another person you believe to be "bad," or some behavior or attitude on the part of another that you believe to be "wrong" or "evil." You believe, or desire, that this person should be different, or should have behaved differently; or perhaps, in an extreme case, you wish that this person did not exist at all. But now reflect that this person's existence, behavior, attitudes, etc., were brought about by the same physical and psychical forces that brought about your own existence, behaviors, and attitudes. To wish that the other person were any different from what he in fact is involves wishing that the forces which produced that person were different. But if those forces had been different, which is impossible, then *you* would have been different too, since you were produced by those same forces. Hence, the judgment that there is something "bad" or "wrong" pertaining to another person necessarily involves the judgment that there is something "bad" or "wrong" pertaining to ourselves. This, I believe, is the real meaning of the biblical injunction to "judge not, lest ye be judged," which would be more clearly rendered as "judge not, for in judging another you judge against yourself."

If it be objected, "What about the Hitlers of this world? Surely they are evil," we reply that the Hitlers of this world, as well as the saints of this world, were produced by these same forces—whether these forces be conceived physically, psychologically, socially, etc.—that produced the rest of us. For have you never, in your whole life, for one instant, hated someone so strongly that you wished he were dead? The only difference, then, between you and Hitler is that his hatred persisted in time, he had the means to act on his hatred and was not restrained, except at the very end, by external forces. We hasten to add that the same can be said about love; we have all experienced moments, usually fleeting, of total unconditional caring for another. The only difference, then, between us and Jesus is that he was able to sustain this caring in time; that is, because he directly experienced "the union existing between his mind and the whole of Nature," he did not experience himself as separate from others and thus had the ability to feel and express unconditional love constantly and continuously. Surely, developing this ability within ourselves is a goal worth living for. Ultimately, it is the only goal worth living for.

Some harmful consequences of believing in "good and bad"

Although our judgments of "right and wrong" and "good and bad" are wholly fictitious with regard to their content, nevertheless, insofar as they are ideas, these judgments are something real and therefore have real consequences. These consequences—the effects of believing in "good and bad," etc.—are obstacles to self-knowledge. We now examine several such consequences.

1. If you believe that some past action of yours is bad or wrong, then you will feel guilty. The feeling of guilt involves a decrease in your power of action. Insofar as that feeling is considered under the Attribute of Thought, it involves a decrease in your ability to understand or to think clearly; and insofar as it is considered under the Attribute of Extension, it involves a weakening of your body, i.e., increased stress and anxiety, lowering of the immune system's ability to prevent disease, etc. Moreover, the feeling of guilt lowers your ability to discover the

causes of those actions you judge to be "wrong."

2. If you believe that some behavior on the part of another is "bad" or "wrong," then you will blame the other. But the emotion of blame, which is a form of hatred, involves a lowering of your power of action and hence a reduction in your power of thinking. The attempt to "justify" your hatred by the belief that what the other person did was "wrong" merely strengthens the connection in your imagination between your lowered power of action and the other person's behavior. But why harm yourself by producing feelings of hate in response to what another does? Reflect over and over again that the emotion of hatred in all its forms, considered both physically and psychologically, is harmful to *you* and *only* to you. And also reflect that this feeling is sustained by the belief that the other's behavior is "bad" or "wrong," that the other "should have" behaved differently.

3. Perhaps you believe that another person has such major "faults," or has committed such grievous sins, that she is beyond forgiveness, and that, in this special case, your hatred is justified. But aside from remembering that your hatred harms only yourself, please consider that everyone who has ever hated, including Hitler, also believes that his hatred is entirely justified. Any attempt to justify your hatred is part of that hatred's endeavor to persevere in *its* being. Are you going to play foolish games of trying to figure out which hatreds are justified and which are not? You will only end up justifying your own hatreds, for those who play the "justification" game always end up justifying their own hatreds and the hatreds of those others who agree with them. So it is that the Israeli believes his hatred for the Palestinians is justified, and vice versa, the Palestinian believes his hatred of the Israelis is justified, all with "good reasons." Similarly, the man in divorce court believes his hatred of his wife is justified and reasonable, and vice versa. Resolve, therefore, because you care for your own being, not to play the justification game—for every reason you find to "justify" your hatred binds you to your hatred and sustains the lowering of your power of action, which lowering constitutes the essence of your hatred.

4. Insofar as you believe that you, or another's, behavior is "bad" or "wrong," you will focus your attention on that behavior. Your mind

will become stuck in first order thinking and will torment itself with endless thoughts about that behavior, how it could have or should have been other than what it in fact was. These thoughts, which are produced by a mind already in a state of lowered capacity for clear thinking, in turn further lowers the mind/body's power of action. The mind, as long as it remains attached to the first order content of its own thinking—the specific behaviors, etc.—has given up its power to that content and lacks the strength needed for self-understanding. It is only when the mind is able to detach itself from thoughts about external things and form second order ideas which have these *thoughts,* not the external things, as their content, that it begins to recover its power of action.

Thus, it is not a question of "good or bad," "right or wrong" in any absolute sense. It is a question only of what you want. If you are seeking a state of consciousness "of which the discovery and attainment would enable [you] to enjoy continuous, supreme, and unending happiness" then you must be willing to strive to relinquish your judgments. For if such a state of consciousness consists of "the knowledge of the union existing between the mind and the whole of Nature," it must follow that our mind is in fact united with all other minds, since the latter are necessarily included in "the whole of Nature." In this state of union, as mystics everywhere testify, all things are experienced as flowing from the Divine Being and as such, are perfect exactly as they are. Our judgments of "good and bad" are therefore incompatible with the attainment of this state of consciousness.

If, on the other hand, you wish to preserve your judgments, then you will either judge against yourself and condemn yourself to lifelong feelings of guilt, unworthiness, and failure; and/or you will judge against others, condemning them as unworthy and hence deserving of all the pain and suffering that lies within your power to confer on them. The first leads to depression and, in extreme cases, to suicide; the second leads to strife among neighbors and nations and ultimately to Hitlers. So what is it that you seek to follow: the example of Jesus or the example of Hitler?

Discernment

It is important to distinguish *judgment* from *discernment.* Whereas the former involves the belief that things, people, behaviors, emotions, etc., are in themselves good or bad, or right or wrong, the latter involves the ability to know what is useful or not useful, what will help or hinder us, as we endeavor to attain to the aforementioned state of consciousness, which we regard as an ideal, or model, for ourselves. Spinoza himself retains the terms "good" and "bad," but explicitly defines them *relative* to our desire to attain the state of conscious union with God, of which Jesus is the main exemplar in Western history. "By 'good,' therefore, I understand in the following pages everything which we are certain is a means by which we may approach nearer and nearer to the model of human nature we set before us. By 'bad,' on the contrary, I understand everything we are certain hinders us from reaching that model" *(Ethics,* pt. 4, preface).

We, likewise, will use these terms in this relative sense; and we will also use synonymous terms such as "helpful," "useful," "hindering," "positive," "negative," and so forth. For example, we may refer to certain behaviors and patterns of thinking, such as guilt, blaming, etc., as "negative," by which we mean not that they are bad or wrong in any absolute sense, but rather that they deter and hinder us from our desire to attain a more complete expression of who we are.

The distinction we wish to make between judgment and discernment may be more easily grasped with a few examples from the Attribute of Extension. (Our thinking with respect to the physical is generally a lot clearer than it is with respect to the mental.) Consider the element arsenic. It exists as a part of Nature and according to the Laws of Nature. In itself, it is neither good nor bad; it simply is, and as such—as a part of existence—it has properties and effects that are worthy of being understood. But in relation to human beings, and with respect to a model of what constitutes physical health, arsenic is bad or harmful, in that the effect of arsenic on the human body involves a decrease in the body's ability to persevere in its own being. Although arsenic may destroy a human body, we do not therefore believe that arsenic is sinful, or that God or Nature made a mistake in creating arsenic.

Similarly, is it good or bad, we may ask, when a lion kills a zebra on the plains of the Serrengetti Desert in Africa? Quite obviously, it is good for the lion and bad for the zebra. If a zebra philosopher were to lament that a good God would not have created a world with lions in it, or if a lion philosopher were to complain that in a perfect world God would not have given zebras the ability to run faster than the lion, we would have to accuse these philosophers of, shall we say, "zebrapomorphisms" and "lionpomorphisms," respectively. And the human philosopher who argues from the fact that not all things in Nature are arranged for the benefit of humans—as evidenced by so much physical and psychological suffering in the world—to the conclusion that Evil is something real, or that Nature is less than perfect, or that there is no order in Creation, or that there is no God, etc., is philosophizing quite anthropomorphically. And yet, we all philosophize in this way whenever we hate, feel guilty, or blame another, and then endeavor to "justify" these emotions.

Nevertheless, the lion, the zebra, and we humans must learn to discern wherein lie our best interests. The lion and zebra know this intuitively, although these instincts can be thwarted even for animals. A lion brought up in captivity does not automatically know, when released in the wild, that it is supposed to hunt zebras; a zebra brought up in captivity might not know that its best interests lie in fleeing from lions. They need to learn to discern what their best interests are. We humans also possess an inner guidance system, which Spinoza calls the "dictates of reason," and which always seeks our true best interests. But, largely through dysfunctional cultural conditioning, our minds have internalized such a perplexing array of emotional and behavioral patterns, together with the beliefs that sustain those patterns, that the voice of reason is all but silent, and we are deeply confused about where and how to seek our true self-interest. Like animals raised in captivity, out of touch with their own inner knowing, we must learn to *discern* what will truly lead to greater happiness.

To further illustrate the concept of discernment, consider once again our previous discussion of hurt feelings. No one enjoys feeling hurt, and everyone endeavors to overcome such feelings. Most people, enacting culturally conditioned programs, endeavor to overcome hurt feelings by fixating on what they believe to be the external cause of such feelings and attempt to weaken or destroy the believed external cause. This they do either in their imaginations—by picturing the other person suffering even more, or dead, or repentant, etc.—or through acts of violence. Thus, we have been conditioned to attempt to remove hurt feelings, to heal our minds, in ways that do not and cannot work. Hence we are ignorant of our true self-interest. Spinoza, on the other hand, teaches us that the way to heal our mind involves becoming aware of our feelings, developing a second order awareness that enables us to detach the feelings from thoughts of an external cause and connect them with other thoughts, etc. This method works, and is a "dictate of reason," which, if we but listen to it, in time and with practice, will heal our minds. Discernment is the ability to know when we are being led by the voice of reason and when we are mechanically executing a programmed response.

Resistance, denial, and emotional bondage
But even discernment, which Spinoza calls the "knowledge of good and bad"— that is, the knowledge of what is truly useful and helpful to us and what is truly not useful and harmful to us—is not sufficient to cause us to follow that which

is useful. For it often happens that "when agitated by conflicting emotions we see that which is better and follow that which is worse" *(Ethics,* pt. 4, preface). Our lives abound with numerous instances in which we engage in behaviors that we know are *not* good for us and resist engaging in behaviors that we know *are* good for us. In the following exercise we suggest a way to become more explicitly aware of our specific resistances.

EXERCISE 22: Begin by resolving not to indulge in judgments against yourself; such judgments harm you more than anything you think you are doing "wrong." Then, in the spirit of nonjudgmental awareness, complete the following sentence: "I know I would be physically and/or mentally happier if I...." Complete the sentence with whatever occurs to you in the moment. Some possible examples are "exercised more," "could stop smoking," "could stop worrying about the future," "did not feel so hurt when criticized," "were not sexually attracted to people I didn't particularly like," "were not so quick to anger," "could express my true feelings to my parents (friends? lover?)," "could stop trying to please everybody," "ate healthier foods," etc.

After you think of several such items, recollect several specific occasions in which this knowledge of what would be in your own best interests was actually present immediately prior to your behavior but was not sufficient to cause you to act on it. For example, "here I am, about to light a cigarette, knowing it will harm my body," or "here I am, not telling my lover what I'm really feeling even though I know I would feel better if I did," or "here I am, about to take my third (or fourth, or fifth) drink at this party, knowing I will suffer from it in the morning," or "here I am, about to have sex with this person toward whom I do not feel emotionally connected, knowing I will feel alone and empty afterwards," and so on.

It is clear that even when we know what is helpful or good for us, we are not consistently able to act on that knowledge. Spinoza calls this "human bondage." "The impotence of man to govern or restrain the emotions I call 'bondage,' for a man who is under their control is not his own master but is mastered by fortune, in whose power he is, so that he is often forced to follow the worse, although he sees the better before him" *(Ethics,* pt. 4 preface). Psychologists will recognize, in the phrase "forced to follow," the contemporary notion of obsessive and compulsive behavior. We will use the term "resistance," recognizing that it has many forms, but interpreting it generally to refer to that in us which prevents us from following the better and avoiding what is harmful. We may be conscious of our resistance, as in the above exercise, or we may not. If we are not conscious of our resistance, then we will also resist any attempt to become conscious. This latter is what therapists call "denial."

Penetrating our own denials and seeing our own resistances as they operate is one of the most difficult things to do, since we generally deny the existence of that which we do not see, and conversely, that the existence of which we have denied, we do not endeavor to see. But, because a denial is really a lack of awareness of some specific way in which we have given up our power of action to some external context, it follows that if we wish to more fully reclaim our power of action, then we must be willing to bring awareness to our own denials.

The human condition, of course, reflects spiritual denial in its ultimate form, in that the mind is not aware of its connection with God and denies the existence of such a connection. But between the mind of man and the Mind of God there are many intermediate levels, and it is enough that each person be willing to explore his or her own "next" level individually. That "next level" involves becoming aware of the culturally conditioned "program" that determines our emotional and/or behavioral responses to external events.

Consider our earlier example of the sports fan. (It is always easier to see these unconscious patterns operating in others.) Suppose his team has just lost, and he is upset and angry. His power of action, that is, his capacity for clear thinking, is lowered, and his mind is filled with thoughts that attempt to place blame for the loss and that attempt to imagine how his team "could have" won had the game been played differently. These mental processes (*blaming* and *imagining*) are efforts that his mind makes as it attempts to alleviate its suffering. If we try to tell him that his anger and sorrow are caused, not by his team's loss, but by his having given up his power to an external event over which he has no control, he is likely to *deny* it and transfer his anger to us. *We* know that the only way for him to remove his feelings of upsetness and anger is to reclaim his power of action, so that his emotions are no longer controlled by the outcome of the game. But *he* regards his emotions as perfectly natural, as caused by the outcome of the game, and will generally deny and resist any suggestion to the contrary.

Even in cases where we know we are allowing our emotions to be determined by external events that are wholly fictitious, such as a movie, we feel a resistance to shifting into second order awareness. The drama on the movie screen, like the drama on the screen of our personal reality, constantly sucks our consciousness into itself; we lose ourself in the external action and resist the awareness of what we are in fact doing, which awareness is necessary for release from what Spinoza calls our "bondage."

Now, quite obviously it is not possible to offer an exercise that will provide any direct insight into the details of our own denials. This is because denial is resistance of which we are not conscious; rather, it is the resistance to becoming conscious of ways in which we give up our power to external events. Nevertheless, we can give some examples of patterns of denial that are common in our culture.

1. A person may have a substance abuse problem and deny it to herself, even though it is obvious to everyone else.

2. A person may be involved in a very dysfunctional ("co-dependent") relationship and yet deny that anything is wrong. (I heard of a case where a women who was regularly beaten by her husband claimed, in his defense, that "he only beats me when I deserve it.")

3. A person, because of security needs, may deny that he is bored with his job and/or unfulfilled by his marriage.

4. Collectively, as a culture, we Americans systematically deny that there is any problem with how we live and will blame anyone and everyone when things don't go our way. In particular, we deny that our addiction to the lifestyle supported by the burning of fossil fuel is destroying the earth's ability to sustain life, and we strongly resist becoming aware, as a nation, of the evidence that this is indeed the case.

5. A person may deny her true feelings toward her parents, because she strongly believes she "should" love them.

6. A person may deny his feelings of hurt, fear, and vulnerability because he believes he "should" be strong and that strength consists in not having such feelings.

In general, we tend to deny any patterns of feeling and behavior that contradict our self-image, as the preceding examples show. But our self-image is just that;

it is an *image,* a fiction, that is mainly the result of our endeavor to survive our childhood. For, as all developmental psychologists agree, the child, adolescent, and young adult adapts various strategies of feeling and behaving in order to extract the maximum amount of nurturing and approval from her parents and other authority figures. Or, as Spinoza would say, these strategies are part of the effort she makes to persevere in her own being, although they are often incompatible with how she truly feels and desires to behave at the time. Over time, insofar as we come to identify with these strategies, our self-image is formed by internalizing others' expectations of how we "should" feel and behave, and we lose touch with the ability to know our true feelings and even to perceive our true behavior.

So to consider a possible example, a child who is harshly criticized or rejected when he makes a mistake or behaves in a way his parents do not like learns first of all to experience fear and anxiety whenever he does something—or even thinks about doing something—he thinks his parents won't like. This learning then transfers over to anyone to whom the person has relinquished power over his emotional well-being. Next, he learns to conceal his anxiety, since he comes to realize that his parents may suspect him of "wrong-doing" if they see that he is anxious. So first he denies his anxiety to his parents, and then, after years of practicing this denial, he denies it to himself—that is, he loses the ability to know that he is afraid of doing something of which another may disapprove; and his self-image will exclude that element of his personality.

EXERCISE 23: The purpose of this exercise is to begin to develop an awareness of feelings and behavior that contradict your self-image. First list several qualities that you believe best describe the kind of person you are. If you wish, complete a sentence like "I am a _____ person." In the blank put adjectives such as "loving," "lazy," "insecure," "angry," etc. Then for each of the words on your list, complete a sentence like "if I see myself as a loving person, then I will not see, i.e., I will deny, those of my feelings and behaviors that are unloving." "If I see myself as lazy, then I will not see the ways in which I behave and feel energetically and industriously." "If I see myself as insecure, then I will not see the ways in which I feel and behave with confidence," etc. Use any resources you may have—groups, friends, and therapists— to help you become more aware of behavioral and emotional patterns that conflict with your self-image.

We cannot alter, or outgrow, any patterns of feeling and behaving unless we first become aware of them. But our self-image is a powerful psychological force that tends to oppose such awareness by denying the existence of any patterns of which we are not now already conscious. It is easier, as we have said, to see denial operating in others, and it may be useful to think about several friends and relatives and consider some of the ways in which their self-image conflicts with their actual behavior. We hasten to add that it is not "wrong" to have an inaccurate self-image, nor are we advocating changing negative self-images to positive ones. *Any* self-image is a conceptual net that accepts certain of our emotions as "valid" and rejects the others. And those emotions that are rejected by our self-image do not, of course, simply vanish; they remain in our minds and bodies, where hidden from the light of conscious awareness, they contribute strongly to all kinds of stress and dis-ease. Since self-knowledge consists first of all in an awareness of our presently occurring feelings and behaviors, *any* self-image is an obstacle to self-knowledge.

EXERCISE 24: Having identified, at least partially, some elements of our self-image, we wish now to catch it in action, to form an occurrent idea—all second order ideas are occurrent—that has our self-image as its content. Such an idea may be expressed verbally as follows (there are, of course, many ways to express an idea verbally, and the reader should find a form which suits her best): "Here I am, my stomach is in knots, my heart is pounding, and my throat is constricted, yet I am refusing to acknowledge that I am now angry because I have identified with an image of myself as always kind and caring," or "here I am, not listening to my own inner knowing, because I have identified with being insecure and believe that the other person knows what is best for me," or "there I go again, arguing some foolish point because my self-image depends on needing always to be right," etc. The difficulty with this exercise will be remembering to do it. But the more we ponder such things and discuss them with others, the more they will affect our imagination and the more frequently we will find ourself spontaneously shifting to second order awareness.

Hence, we are not trying to "correct" our self-image; rather, we wish to bypass it altogether. In a way, the same thing that we said about our emotions and behaviors—that we must develop a second order awareness with respect to them—applies to our self-image. For our self-image, although its content be fictitious, nevertheless has real effects, insofar as it is an idea. We cannot free ourselves from its influence until we catch it in the act; that is, until we form a second order idea that has our self-image as *its* content.

Hopefully, we have now gained some insight into some of our own resistances and denials. Although we have described them and experienced them more consciously, however, we have not yet fully explained them in terms of their causes. For to abstract from our personal dramas for a moment, it is certainly most interesting, if not amusing, that such phenomena as resistance and denial exist. How is it possible that we can resist our own self-interest, that we so often "see the better but follow the worse," that we can deny having feelings and behaviors that are obvious to everyone except ourselves? We wish to address this question now, not only because they are interesting in their own right, but also because when we understand that resistance and denial, like everything else, arise from the natural order of things, we will perhaps become a little less judgmental and a little more forgiving and loving, both of ourselves and of others.

The cause and structure of human bondage

As we have seen, we are in what Spinoza calls "bondage" to conditioned and repetitive patterns of feeling and behaving, to our self-image, to our memories, to our fears and anxieties, etc. Our resistances and denials are the dynamic psychological forces in our mind that keep us in bondage. To give an explanation for our resistances and denials in general is also to give an explanation for human bondage in general; the specifics of course will vary from one individual to the next. The explanation for the fact of human bondage—for the fact that we are not able to do what we know is in our best interest and that we are blind to many things about ourselves that are so apparent to everyone else—is not to be found in any obscure theological or psychological doctrine of sin, original or otherwise, which teaches that some aspects of our being are bad or evil and hence need to be repressed and resisted; nor is it to be found in any equally obscure romantic doctrine which holds that human nature is "flawed," or "weak," or "imperfect." On the contrary, the human being is a part of nature. Her existence follows from the Laws of Nature, and therefore the fact of bondage must be understood in terms of the Natural Order of things. In other words, we wish to show that bondage is a natural phenomenon and as such, it must be understood, not lamented over.

We begin by recalling a number of metaphysical principles that we have discussed earlier.

1. Every mode of Substance (or of God or of Nature), whether it be conceived as physical or as mental, endeavors to persevere in its being.

2. The human body is a mode of Nature, conceived under the Attribute of Extension.

3. The human mind (or the imaginative portion thereof) is that same mode of Nature, conceived under the Attribute of Thought.

4. The human body is composed of many other bodies (e.g., organs), which in turn are composed of many other bodies (cells), which in turn are composed of many other bodies (molecules), etc. The human body is thus composite to a high degree

5. For each mode conceived as existing in the Attribute of Extension, there exists a correlate in the Attribute of Thought, which latter we call the idea or the mind of the thing.

6. For each part within the human body—for each organ and system of organs, for each cell and system of cells, etc.—there exists within the human mind a mode that is the idea or mind of that organ, cell, etc. Thus, the mind, like the body, is composite to a high degree.

7. From (1) it follows that each part within the body and each part within the mind endeavors to persevere in its being.

8. The endeavor or force by which a given part of the body (or mind) strives to persevere in *its* own being may conflict with the endeavor of other parts of the body (or mind) to persevere in *their* own being.

9. The endeavors of the various parts of the body and mind may also conflict with the endeavor of the body and mind *as a whole* to persevere in *its* own being.

To illustrate (8), consider an individual molecule within our body. The endeavor, or force, by which it perseveres in its being has to do with the physical and chemical forces that hold its atoms together. It does not, as Spinoza might put it, pertain to the essence of the molecule that it belongs to our body. Similarly, the idea, or mind, of the molecule does not care whether or not it belongs to the mind of the body as a whole. A given molecule actively resists, through the binding energy of the forces that hold its atoms together, any attempt to alter its form. But such efforts are made all the time by other molecules and systems of molecules; that is, chemical transformations occur continuously within the body (digestion, respiration, etc.). This also illustrates (9): the effort which our body as a whole makes to persevere in its being involves the continuous creation and destruction of molecules within it, and so the endeavor of the body as a whole to maintain its form by, say, breaking up a given sugar molecule, will be contrary to the striving of that sugar molecule to maintain *its* form.

Let us continue with this line of reasoning. A given atom or simple molecule existed prior to becoming part of our body and will exist after our body has perished. For that matter, atoms and some molecules existed prior to the formation of the earth itself, and so, being part of this or that body, or of the earth itself, is not something relevant to the being of the atom. But there *are* parts within our body, e.g., the cells, whose existence very much depends on the larger whole, i.e., the body, in which they are embedded. The cells are created by processes going on in the body as a whole, they are sustained through continuous interaction with other cells, and they are eventually destroyed by the same natural forces that created them. To put it metaphysically, the Order of Nature, insofar as that order manifests as a human body, creates, sustains, and destroys the cells that constitute that body.

This way of thinking also applies to the human body as a whole. The human body depends for its existence on a larger ecosystem which creates it, sustains it, and eventually destroys it. Just as the human body is the larger ecosystem in which the various cells enjoy their existence, so the earth as a whole is the larger ecosystem in which each human body has *its* existence. This is meant not metaphorically, but literally. It is therefore no more a fault of Nature that human bodies should be overcome by external causes and suffer and die, than it is a fault of Nature that a given cell within our body should weaken and die. Just as the death of a cell is a part of the natural process by which our body endeavors to persevere in its being—for the body would perish if its cells were not continuously created and destroyed—so the death of our body is part of the natural process by which the larger ecosystem in which we exist and which created our bodies in the first place perseveres in *its* being. This also illustrates (9) above, for clearly the striving of the human body to persevere in its being is eventually overcome by the striving of the earth, which we regard as a living, conscious organism, to persevere in *its* being.

We have seen how the striving of a whole may overcome the striving of its parts. The converse is also true. Cancer cells are a good example of how the striving, or endeavor, of one part of the body to persevere in its existence by conflicting with, and often overcoming, the striving of the body as a whole to continue to exist. Similarly, the striving of the human body as a whole to persevere in its existence by multiplying is destroying the earth's ability to continue to exist in its present form. Quite literally, the human body is now a cancer upon the body of the planet, reproducing uncontrollably and consuming everything it can. And just as the striving of cancer cells may destroy the very ecosystem on which its existence depends, so also the present striving of human bodies may very well destroy the earth's ability to sustain the rich diversity of life, including our own, that presently exists.

Reason and rationality
This example shows very clearly the need to distinguish (1) what an individual *believes* to be in his best interests and (2) what is truly in his best interests, for it is certainly not in the best interests of any individual to act in a way that undermines the conditions necessary for his own existence. An individual may thus be mistaken about what is truly in his best interests. So we will distinguish between (1) an apparent good—that which appears to be good in the moment—and (2) a true good—that which is truly beneficial to us. Clearly, no behavior or striving of a given individual, whether cell or human, that weakens the ability of the larger whole, upon which the individual's own existence depends, to persevere in *its* existence, is in the best interests of the given individual. And this is so regardless of whether or not the given individual is aware of the consequences of his behavior.

We will use the term "rational" to refer to any behavior, together with the mental correlate of that behavior, that is, the thoughts and emotions and desires which accompany the behavior, that is *truly* in our best interests. We use the term "irrational" to refer to any behavior and/or thinking which is *truly* bad, or not in our best interests. Thus, cells that reproduce without limit are behaving irrationally; and humans who reproduce without limit, who burn fossil fuels that destroy the environment, etc., are also behaving, collectively, irrationally. We shall use the term "reason" to denote the ability, or power, of the mind to discern its true best interests, that is, to distinguish between rational and irrational emotions, behaviors, and desires. The "man of reason," who Spinoza describes in part 4 of

The Ethics, is one who is always able to feel and act in accordance with his own best interests.

We remark that our usage of these terms, "rational," "irrational," and "reason," differs greatly from what is taught in schools and universities today. There the term "reasoning" is used to describe the mental process by which an individual figures out the best means to accomplish some end, or goal, or desire, without regard for whether or not that goal is in the true best interest of the individual. Of course, given any particular desire—for wealth, for fame, for pleasure, etc.—there are more or less expedient ways to accomplish it. But once we have seen that we can and do have desires that are *not* in accord with our best interests, then it seems rather inappropriate, if not a bit perverse, to use the word "reasoning" to describe the mental process by which an individual strives to achieve some goal without regard for whether that goal is truly useful to her. It also seems perverse to use the word "reason" to describe the mental process by which, for example, a drug addict calculates how to rob a store to support his habit, or a politician plots a military adventure to serve his lust for power, or a business executive plots how to skimp on the quality and safety of a product to satisfy his addiction to money. Hence, we will use the term "cleverness" to describe this latter mental process and follow Plato and Spinoza in reserving the term "reasoning" to refer to that mental activity which discerns which of our goals and desires are good.

Again, we wish to emphasize that we are not using the terms "good" and "bad" in any objective sense. It is not objectively bad or wrong that a person destroy herself, or live miserably through an addiction to drugs, greed, a certain self-image, etc.; it is bad simply relative to the person's true happiness. Neither is it bad or evil for the human race to destroy itself through its addiction to fossil fuels; it is bad simply relative to our collective desire to persevere in our own being. Or in other words, it is not rational to burn fossil fuels, pollute the environment, etc.

To be sure, if we wish to conceive things more theologically, we may truthfully believe such things as "God will punish us for our sins." For by "sin" we understand a behavior or thought that is not in our true best interest. By "punishment" we understand the adverse effects that such behavior has on us individually and collectively. And by "God" we understand here that portion of the Order of Nature in terms of which the adverse effects are necessary consequences of such behaviors. Thus, religions' admonishments that we shall be "punished" for our transgressions has the same meaning for us as a mother's warning to her child not to eat too much cake. The child may be ignorant of the causal connection between eating too much cake and the ensuing stomach ache, but the latter is a necessary consequence of the former in virtue of the Order of Nature that has manifested as the body of that child. The child's appetites, like our own, pertain to "things which are sweet in the moment" *(Ethics,* pt. 4, prop. 16) and do not take into account the larger picture, which is the province of reason.

So although we human beings are not "evil" or "sinful" as theologians usually understand these terms, we are, nevertheless, largely ignorant of which goals and desires are rational and worth pursuing. Cancer cells are ignorant of their connection with the larger whole in which they have their being. They are ignorant of the fact that their best interests lie in maintaining a certain balance between themselves and the other cells that collectively constitute the body; they are ignorant of the fact that if this balance is upset, the body as a whole will perish and so will they. So also, irrational human behavior and desires, both individually and collectively, arise ultimately from our ignorance of the connection that exists between ourselves and the Whole of Nature. And although irrational human behavior cannot destroy the Whole of Nature, it can destroy the ability of that whole to support human life, which is all we need care about.

We can now give a fuller account of the structure of resistance and denial. The body, as we have said, is constituted by many parts or subsystems, each of which has its own *striving,* often without regard for the other subsystems or for the body as a whole. A subsystem that has been relatively strengthened, as is the case with addictive behavior, will not endeavor to lose its strength in order that the body/mind as a whole be restored to balance, any more than a wealthy person will endeavor to lose his wealth in order that society as a whole be restored to balance.

Suppose, for example, that a person has an addiction to alcohol, or to the accumulation of wealth, or to fame, etc. The person then suffers from incessant desires, or compulsions, to consume alcohol, acquire wealth, be admired, etc. This desire comes from a subsystem that has been relatively strengthened from past use, and it is not uncommon to find that in some people the subsystem is so strong that it dominates the entire personality and the individual's mind is entirely controlled by thoughts of alcohol, money, and praise.

Psychologically, a subsystem may be thought of as a nexus of emotions and thoughts, conscious or unconscious, together with the desires that spring from this nexus. The given nexus has gained a position of strength over other systems within the body/mind, through repeated past reinforcement and strives to maintain its control over the body/mind as a whole. In order to persevere in its being, the nexus will generate many thoughts, for example, *memories* of how good it felt to drink, make money, be praised, etc., *plans* to repeat those behaviors in the present and future, *"arguments"* to the mind as a whole that appear to justify its desire to repeat these behaviors, and *emotions* of anxiety, fear, loneliness, and panic that it promises to remove upon repetition of the past behavior.

Any repetitive pattern of feeling and/or behavior constitutes a subsystem within our mind and, together with its counterpart in the body, strives to persevere in its being without regard for the overall well-being of the mind and body as a whole. The mind/body, considered as a whole, endeavors to balance the various subsystems within itself, so that *it* is in control of them, rather than vice versa, which latter is what Spinoza calls "bondage." Insofar as it is successful in this endeavor it is using reason and is active; insofar as it is unsuccessful in this endeavor, it is passive and suffers from its bondage to the imaginative thinking and feeling produced by one or more of its subsystems.

Now, if any given subsystem, for the continuation of its own existence, requires that the mind as a whole be unaware of it, then, as part of its (the subsystem's) striving to persevere in its own being, it will attempt to conceal its existence from the mind as a whole. This is the cause of *denial*. For clearly, if a pattern, or subsystem, of feeling and behavior is not in the best interests of the mind as a whole, then insofar as the mind as a whole is aware of the pattern, it (the mind) will endeavor to remove or modify it. But the mind cannot strive to remove a pattern of which it is unaware. Therefore, insofar as a given pattern would be weakened or destroyed by the clear light of awareness, it seeks to hide from this light and seeks to control the mind as a whole by producing many thoughts ("arguments," "justifications," etc.) that deny the existence of any such pattern. That is why the first and most difficult step for any addict is to acknowledge his addiction and to acknowledge that his addiction is harmful to his overall well-being.

Repetitive patterns that manifest in obvious physical behavior, e.g., alcoholism, compulsive eating, compulsive talking, gambling, material acquisition, etc., as difficult as they may be to acknowledge, are generally easier to see than emotional repetitive patterns. Perhaps this is because the latter are closer to who we take ourselves to be, and their exposure would threaten our concept of who we actually are. According to our metaphysics, if we experience ourselves as anything less than what we *really* are—a holy thought in the Mind of God—then our concept of who we are is produced by a nexus of such patterns that seek to make us believe that we shall die without them.

PROGRAMMED PATTERNS OF FEELING AND BEHAVIOR

Identifying our patterns
To illustrate (a), notice how readily these emotions come into play merely by *imagining* the programmed stimulus. Merely imagining, for example, that your lover is enjoying sex with another person will activate the "jealousy" pattern

 EXERCISE 25: Begin by identifying one or more emotional patterns that you can see operating in your life. We will list several patterns that are common in our culture:

1. You feel *upset* when things do not happen as you wish.
2. You feel *hurt* or *angry* when criticized.
3. You feel *envy* toward those you believe have been more fortunate than yourself.
4. You feel *jealous* with regard to your lover.
5. You feel *guilt* when you think you have not behaved as you should.
6. You feel *anxious* when you contemplate expressing what you really think and feel.
7. You *worry* or feel *fear* with respect to the future.

Everyone has doubtless experienced all of the above in varying degrees, but probably a few will be more prominent to you, more a part of your "modus operandi," than the others. After you have identified a few, remind yourself that the feelings are *never* caused by the external events that trigger them. Rather, your body and mind have been programmed to produce these feelings as a response to external stimuli. This program constitutes a pattern in your mind/body, which pattern strives to persevere in its existence without regard to your overall well-being. As part of their striving, these patterns (a) constantly seek opportunities to express themselves, (b) generate to your conscious mind arguments, thoughts, and rationales to convince you of the appropriateness of their existence, (c) cause you to believe that the only way to alleviate these emotions is by controlling the external events that trigger them—and since this is virtually impossible, this belief guarantees the perpetuation of the pattern, and (d) cause you to *deny* that it is the pattern itself that is the problem.

within you. Just thinking about telling your boss, or your mother, how you really feel about them can activate the anxiety response. Imagining doing something you believe to be wrong will activate the guilt response, and so forth. The fact that merely thinking about, or imagining, the stimulus can activate the response should be sufficient to show that these emotions are not caused by external events. Rather, they are caused by the patterns themselves, which constantly strive for opportunities, real or imagined, to express themselves.

If a pattern is strong enough to dominate the personality, then we often describe the person by the pattern. An angry person (where "anger" is used in its dispositional sense) constantly looks for things to become angry (occurrent sense) about. A guilt-ridden person constantly looks for opportunities to feel guilty. A worrier constantly looks for reasons to express and justify his worrying; an insecure person is always on the lookout for things to feel hurt about, etc. In each case, we believe we have "good reasons" to feel the way we do. To illustrate (b), the worrier will produce many arguments to justify his worrying. The angry person believes his anger is righteous and justified by the "bad" behavior of someone else. The envious person believes that he has a right to feel the way he does because life has treated him unfairly, etc. All these "reasons" and "justifications" are merely thought-forms created by the emotional patterns themselves and serve the sole purpose of perpetuating and strengthening the patterns, and form a major portion of the individual's system of *denial*.

To continue this exercise, notice how you justify these feelings to yourself—how you tell yourself you have a "right" to feel this way, that you "have to" feel this way, that you "can't help" feeling this way, etc. Write down the specific arguments and rationales that have as their conclusion that under *these* circumstances you *must* have these feelings. For example, you may find yourself thinking like this: "of course I should worry; I don't know if I will get the job" (as if worrying has anything to do with whether or not you'll get the job), or "I have good reason to be upset because my car just broke down" (as if becoming upset is necessary to fix the car), or "I can't help feeling angry; my lover just left me" (as if feeling anger will bring your lover back, or punish him or her for leaving you) . Now tell yourself that such thinking, or rather, the content of such thinking, has nothing to do with reality, and that the thinking itself is generated by the emotional pattern which strives only to create and re-create the emotions of worry, anger, etc.

Thus, this thinking, this endeavor to justify our emotions, is actually part of a pattern of denial, (c) above. For when we are engaged in such thinking, our attention is focused, not on the emotion itself, not on the feelings within our body, but rather on some external event. But as long as we fix our awareness on external events we deprive ourselves of the most effective tool for healing, namely, our awareness. As part of their striving to sustain their own existence, these patterns divert our awareness away from them and cause us to focus instead on external events and to deny that the emotions themselves are the problem. The mental energy that we dissipate planning how to control external events could be used to heal ourselves.

To conclude this exercise, imagine some external event that usually triggers a specific emotional response in you. If, for example, you tend to feel hurt when criticized, then imagine yourself being criticized by someone whose approval you believe you need. Or, if you tend to be jealous, imagine your lover enjoying sex with another person, and so forth. First focus your awareness on the external event; then shift your awareness to the feeling in your body. Remind yourself that to be aware of an emotion is to be aware of it in your body—as a definite sensation in some part of your body, e.g., throat, stomach, chest. Insofar as the content of your awareness is the outer event, you are not aware of your emotions, which are always in your body.

Notice any resistance to shifting your awareness to the feelings themselves. The pattern or subsystem within your mind/body that causes you to create these specific feelings in response to those specific outer events seeks to keep your awareness on the outer events, thereby strengthening their hold on you. It is as if it "knows" that as long as it can get you to look for the solution to your problems where it can't be found—in the external events—and cause you to deny that the problem is in the feelings themselves, then it is itself safe, hidden from the natural light of your own understanding, able to persevere in its being and keep you in bondage to it, so that your whole life is a series of reactive, or conditioned, responses to external events that you believe "make" you feel the way you do.

Infections of the mind, or the power of conditioned patterns
We have explained *denial* in terms of the endeavor, or *striving* of various physiological and psychological patterns or subsystems to persevere in their being by keeping their existence hidden from our *reason,* which latter, as we are using the term, is the striving of our mind as a whole and always seeks our true best interests. But yet, even when we are able to penetrate our denials and see our patterns clearly, they are still able to control us so that quite often it happens that "we see the better but follow the worse." Would that it were so easy that the mere knowledge of what is good for us and what is bad for us were sufficient to cause

us to follow the good and avoid the bad! To be sure, from the knowledge of good and bad arises the desire or striving to seek the former and shun the latter; but the strength, or force, of this desire is often weak compared with the desires that arise from the striving of the various patterns and subsystems within us. So the tobacco addict may know that smoking is not good for him and from this knowledge arises a desire to stop smoking, but this desire, which, as Spinoza puts it, springs from reason, will be weak compared to the desire which springs from the striving of the addictive pattern to perpetuate itself.

Now, our emotional patterns, we must remember, are as physiological as they are psychological. For each of these patterns, deep pathways have been grooved into the brain itself, so we must not expect that an emotional addiction—to greed, to guilt, to anxiety, etc.—is any easier to correct than is a physical addiction. For all patterns within us exist as modifications both of our mind *and* our body. Just because we tend to conceive of chemical addictions as physical doesn't mean they are not also psychological, and just because we conceive emotional patterns as psychological does not mean they are not also physical. The person who is addicted to greed, anxiety, guilt, etc.—or to put it another way, the person in whom the physical and psychological patterns that produce these emotions are very strong—strives to create and re-create these emotions with as much force and intensity as the chemical addict constantly strives to recreate the "high" he gets when he indulges. Indeed, we often speak of a person being "consumed" or "ravaged" by greed, guilt, anxiety, etc., in the same way that a person may be consumed by an obsessive desire for drugs.

So how does a part within us get to be so strong that it dominates the rest of us, even to the point of destroying us? Spinoza's answer to this question is, basically, that these patterns are grooved into our body/mind by means of our interactions with the external world, whose strength exceeds our own. We are not born, or at least, we are not conceived, feeling anxious, envious, guilty, etc.; hence, these are responses that are conditioned into us from conception through adolescence by our environment. These patterns are how we responded to the environment in which our personality was formed. Therefore, the strength of any such pattern, once formed, will involve the strength of the particular environmental forces that caused the formation of that pattern in that individual. Since such external forces—parental, religious, economic, cultural, etc.—can be indefinitely strong compared with the force with which a single individual strives to persevere in his or her own being, it follows that an individual, especially as a child, may internalize and be overcome by thinking and feeling just as easily as he may be overcome by ingesting poison. In either case, the individual endeavors, insofar as he is able, to persevere in his own being. In either case, this endeavor is limited by external forces, the strength of which exceeds his own.

It is easier, I think, to understand the structure of Spinoza's explanation by first seeing how it works with respect to the physical body. As we have noted, each body strives to persevere in its own being. This striving manifests not only overtly, in seeking for food and water and avoiding pain, etc., but also in protecting us from forces that seek to destroy us from within. For example, the striving of a bacterium that enters our body may or may not be compatible with the striving of our body, by means of its immune system, to persevere in its being. Although there are many kinds of bacteria and viruses whose striving is compatible with our own striving, such as those that assist with digestion, there are also many kinds whose own striving in the human body is incompatible with the continued existence of our body, as, for example, in infectious diseases.

Just as there are organisms living in our body whose *striving* is different from our own and which seek to modify our body to suit its own purposes, even to the extent of destroying our body, so also there are ideas, or psychological structures "living" in our mind, whose striving is different from that of our own and which seek to modify our mind to suit *its* purposes, even to the point of weakening and destroying the (imaginative portion of the) mind. Such an idea, like a bacterium or virus, may be *in* us, but it is not *of* us. Our minds contain very many such ideas, some of which are compatible with us and others of which may be said to infect us in the same way that a virus infects us. As a viral infection can lessen the body's power of action by weakening or overcoming the immune system, so an external idea, once internalized, can infect the mind and lessen its power of action. That is to say, it can weaken and overcome the mind's natural ability to reason, to know what is truly in its own best interests.

Consider, if you will, the human being at the moment of conception. The fertilized egg, through its genetic material, is the seed from which the human body grows. The seed contains within itself the blueprint, or plan, for making a mature human body. Corresponding to the genetic material there exists an idea that we may conceive as the "seed" or essence of the (imaginative portion of the) mind. It contains the plan or blueprint for the mind in the same way that the DNA constitutes the plan for the body. This essence is an idea in the soul that contains the plans to grow a specific personality associated with a specific body.

How these plans are actualized, however, depends not only on itself—not only on the nature of the plans—but also on its relationships with an external environment. Two genetically identical seeds, for example, one of which is planted in fertile soil, watered regularly, etc., and the other of which is planted in impoverished soil, uncared for, etc., will grow or manifest quite differently. In the former case, the plan encoded in the genetic materials is assisted by its interactions with its environment; in the latter case, it is hindered or thwarted altogether. The actualization of any given human seed, considered physically *and* psychologically, thus depends on whether, and the extent to which, its interactions with its physical *and* psychological environment help or hinder the plan encoded in its physical *and* psychological essence. A fertilized egg placed in the body of a woman addicted to cocaine will not be able to actualize the plan of its genetic material. And neither will a child raised in an environment of chronic fear, anxiety, greed, guilt, etc.

What we are here calling "psychological infections" are ideas or thought-structures that we naturally ingest in the process of growing up and that hinder or thwart the blueprint for, or essence of, our personality in its striving to actualize its full potential. This is completely parallel to saying that the plan for growing a body, which plan is contained within the DNA, can be hindered or thwarted in its striving by the absence of things that it needs and the presence of things that are harmful to it. And a psychological infection, like a physical infection, may be so strong that it completely overcomes the individual, resulting in death. Suicide is such an example.

Principles for a mentally healthy culture
As a culture, we are beginning to have a fairly adequate conception of what the body requires in order to maximize the potential contained within its genetic structure. We are learning to conceive of physical health as something positive in itself, rather than as a mere absence of disease or as adaptation to a certain cultural norm. Indeed, a positive conception of physical health gives us a platform from which to discern that the norm of a given culture may itself be unhealthy—for example, a norm that consists of fatty foods, little exercise, excessive sugar, and a lot of processed foods. No one for a moment would think to define physical health as conformity to such a norm.

Yet, almost everyone follows Freud in believing that mental health consists in conformity to the psychological norms of our present culture, without examining whether these norms themselves may be unhealthy. We have, in fact, already given a few reasons to question the healthfulness of the psychological norms of our culture: (1) to adapt to our culture, to be "successful" in our culture, generally requires us to separate our "personal" life from our "professional" life, that is, it requires us, in clinical terms, to become disassociated; and (2) our culture, insofar as its various norms and values are leading to the destruction of the earth's ability to sustain human life, is on the verge of suicide; thus it is as psychologically unhealthy as is any individual on the brink of self-destruction.

The basic principles of a mentally healthy culture, of a *rational* culture, may easily be derived from metaphysical first principles: every human being, mind and body, is a part of the Divine Being. In a mentally healthy culture this metaphysical fact would be taught *and lived* (for children learn only from the *lived* examples of their elders). More specifically, children would be taught by word and by deed, first of all to foster within themselves an attitude of acceptance, what Spinoza calls *lovingkindness* toward themselves, the only appropriate attitude toward something that is divine. Second, they would be taught by the example of their elders to extend this attitude toward the forces that created them—they would be taught to love God, to understand Nature, and to know themselves as a part of the Natural Order of things. And third, since this Divine Order that created them also created all other human beings and all things whatsoever, they would be taught, also by example, to extend this attitude of lovingkindness toward all other human beings and generally to all created things.

No culture that fails to embody these three principles—self-acceptance or self-love, love of God or Nature, and acceptance or love of all others—and manifest them in *all* of its aspects, from personal relations to commercial and political institutions, can be regarded as mentally healthy. Insofar as we have ingested the norms and values of an unhealthy culture, we become psychologically unhealthy ourselves.

The irrational and unhealthy nature of contemporary society
We wish to give some specific examples to illustrate some of the ways in which our culture as a whole is psychologically unhealthy and also indicate some of the ways in which a given individual may become mentally infected with unhealthy thought-structures; that is, infected with values, beliefs, goals, and other ideas that hinder the actualization of his or her full potential.

1. Competition vs. Cooperation. We live in a very competitive society that rewards people, not for doing their best, but for being the best, or at least, being better than others. *Greed,* the desire to have more money and possessions than others, and *ambition,* the desire for fame and reputation, that is, the desire to be thought better than others, are the psychological qualities necessary for success in our culture. These emotions are, as Spinoza puts it, "really species of madness" (*Ethics,* pt. 4, prop. 44, note). Anyone who is motivated by the desire to be better than others is deeply disassociated from the connection that exists between himself, other human beings, and, indeed, from the "Whole of Nature."

A healthy society would regard greed and ambition as a pathology, a mental illness that should be corrected with love and kindness. For those who experience themselves as so disconnected from other human beings that they believe their happiness can be purchased at the expense of others (i.e., by "winning") are in great mental distress, and their whole life is an acting out of this distress. Yet, instead of regarding greed and ambition as mental aberrations, our society selects for those qualities.

Thus many people compete for a goal that only a few can achieve, whether that goal be money, reputation in some profession, power and authority over others, etc. This is a recipe for misery, for many more people necessarily will fail to achieve such ill-defined "success" than will achieve it. Social conditioning that includes a so-called educational system in which children compete for grades (as if learning can be quantified), infects our minds with the idea that our self-worth depends on being better than others, and since this is logically impossible for the majority of people, it guarantees that the majority of people will judge themselves to have "failed" and will feel insecure and unworthy.

The consequences are even worse for those who succeed, because pride and arrogance, being relative strengths, are more difficult to overcome than despondency (*Ethics,* pt. 4, prop. 50, note). But these relative strengths accrue to only a portion of the person and are actually harmful to the person as a whole. The proud man, for example, believes himself to be better than others and will not strive to understand his connections with the larger social whole in which he has his being and which alone makes possible his so-called success. For the proud and arrogant construct ideologies according to which they "deserve" and "merit" their success because of their "superior" intelligence, hard work, etc., and where those who fail "deserve" to fail because of their stupidity, laziness, etc. Such ideologies, it should now be apparent, are merely thoughts produced by the very emotions of pride and arrogance, greed and ambition, that they seek to justify. Therefore those who succeed are easily caught in a web of denial that is very difficult to penetrate.

If it be objected that such emotions are necessary for the conduct of life, that without the competitive desire to be better than others, or without the desire to make more money than others, there would be no incentive for business and commerce, or that without the desire to "win" people would lack the motivation to excel, we reply, as does Spinoza *(Ethics,* pt. 4, prop. 50, note), that any action or behavior that is done from a desire that springs from an emotion could also be done from a desire which springs from reason, from an attitude of lovingkindness. We are being very serious here. What better motivation could there be for business and commerce than one of lovingkindness toward all the people of this world? From this motivation would come a desire to distribute resources fairly, to share with others inventions and products that increase the quality and ease of life, etc. With regard to science, the best motivation for doing research is (1) the love of God, for from this love springs the desire to know God insofar as God manifests as the various domains of nature, e.g., the heavens (astronomy), living systems (biology), the earth (geology), human behavior (psychology), etc., and (2) love of humanity, from which springs the desire to discover and apply new ways to utilize the materials of the earth for the benefit of all. The absence of these motivations and the presence of other motivations, such as greed and ambition, is the cause of the corruption and disintegration of the institutions of our culture.

Those who mindlessly pursue money, fame, and other forms of self-aggrandizement do so because they have been programmed to believe that their happiness, self-worth, and security depend on so doing. They are oblivious to the simple fact that those who have fame and wealth are on the whole no happier than those who don't. Greed is especially harmful, because the "high" that the greedy person experiences depends on *making* money, not on *having* it. Like an addictive drug, the more such a person has, the more he needs in order to experience the same high. Because most of the institutions of this culture are driven by such powerfully addictive psychological forces, like a cancer, they will continue to expand, unless checked by external forces, until they exhaust the ability of the earth to sustain human life. We must say to such people, "we will love and accept you, and we will teach you how to love and accept yourself, but we can no longer allow you to run amok, acting out your addiction to money, self-aggrandizement, and power over others, for such behavior is rapidly becoming the destruction of us all."

It is not, however, just the more extreme cases of this madness that concern us. All of us have been infected with the idea or value that our self-worth depends on our place within some hierarchical system, so we think we are "better" than some, toward whom we feel superior, and "worse" than others, toward whom we feel envy. The strength of this infection may far exceed the ability of our reason to overcome it. We partially succumb to it whenever we feel envious, proud, unworthy, etc. We succumb to it totally—that is, we are completely mad—when our mind is completely obsessed with thoughts about how to make money, become famous, and gain power and control over others.

EXERCISE 26: In order to become more aware of the extent to which your own mind is presently infected with such ideas, make a list of ten or twelve people, half of whom you believe are better than you and half of whom you believe are inferior to you. For each person on your list, write down *why* you believe he or she is better or worse than you. These "reasons" reflect society's judgment of what is good and bad, better and worse; they are mental infections that have been programmed into you by society.

The best antidote to this mental infection is to develop a second order awareness of the emotions as they occur. Whatever assists in doing this is good, such as therapy, discussion in groups and with friends, and, above all, constantly affirming to yourself that everyone is equally a part of the Divine Being, and that one's self-worth, and the worth of everyone else, is intrinsic to one's existence, guaranteed simply and only by one's existence as a mode of the Divine Being.

2. Advertising, or the Unhealthy Programming of Desire. In our culture, one of the chief mechanisms for spreading this infection into the minds of people is the advertising industry, whose purpose is to manipulate our minds so that we will want and desire things that we would not otherwise want and desire. The way it accomplishes this is by conditioning our minds to associate their product with something that is natural for us to want, e.g., food, sex, safety, friendship, community, etc., so that whenever we feel lonely for lack of friendship we immediately think of that product and attempt to satisfy the natural desire for friendship by buying something, or eating something, or drinking something. Aside from programming into us desires for specific material things, the advertising industry conditions us to believe and feel that we are *not* o.k. as we are and that our happiness depends on material acquisition. This is the opposite of our principles for a sane society, which teaches that we *are* o.k. as we are and that our happiness depends on experiencing our connection with God and hence, with each other.

Because advertising is such a powerful and insidious form of mind control because its victims do not believe their desires are under the control of external forces, it is easy to see how we can want and pursue things that we know are not good for us. Suppose, for example, a person desires a cigarette, knowing that it is harmful to him. This desire, although it is *in* him, is not *of* him, since it quite obviously does not serve his best interests. And much the same could be said for other industries that manufacture things that are harmful to human beings, such as soft drinks, junk foods, guns, and so forth. Where, then, does the desire originate? It originates in corporate boardrooms where individuals motivated by greed and ambition think of ways to manipulate people into buying their product. As part of their striving they produce numerous commercials showing people enjoying themselves while smoking or eating a hamburger. The individual sees these advertisements repeatedly, and they take hold of him, especially if he was exposed to them as a child, and cause him to associate the natural desire for friendship and community with cigarettes or soft drinks. Then, as soon as he thinks of the one he thinks of the other.

Of course, as soon as the person comes to understand that smoking is harmful to him he automatically forms a desire to stop. But this desire that "springs from a true knowledge of good and bad" will be much weaker than the former desire that has been programmed into him and has etched deep pathways in his brain and psyche. This desire (to smoke) serves the interests of the tobacco industry, not that of the individual. For the mind of any given individual can be overcome by the minds—the desires and emotions—of other individuals in the same way that the body of a given individual can be overpowered and destroyed by the collective action of the bodies of other individuals. Thus, the desire to smoke, although *in* the mind of the individual, is not a part of the striving *of* the individual *as a whole*; it is rather, as we have said, a part of the striving of the tobacco industry to persevere in *its* being, which involves infecting the minds of large numbers of people with the desire to consume their product.

We do not claim to have given the full causal story of how a person comes to desire things that are not good for her. A fuller story must explain why not everyone is infected by the advertising industry in the same way. But this is easy to sketch. Consider this analogy: disease causing bacteria and viruses are around us all the time, yet not everyone is infected by them. The difference between those who succumb to the disease and those who do not lies in the relative strength or weakness of the individual's immune system, which renders it more or less susceptible to this or that bacterium or virus. Similarly, any given individual, depending on her psychological strengths and weaknesses, is more or less susceptible to this or that form of advertising. And the relative strengths and weaknesses of any given individual in turn depend on the particularities both of her upbringing and of the "plan" for the unfolding of her mind. We see also, from this example, why most emotions and the desires that follow from them are inadequate ideas; their cause lies partly within the individual and partly outside the individual, e.g., in the corporate boardrooms and the various other institutions whose greed is served by such emotions.

Indeed, the analysis here is quite the same as was given earlier for religious and nationalistic fanaticism. For these are psychically active thought-structures that seek to persevere in their being by infecting and controlling the minds of large numbers of individuals, causing them to desire the destruction of all who are different from them. The natural striving of such a mind, infected and ravaged by envy and hatred, has been virtually overpowered by the striving of the ideology that controls them. But the gods we worship in our present culture—material acquisition, fame, power, etc.—are no less damaging to us than are the gods of fundamentalist religion and mindless nationalism to those who worship them. We believe, for example, that it is only "right" or "natural" to want to become famous or to want material things as an end in themselves, in the same way that the various religious zealots in the Middle East and elsewhere believe it is only "right" or "natural" to desire the destruction of those who are different from themselves. In each case, the respective beliefs are part of the system of "justification" created by the respective ideologies to persevere in their being. If people in the West did not believe that their self-worth depended upon material acquisition, our whole way of life would collapse overnight.

3. The Avoidance of Nurturing in Contemporary Society. We have discussed several ways in which our culture actively inhibits our ability to live in accordance with what Spinoza calls "the dictates of reason." On the whole, our culture opposes, rather than assists, the actualization and unfoldment of our full creative potential. We wish to discuss this further by considering the unbalanced value that our culture places on so-called masculine psychological qualities, at the expense of the feminine. We take it as obvious that a healthy culture must value both male and female qualities. After all, one cannot have a culture without male *and* female bodies. And since the male and female bodies are different, it follows that the respective ideas, or minds, of the male and female bodies must also be different.

We do not wish to enter into any controversy as to what is the difference, psychologically speaking, between the male and the female. It suffices to say that any mode, whether conceived under the Attribute of Extension as a body, or under the Attribute of Thought as a mind, is embedded within a larger whole, with which it continuously interacts and which incorporates both masculine and feminine qualities. Hence, it necessarily both receives from, and is acted upon by, the environment in which it has its being *and,* in turn, acts upon and affects that environment. We use the expression "female psychological qualities" to refer to that aspect of the mind that receives from its environment, and the expression "male psychological qualities" to refer to that aspect of the mind that acts upon its environment. A balanced society is one that, as a reflection of the Divine Mind, encourages and values the development and expression of *both* male and female qualities. We also note that the human mind, or the idea of human body, is not rigidly tied to the sex of its body, so that, although on the whole we would expect the mind that is correlated with a female (male) body to exhibit a preponderance of female (male) psychological qualities, the mind of a healthy individual will contain a balance of both masculine and feminine qualities.

It does not take much acuity to see that our present culture is way out of balance. One main consequence of this imbalance—that our self-worth is made to depend on position within some externally given hierarchy—we have already examined. In what follows, we will continue to discuss this imbalance insofar as it manifests as a resistance and aversion to nurturing and caring, and also insofar as it is embodied by our present educational system.

Nurturing and caring are most directly and powerfully expressed physically through touch. Scientific studies have shown beyond any possibility of doubt that touching is vitally important for the physical and mental health of human beings. We mention three here.

(a) The famous Harlow experiments with primates show that if a primate does not receive sufficient touching, caressing, nurturing, etc., in infancy and childhood, then later, as young adults, they exhibit severe depression and/or react with violence toward any other "normal" primate who approaches them. Since depression and violence are the two most significant social diseases in our culture, one would think that psychologists and social scientists might put two and two together and see that a major causal factor in depression and violence is lack of touching, a lack of nurturing expressed physically.

(b) There are studies that detail some of the ways in which touching and caressing babies affects the physiological development of their brains. Touching a baby stimulates the nerves under their skin, which stimulation is transmitted to the brain and appears to be necessary for the brain itself to develop. Lack of touching leads to retardation and, in some cases, to death. (The "analytic" mind, which we discuss below, might need a scientific study like this to impel it to touch a baby; fortunately for us, our mothers usually did not need to wait for science to "justify" their inner knowing that babies need to be touched.)

(c) Post-operative recovery rates are faster for patients who are touched by their doctors and nurses than for patients who are not touched. It seems reasonable to infer from this that touching is necessary and beneficial for our well being, even if we are not babies or sick.

Lack of touching thus has known physiological and psychological effects, not only for infants and babies, but also for adults. If touching promotes a sense of calm, well-being, and connectedness, then lack of touching promotes a sense of chronic anxiety, nervousness, and isolation from others. These feelings of lack-of-ease, or dis-ease, are so pervasive in our culture that we hardly notice them; they constitute the psychological norm. And, we wish to emphasize, these feelings constitute the psychological and physiological foundation that supports our entire social, economic, and political way of life. For why would anyone desire to compete against his fellow human beings, why would anyone want to benefit at another's expense, unless he already experienced himself as disconnected from, other than, and alienated from, his fellows? Lack of nurturing in general, and of touching in particular, serves the function of creating and sustaining a feeling of alienation and neediness in the individual, which he futilely attempts to overcome by competing and "winning" in some hierarchical system. It is not possible to play such harmful games, however, which only increase the feeling of alienation and make the problem even worse, if one feels connected with his fellow human beings.

The desire to compete against others (which, we hasten to add, is a very different thing from the desire to do good and to fully develop one's abilities), like greed and ambition, is a form of mental illness caused and sustained by feelings of alienation and disconnectedness from others. These feelings are in turn caused, at least partially, by powerful taboos against touching. Indeed, the desire to compete, to win, etc., is part of the *striving* of these deep-rooted feelings of alienation to persevere in *their* being and do not spring from reason, which teaches that our interests are best served by cooperatively joining with others rather than separating from them. "To man, then, there is nothing more useful than man. Man, I say, can wish for nothing more helpful to the preservation of his being than that all should so agree in all things that the minds and bodies of all would compose, as it were, one mind and one body; that all should strive together, as far as they can, to preserve their being; and that all together, should seek for themselves the common advantage of all" *(Ethics,* pt. 4, prop. 18).

In our present culture, males are especially fearful of nurturing and touch. Part of the epidemic abuse of women by men derives from this fear of nurturing combined with a general association of sex with violence, which latter are the only two socially accepted forms of touching for males. This *fear* of nurturing, itself caused by a lack of nurturing, seeks to sustain itself (1) by avoiding and striking out against that which would weaken it, namely caring and nurturing as symbolized by the feminine; and (2) by seeking that which would strengthen it, namely participating in competitive games against one another.

But how can one receive the love of God if one is not able to receive nurturing from other human beings? Indeed, one way to allow ourselves to feel more closely connected with God is by allowing ourselves to feel more closely connected with other human beings. Nurturing touch, touch that is nonviolent and nonsexual, is a most powerful way to generate feelings of connectedness with others. It soothes the body, calms the mind, and creates conditions within the body/mind favorable for healing. Let us make of this an exercise.

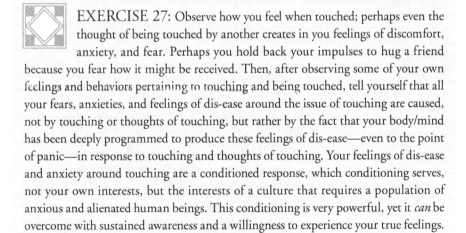

EXERCISE 27: Observe how you feel when touched; perhaps even the thought of being touched by another creates in you feelings of discomfort, anxiety, and fear. Perhaps you hold back your impulses to hug a friend because you fear how it might be received. Then, after observing some of your own feelings and behaviors pertaining to touching and being touched, tell yourself that all your fears, anxieties, and feelings of dis-ease around the issue of touching are caused, not by touching or thoughts of touching, but rather by the fact that your body/mind has been deeply programmed to produce these feelings of dis-ease—even to the point of panic—in response to touching and thoughts of touching. Your feelings of dis-ease and anxiety around touching are a conditioned response, which conditioning serves, not your own interests, but the interests of a culture that requires a population of anxious and alienated human beings. This conditioning is very powerful, yet it *can* be overcome with sustained awareness and a willingness to experience your true feelings.

4. Education: Analysis vs. Appreciation. The imbalance between masculine and feminine polarities in our culture strongly affects the educational system to which we are all subjected. It manifests most generally in an overemphasis of *analysis* at the expense of *appreciation.* Our educational system regards only that which is quantifiably measurable, that can be given a grade, as real. And so, because it cannot be graded, the ability to appreciate is ignored and allowed to atrophy. Consider how things might be different if our schools and universities valued appreciation as much as analysis—if the "best" student in a poetry, literature, or music class was the one who was most deeply moved in his heart by the poetry, rather than the student who produced the "best" analysis of the poetry, etc.. What if psychologists and sociologists valued and taught the appreciation of human behavior and relationships, rather than merely analyzing them according to semi-arbitrary conceptual systems; or if students were taught to see and be moved by the beauty of Nature and our connections with it? The overemphasis on developing analytic abilities, as if those alone were the epitome of intelligence, has had numerous unfortunate consequences.

(a) Since analysis is almost always defined in terms of constituent parts, the exclusive emphasis on analysis fosters the belief that the whole is nothing more than the sum of its parts—that the body is nothing beyond the molecules which constitute it, that a symphony is just a bunch of notes, that a poem is no more than some words strung together. Analysis alone is unable to see how a given whole relates to other wholes and leads to the discovery of the interconnectedness of all things. Thus, the feeling of separateness is strongly reinforced by this imbalance in our educational system.

(b) Analytical thinking, also referred to as "critical thinking, assumes that everything can be broken down into its constituent parts. For example, a typical assignment in a philosophy class might be to "critically evaluate" (not "appreciatively evaluate") such and such an argument in Plato, Descartes or Kant, etc. The student learns that nothing is above criticism, and if the greatest minds of Western thought can be criticized, then certainly nothing that he could think for himself could possibly escape the sharp knife of criticism. The student thus comes to believe that his own thinking is not good enough, feels inadequate, and fears to express himself. Or what is worse, the student becomes proficient at critical analysis and comes to believe that because he can criticize everybody, he is therefore superior to everybody else; hence creativity and honest self-expression are stifled. For creative self-expression flourishes best in an atmosphere of acceptance, appreciation, and encouragement; it withers and atrophies in an environment where everyone fears saying anything lest it be criticized.

Only someone who enjoys analyzing for the sake of analyzing and criticizing for the sake of criticizing can prosper in such a negative, fearful environment. It is no accident that most of the truly creative individuals in our culture—poets, novelists, musicians, artists—are only rarely found within our academic institutions. (Spinoza himself, incidentally, refused such an appointment). For in order to "succeed" within the academic hierarchy, the student must stifle her creativity and adapt her thinking to what her professors want. But the professor got to be a professor by adapting *her* thinking to what *her* professor wanted and continues to adapt her thinking to what her external authorities (colleagues, journals, tenure committees, etc.) define as "sound" or "proper" thinking. And so the system perpetuates itself, "justified" by an ideology according to which those at the top of the academic ladder are more intelligent and/or worked harder than everybody else, and hence "deserve" to be at the top. This is the same circular and transparently self-serving rationalization by which the wealthy "justify" their wealth, the politicians "justify" their power, etc.

(c) Those who succeed in such a system (as well as those who fail) fall victim to this ideology. That is, they judge themselves according to it. They suffer from pride and arrogance insofar as they succeed—emotions that are very difficult to overcome since the person who suffers from them usually has no desire to remove them. This pride sets them apart from their fellow human so and increases their feelings of separation and alienation.

(d) Students are affected as much by what is *not* taught as by what is taught. Since the spiritual values of which we speak—that we are part of a larger whole, that we must aspire to desire for ourselves nothing that we would not also desire for all others, and that desires which follow from greed and ambition are errors that need to be corrected—are rarely taught and exemplified in our universities, then students will come to believe that such values are not important and may come to feel that their own natural and spontaneous feelings of caring and empathy for others cannot be justified and are therefore symptoms of "fuzzy thinking" and "soft-headedness." Indeed, epithets such as "hard-nosed" and "tough-mindedness" are regarded as compliments among academics.

(e) This belief is further reinforced in the minds of students as they observe their professors in practice. If professors are selected only on the basis of cleverness (that is, on the basis of highly developed analytical skills), rather than on the basis of moral development, then the ability to feel kindness and compassion toward others, or the ability to use reason (which is the ability to discern what is truly good and to place analytical skills in the service of what is good) cannot effectively be communicated to their students.

I should qualify this by saying that it is not true for everyone and in every case. For example, it is well known that on average, the highest paid professors do little or no teaching, because they usually get paid for their ability to raise money for the university by getting research grants, which reflects the values of the universities. This "research" is justified by an ideology according to which those who are rewarded for their research are "advancing knowledge," "contributing to the field," and so on, an ideology contradicted by the fact that the overwhelming majority of academic publications sit on library shelves, uselessly gathering dust. Since the student believes that intelligence is embodied by what their professors *do*, as indicated by the number of their academic publications, she comes to believe that love and compassion have nothing to do with reason and intelligence, and that greed, ambition, and the desire to "get ahead," are compatible with the desire to know.

(f) If it is true that the "kingdom of heaven lies within," then the analytical mind can never find it, because the analytical mind has been taught to reject anything that cannot be broken down into parts. But intuitive knowledge is an insight that comes as a whole and cannot be broken down without being destroyed. Despite the scientific evidence, described earlier, that babies need to be held, touched, and caressed to promote healthy development, the analytic mind rejects intuition as a source of knowledge,. This knowledge has always been experienced as an inner knowing, in the same way that we know we must drink when thirsty. For example, the powerful impulse to touch and caress a baby in distress, constitutes knowledge that the baby needs to be touched, in the same way that our impulse to drink when thirsty constitutes knowledge that our body needs water. But the analytic mind claims that it did not know that babies need touching until the effect of touching on the development of the baby's brain and nervous system was demonstrated by science. Such a mind is deeply disassociated with its own inner knowing—which it denigrates as "mere instinct," as if instinct were not itself a manifestation of intelligence in Nature—and attempts to influence others to doubt and disdain their own inner knowing.

It has been said that analysis without appreciation is blind. But it is actually worse than blind. For without the ability to appreciate, critical analytical thinking forever goes in circles, creating ideologies that merely seek to justify the emotional and behavioral patterns that were programmed into the individual in childhood and adolescence. Cleverness is a sharp-edged tool, to be sold to the highest bidder. Instead of being guided to self-healing by the cultivation of its ability to appreciate and receive (a prerequisite for self-knowledge), this aimless, programmed mind is allowed to run amok, destroying everything that pertains to the quality of life. As Jung says in his autobiography, "the more critical reason [i.e., cleverness] dominates, the more impoverished life becomes." And also, "the phenomenon of dictators and all misery they have wrought springs from the fact that man has been robbed of his transcendence by the shortsightedness of the superintellectuals" (Carl Jung. *Dreams, Memories, and Reflections,* p. 326). Thus, cleverness, or analysis that is uninformed and unguided by appreciation, is a major cause of the alienation of ourselves from our inner life, and because of that, becomes a major cause of the destruction of the earth's ability to sustain human life.

Summary, and a step toward freedom
Let us now summarize our discussion of some of the ways in which our culture causes us to internalize behavioral and emotional patterns that are opposed

to self-knowledge, and thus to our own happiness: (1) it is competitive, rather than cooperative, making our self-worth dependent on status, position within some hierarchy, being "better" than others, and on "winning"; (2) it teaches us that our happiness consists in material acquisition; (3) it conditions us to be fearful of touching and nurturing; and (4) it teaches that intelligence consists solely in cleverness, denying the existence and/or importance of intuition and the ability to appreciate, without which life cannot be fulfilling. The first steps toward freedom from socially conditioned patterns of feeling and behavior lie in becoming conscious of how these patterns operate within our own mind and body. The reader might reflect on her personal history and consider the extent to which her mind has been infected by these negative beliefs and values. Recalling the earlier analogy with a seed that could be planted either in good soil that helps its striving to grow, or in poor soil that hinders its striving to unfold, it is useful to consider how *we* might have unfolded differently had we been "planted" in an environment that more fully supported and nurtured our growth. Having been already damaged by our culture, it is not possible to go back in time and "replant" ourselves in a more positive culture. Indeed, such a culture nowhere exists. But we can strive to root out the negative programming by applying and practicing the techniques developed in this book, especially what we have called "second order awareness." Above all, we can develop an attitude of lovingkindness toward ourselves. We must learn to appreciate ourselves, for, like a quality seed forced to grow in impoverished soil, each one of us has made the very best effort possible to persevere in our being in an unsupportive environment, and we must continually acknowledge and appreciate ourselves (and everyone else) for having done the very best we could, even when lacking the power to fully penetrate our denials and overcome our resistances. For our denials, resistances, repetitive patterns of feeling and behavior, etc., were our best response to a mentally unhealthy environment whose effort to persevere in *its* being may far surpass our own. The necessary lovingkindness, appreciation, and support for our inner life that we may not have gotten when we were children, we must now give to ourselves.

All our present denials, resistances, and dysfunctional behaviors have their roots in this child who was making his best effort to extract whatever nurturing he could from a spiritually impoverished soil. All our dysfunctional emotions and behaviors are the residues of that child's way of adapting to a lack of nurturing and support, and they will remain with us until we give that child—who exists within us in the form of those behaviors and emotions—the support, nurturing, and understanding he failed to get years ago. That is why we have repeatedly urged that the exercises here be practiced gently, with an attitude of nonjudgmental awareness. For, whenever we judge and criticize ourselves, we contribute to and recreate the causes that sustain the very emotional and behavioral patterns we wish to alter.

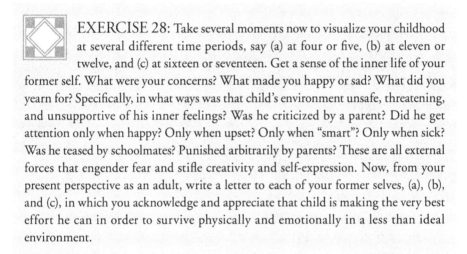

EXERCISE 28: Take several moments now to visualize your childhood at several different time periods, say (a) at four or five, (b) at eleven or twelve, and (c) at sixteen or seventeen. Get a sense of the inner life of your former self. What were your concerns? What made you happy or sad? What did you yearn for? Specifically, in what ways was that child's environment unsafe, threatening, and unsupportive of his inner feelings? Was he criticized by a parent? Did he get attention only when happy? Only when upset? Only when "smart"? Only when sick? Was he teased by schoolmates? Punished arbitrarily by parents? These are all external forces that engender fear and stifle creativity and self-expression. Now, from your present perspective as an adult, write a letter to each of your former selves, (a), (b), and (c), in which you acknowledge and appreciate that child is making the very best effort he can in order to survive physically and emotionally in a less than ideal environment.

5 TRANSCENDENCE

SEXUALITY: TRANSCENDENCE OF THE BODY

One of the more positive aspects of our culture is the relative freedom granted to both men and women to explore sexuality for themselves. As a culture, we are finally emerging from hundreds of years of religious dogma that taught that sexual pleasure is inherently sinful, and which dogma engendered in the psyche of individuals countless fears, anxieties, and guilts pertaining to a necessary aspect of their own biological nature. It is characteristic of "new age" spirituality to attempt to reconcile sexuality with spirituality and to see nothing in the latter that would preclude a healthy enjoyment of the former.

The phrase "healthy enjoyment" is important here, for, although our culture grants us the freedom to explore sexuality, it does not teach us what is involved in a healthy enjoyment of our sexuality; that is, it does not teach us how to experience sex in a way that is maximally conducive to increasing the mind/body's power of action. Consider the following analogy: through conditioning, by advertising, etc., our natural appetite for food can be misdirected, so that we end up desiring foods that contain little or no nutritional value and/or actually weaken our body. Although we have the freedom to buy whatever foods we want, our very wants and desires have been manipulated by the food industry, whose interest is financial gain, not our health. Our desire for junk food is, therefore, an infection in our mind; it is part of the striving of various corporations and advertising agencies to persevere in *their* being without regard to our best interests.

Similarly, although we have the freedom to experience sex in whatever way we want, our very wants and desires have been manipulated by the same forces that have manipulated our natural desires for food, companionship, etc. The appetite for sex, like the appetite for food, is innate, that is, it is biologically hardwired into us; but the expression of that appetite, the behaviors and emotions that come into play around sex, is dependent on the particular psychological forces, parental and cultural, present in the environment as we were growing up. And these forces can and do compel us to emotions, desires, and behaviors that are unhealthy, that decrease our power of action and alienate us from the knowledge of what is in our true best interests.

Sexuality and the metaphysics of holism

In the history of Western philosophy, only Plato and Schopenhauer attempted to explain sexuality in terms of their metaphysical systems. Although their respective analyses are insightful and not, I believe, incompatible with what we shall present below, neither philosopher attempted to derive a practice based on their metaphysical analysis (although Plato hints at one). We note that the situation is quite different in Eastern philosophy, in that Tantric Yoga is a specific practice following from a metaphysical analysis of the nature of the sexual energy. We desire, therefore, to derive from our general metaphysical principles an ideal toward which we may strive, one that teaches us the maximally beneficial use of our sexual energy.

Although Spinoza himself does not discuss sexuality explicitly, I believe that his metaphysical principles can readily be extended, or I should say, applied, to this important area of life. It is obvious that sexuality constitutes a necessary part of the essence of the human species, for without sex no species could either come into being in the first place, nor could it endure for more than one generation. Thus, the idea of a species must contain the idea of a force that compels members of one generation to participate in the creation of the next generation.

Anything that may be conceived *as a whole* must contain within itself the power to create and/or organize the "parts" that constitute it into the whole that it is. Earlier, when we discussed *holism,* we said that a whole is something over and above the parts that constitute it. This "something over and above" is what we mean by the "power to create and/or organize." We will use the terms "transcend" and "transcendent" to refer to any property or power of a whole that is not reducible to the properties or powers of the parts considered individually. We give several examples to make our usage of these terms clear.

1. The human body as a whole has the power to create and organize the cells that constitute it. That this power is transcendent—that it cannot be understood in terms of the cells considered individually—is made strikingly apparent by the "problem" of morphogenesis. Given that the human body grows from a single cell and given that each cell that divides creates an exact replica of itself, how does differentiation occur? How do cells differentiate into nerve cells, muscle cells, blood cells, fat cells, etc.? How does the embryo "know" where to grow limbs, organs, etc.? Since this knowledge or power does not, it would seem, reside in the cells considered individually, we say that it *transcends* the individual cells and can be understood only in terms of the body as a whole.

2. We have given many examples of the power of a culture to shape, structure, and control the imaginations of the people who constitute that culture, so that people are determined to think, feel, and behave in ways considered appropriate by the culture as a whole. The power, or striving, of a culture cannot, therefore, be understood in terms of the individuals who constitute that culture and hence is a holistic property that *transcends* its members considered individually.

3. We have also given examples from physics, especially the quantum theory, according to which any system of interacting particles, such as an atom or molecule, exhibits holistic or *transcendent* properties that cannot be understood in terms of the constituent particles considered separately.

4. The human body is part of an ecosystem, whose power sustains, or continuously creates, us. The body is in dynamic interaction with its environment; therefore a complete understanding of the body involves understanding the laws according to which the earth as a whole creates and sustains us. The body, as we have said, is created and sustained by the power of the earth (and sun) and thus this power cannot be understood in terms of our bodies considered individually. The power of the earth *transcends* our own.

Likewise, when we consider the human body as belonging to a species that extends temporally over numerous generations, it is clear that the power or force by which the species creates and organizes the individuals that constitute it must transcend that of the individuals considered separately. Sexuality is the glue, so to speak, that holds the members of a given species, extended over time, together so as to form a single species—that is, a single organic whole that is something over and above a mere aggregate of individuals. Sex is the power that enables a species to *be* a species—to be temporally extended over many generations

Perhaps this will become clearer if we consider the efficient cause of the existence of our body. Each body grows and develops from a single cell, which in turn came into being as a result of the union between a sperm and an egg. The sperm and egg cells in turn were created by mature human bodies, each of which itself grew from a single cell, which was itself formed from the union of a sperm and an egg. This process goes back *continuously* in time, to the first beings that could be called human. We are thus causally united to these first humans and to all intermediate and subsequent generations. This causal union, through the power of sexuality, constitutes our species.

We note that this way of considering the matter enables us to see that we are connected with *all* living beings, since the first humans were themselves created, through the power of sex, from other species, etc., and this process can be traced continuously to the first single-celled organisms, from which all life sprang. Thus, the earth may be considered as a single living organism, constituted by many species, which in turn are constituted by many individual bodies, which in turn are constituted by many cells. It is with good reason, therefore, that many authors have considered sexuality to be the Life Force.

The sexual experience is one in which we transcend the boundaries of finite individuality and merge physically with the Life Force itself, with the biological energy that holds together our own species, and indeed, all living things. For during sex, our body is taken over by this force and we are compelled to surrender to it. It is an experience of our body's connectedness—its union—with the earth itself.

The question we wish to raise now is whether anything can be derived from this analysis that could guide us to greater health, happiness, and well-being with respect to our experience of sex. One of our constant themes in this book has been to bring our imagination (knowledge of the first kind) into harmony with our metaphysical understanding (knowledge of the second kind); this harmony constitutes our true happiness, our freedom, and also the conditions for what Spinoza calls our salvation, or blessedness (knowledge of the third kind).

Let us consider this question by comparing the desire for sex, a desire that is part of the striving of our species to persevere in its being, with the desire for food that is a part of the striving of our individual body to persevere in its being. The following are points of similarity between the two:

1. In both cases, the desire is a part of our essence, without which the body could neither come into being nor continue to be. That which pertains to our essence can only be of benefit to us; it is therefore our right to enjoy the pleasure obtained from the satisfaction of these desires.

2. Anything in us or outside of us that detracts from our ability to enjoy food or sex, making these things into sorrows instead of joys, originates in forces that do not serve our best interests. Any religion

or psychology, for example, that teaches people to feel shame or guilt for experiencing and delighting in the joy inherent in our biological nature, is a force that is truly harmful to us.

3. Our natural appetite for sex, however, like our appetite for food, can be and has been grossly distorted by our culture. For just as we can be conditioned to desire foods that are unhealthy, and to consume them in ways that are unhealthy, we can also be conditioned to desire and "consume" sex in ways that are less than fulfilling. For example, many men in our culture have been programmed to respond sexually to pornographic or even violent images of the female body, and many women have been programmed to respond sexually to their projections of "romantic" images and stereotypes.

4. Related to this is the fact that external conditioning generally strengthens one part of our body/mind at the expense of our body/mind as a whole. For example, the satisfaction of a desire for sugar strengthens those neural pathways associated with the pleasure derived from consuming sweets, but it weakens the body as a whole. Similarly, most of us have experienced sexual attraction to people with whom, on the whole, we know are not good for us to associate. Sex under such circumstances strengthens that portion of our body/mind that has been conditioned to respond sexually to whatever qualities the other embodies, but it weakens our mind/body considered as a whole.

5. The manner in which food is consumed is as important for our well-being as is the food itself. In some cultures, eating is a sacred act. People reflect on what they eat and on the process by which their food was harvested, or slaughtered, and prepared. Eating becomes a meditation on the connection that exists between the body, the food chain, and the whole of nature. The food is maximally beneficial when eaten with this attitude of awareness, appreciation, and thanksgiving. I doubt if many people could continue to eat "fast foods" if they took the time to reflect in detail on the process by which the food comes to them: the cruel conditions under which the animals are raised and killed, the hormones and other chemicals injected in the animals, etc. Eating with conscious awareness would radically alter what we eat, and eating

would become a joyous, healthy experience, and our sense of taste would become naturally aligned with what is in the best interests of the body. Similarly, sex is maximally beneficial insofar as we participate in it, not as a means to escape from ourselves, but with conscious awareness and appreciation for our own body, our partner's body, and the Life Force that unites us, momentarily, into a single being.

Exploring our programmed sexual patterns
We have seen how the striving of a culture, or of institutions within a culture, may be at variance with the striving of individuals within the culture. It is not necessary to trace *all* the ways, although some are very obvious, in which these institutions have adversely affected our capacity for healthy sexual enjoyment. *Some* of these adverse effects are: (1) we have been programmed to associate emotions of guilt, fear, and anxiety in conjunction with sex; (2) we have been conditioned to regard sex as something to "get" or to "have," as if it were a commodity—and this belief in turn creates the emotions of envy and jealousy; and (3) we have been programmed (especially men) to experience sex in terms of control, domination, and conquest of another person, which is a major contributing factor of the widespread violence by men against women. Below we will offer an exercise to examine some of the emotions which we have been conditioned to associate with sexuality. But first, we wish to address briefly the general question of why it is that the institutions of our culture, and indeed, of almost all cultures, seek to control, limit, and reduce the individual's capacity for sexual enjoyment.

Whenever an institution, whether it be a church, a nation, an economy, etc., is organized and administered by men who are motivated, not by lovingkindness, but by a need born out of their own weaknesses and insecurities, to manipulate and control others, then that institution will necessarily strive to alienate people from their own inner knowing and power. As a result, the people thus alienated will willingly look to the authority of the institution and its priests for instructions about how to live. For example, suppose a child is experiencing pleasure playing with his or her genitals. The parents see this and feel uncomfortable, a discomfort that reflects the parents' own negative upbringing with respect to sex and which they convey to the child, verbally or otherwise. The child learns that something he knows feels good is "bad" or "wrong." Since the child needs his parents' approval in order to survive as an individual, he gives up his inner knowing of what is good and bad to what his parents tell him is "good" and "bad," and thereby becomes alienated from his own biological nature.

And if the child cannot trust in the goodness of his own biological nature, his very essence insofar as he is a mode within the Attribute of Extension, then there is nothing about himself that he can trust. He thus reaches adolescence disassociated from his inner knowing and ready to give up his power of action and control over his life to the institutions of his culture. For just as a mystic who knows God directly has no need of a church to tell him what God is, so a "man of reason," in touch with his own inner knowing, cannot be tricked into thinking that his happiness lies in material acquisition or being thought "better" than another, etc., and hence has no need of the institutions whose own striving requires that people believe these things.

EXERCISE 29: The purpose of this exercise is to bring conscious awareness to some of the specifics of your own sexual conditioning. What are some of the images that, for you, are associated with and elicit sexual feelings? You can best answer this question by observing what you are thinking about (the content of your inner dialogue) while masturbating. Does your mind fixate on images of body parts? Do you imagine some romantic fantasy? Do you imagine scenes of domination? See if you can move into second order awareness while masturbating; for example, "here I am, imagining such and such in order to summon forth my sexual energy." Write down, in as much detail as possible, the content of your fantasies. For this is how you have been programmed with respect to experiencing your sexuality. That is, whatever images "turn you on" sexually, constitute the content of your sexual conditioning; your mind/body has been programmed to associate these specific images with sex, and you bring this program with you, consciously or not, to all sexual encounters with others. Notice any resistance to moving into second order awareness. For the awareness that we are fantasizing in order to experience sex, deflates the fantasy *and also* the sexual feelings that have been programmed to come into play in response to those fantasies.

So, to continue with this exercise, if we wish to experience our sexuality more deeply and authentically, we must allow the content of our awareness to shift from an unreal fantasy to the reality of what is happening. And what is happening when we masturbate is that we are using our hands to stimulate our genitals to give us pleasure. Let the content of your awareness be the sensations in your hands and genitals, and the feelings throughout your body. Any resistance you experience to doing this—such as emotions of guilt and anxiety—is part of your lack of acceptance of your right to enjoy your own biological nature as it is in itself, unmediated by socially conditioned thought-forms. Moreover, these emotions themselves (guilt, fear, anxiety, etc.) constitute an actual *decrease* in your power of action, and their presence during sex, with yourself or with another, inhibits a fuller participation in and enjoyment of the Life Force as it manifests through you. Remind yourself that such emotions have been programmed into you by outside forces that do not seek your own best interests. Affirm to yourself your right, insofar as your body is a part of the Divine Being, to enjoy with full consciousness all the pleasures that lie within the power of that body to experience.

Union with the earth

Now most of what we have said about sex could be said about any interaction that benefits the body and in which it is our right to take pleasure. For any such activity—eating, exercising, music, etc.—is more beneficial to us if done in an attitude of receptive appreciation with full conscious awareness and without the negative emotions of guilt, anxiety and fear that decrease our power of action and leave us confused. But there is something very special about sex, because unlike other bodily pleasures, which pertain to the body individually, sex pertains to the body insofar as the body is a part of a larger organismic system: namely, the species as a whole, or more broadly, the system of all living things on earth. During the sexual experience, at the moment of orgasm, we cease to experience the body as a separate organism. The illusion of individuality dissolves and we experience directly the union that exists between our body and the earth as a whole. So how can we best align the imaginative portion of our mind in order to gain maximal benefit from this experience of union?

Strictly speaking, the best way to align the imagination is to let go of it altogether. The imagination, after all, is that part of the mind which follows the body's experience: it consists of sensations, emotions, and a constant background noise called the inner dialogue. It is this inner dialogue that is transcended during the sexual experience. Indeed, by "transcendence" we mean the experience of ourselves as something more than the idea of a body that is isolated, separated, and unconnected with other things. For just as the *body,* during sex, "becomes" united with the forces that created it, so the *mind* "becomes" united with the idea of those creative forces, or, if you will, with the mind of the earth.

The imagination, therefore, must be willing to surrender itself to these transcendent forces. Insofar as it attempts to control these forces, by fantasizing, fixating on images, clinging to emotions, etc., it resists the experience of transcendence. At best, it will experience sex only partially or confusedly; at worst, the sexual energy will be used to strengthen and reinforce emotional and behavioral patterns that are harmful to the body/mind as a whole. In order for our mind as a whole to experience union with another fully, it is necessary that our whole mind be fully present—that is, surrender to the sexual experience. Then, at the moment of orgasm, the inner dialogue ceases, our imagination is transcended, and our mind consciously joins with the mind of the earth.

This love for the earth is the same as the earth's love for us. What we surrender at the moment of orgasm is the illusion that we are separate from the earth that created us. Strictly speaking, there is no "I" who is distinct from the earth, and hence, no "I" who could love the earth. There remains only the experience of transcendence and ecstasy. Insofar as this experience is a joy that is caused by the earth, we may be said to experience love for the earth, and also, insofar as at that moment we are one with the earth, we may also be said to experience the earth's love for us.

We emphasize that what we have outlined here is a model, or ideal, that describes the maximum benefits to our well-being, which derive from a healthy use of the sexual energy. We cannot expect to cease immediately from those patterns of thinking and feeling that keep us from a fuller participation in our sexuality. That is to say, we cannot immediately let go of our habits with respect to fantasizing, to feeling guilty about pleasure and anxious about performance, to using sex to manipulate and control, to feeling fearful of direct, honest communication with our partner, etc., all of which limit and inhibit our ability to fully participate, with our whole body and mind, in the ecstasy of sexual union. These habits of thinking and emoting did not come to us overnight, and they will not disappear simply by reading a book and wishing they would go away.

BLESSEDNESS: TRANSCENDENCE OF THE MIND

Imagining the temporal, understanding the eternal

If it were the case that we were identical to our body, or that our mind were limited to the experiences of the body and had no existence beyond that of the body, then the ecstasy of sexual union would be the highest possible human joy. In that case, the materialist psychologists and philosophers would be correct, and their program of trying to explain all human behavior as deriving from the bodily instincts of self-preservation and species preservation would be the only program possible. Yet, their efforts to account for common humanistic and spiritual phenomena—such as our moral sense of fairness, empathy for others, the aesthetic sense of beauty, and the experience of the divine, etc.—in such narrow terms are dismissed with ridicule and indifference by everyone but themselves.

Although we shall never be able to convince the committed skeptic, "nevertheless we feel and know by experience that we are eternal" (*Ethics,* pt. 5, prop. 23, note). That is, at some level we intuit that we are more than what we have been calling the imagination, that portion of the mind which follows the body's experiences. It is only because we are more than our body that we are able to feel great happiness, and create feelings of peace and well-being through non-sensual experiences, e.g., being moved deeply by music and poetry, understanding something new, feeling compassion for another, and so forth. Although, as all commentators agree, Spinoza's demonstration and discussion of the mind's eternity is difficult to follow, it is nevertheless well worth the effort, for it is greatly beneficial for the mind to allow itself to understand that it is eternal and cannot perish when the body dies.

To consider one such benefit, psychologists generally agree that most, if not all, of our fears are projections to the surface of our consciousness of a root fear of death. If the mind could become convinced that the death of the body is not also the annihilation of itself, then this root fear would be eliminated, or at least greatly reduced, and would remove or reduce all other fears. Therefore, it seems immeasurably worthwhile for the mind to make every effort to *understand* its own immortality.

We emphasize the word "understand" here, to call attention once again to the distinction between the understanding and the imagination. For it might be objected that most people who believe in an afterlife have as much, if not more, fear in them than atheists, so that the mere belief in an afterlife is not sufficient to reduce fear. And this objection is quite correct. Most religions are in fact fear-based, conditioning all sorts of fears into the minds of their adherents, from fears pertaining to the enjoyment of the body's pleasures to, in extreme cases, such intense fear of differences of opinion as to lead to murder and war. But all such beliefs in immortality that engender fear are based in the imagination, not in the understanding. There is as much difference between *imagining* immortality and *understanding* it, as there is between *imagining* God to be a bearded white male and *understanding* God to be the Whole in which all things have their being. Thus, insofar as we *understand* that we are immortal, the fear of death must subside.

This is demonstrated empirically by studies of people who have had a so-called Near Death Experience, or NDE. This experience, in its deeper aspects, is an example of what Spinoza calls "knowledge of the third kind," for people who return from an NDE report that while immersed in the experience they know themselves to be united with God, feel themselves bathed in an infinite and eternal love, and know that their consciousness is eternal. The Near Death Experience permanently transforms the personality, causing it to lose all fear of death and resulting in a significant decrease in fear-based worries and anxieties, leading to an increased capacity to live life fully and joyfully.

Of course, we cannot expect that reason alone—knowledge of the second kind—in the absence of direct experience can produce the degree of certitude that only the latter can produce. For only the mind's direct experience of its own eternal nature—which Spinoza calls "blessedness" or "salvation"—is sufficient to remove all its doubts and fears that it may perish with the body. So long as we lack this perfect knowledge, we cannot help but be affected by the imaginative portion of our mind, which has identified with the body and knows the body must perish. That is to say, the imagination knows that what it has identified with, what it thinks it is, must perish, and this identification engenders great fear. Although, as Spinoza puts it "reason has no power to bring us to our well-being," it can, nevertheless, point us in that general direction. In other words, even though reason cannot give us the direct experience of our immortality, which experience alone removes all fear and constitutes our "well-being," it can convince us of the general possibility of such direct experience. "Reason," Spinoza tells us, "is not the principle thing in us, but only like a stairway, by which we can climb to the desired place, or like a good spirit which without any falsity or deception brings tidings of the greatest good, to spur us thereby to seek it, and unite with it in a union which is our greatest salvation and blessedness" (*Treatise on God, Man, and His Well-Being*).

These "tidings of the greatest good," which reason *can* demonstrate to us, are (1) an *understanding* that our mind or consciousness is eternal and hence does not perish with the body, (2) an *understanding* that our mind can obtain direct experience of its eternal nature, and (3) an *understanding* that in this direct experience lies our greatest happiness and freedom. This demonstration, we note, is being offered, not to that aspect of our mind by which we "know and feel we are eternal" and which therefore needs no demonstration, but rather to that aspect of our mind, the imagination or personality, which has identified with the body's experiences. And this presents a problem: for just as thought-structures *within* the imagination—e.g., particular ideas and emotions, as well as complexes or patterns of ideas and emotions—endeavor to persevere in their being, so also the imagination as a whole is itself a pattern of organization within the Attribute of Thought and, as such, endeavors to persevere in its own being. This endeavor can cause the ego to resist and deny any suggestion that there exists anything "more than" itself, which suggestion it experiences as a threat to its own autonomy. This resistance, which is a kind of arrogance, leads to two kinds of errors that we commonly make when we contemplate the possibility of an afterlife.

The first error involves the ego's great difficulty in conceiving that anything can exist that is not in time. Most people who believe that consciousness survives the death of the body believe that it is the imagination or ego that survives and continues to exist in time "forever and forever." They believe that they, as they now experience themselves to be, will survive the death of their body and continue to have temporal experiences. As Spinoza puts it, "if we look to the common opinion of men, we shall see that they are indeed conscious of the eternity of their minds, but they confound it with duration and attribute it to imagination or memory, which they believe remain after death" (*Ethics*, 5, prop. 34, note). It is this kind of error that is caricatured in the popular image of heaven as a realm of terminal boredom, where its inhabitants play their harps and sing God's praises, forever and forever in time.

On the other hand, a more serious error arising from the ego's arrogance is committed by those who believe that nothing survives the death of the body. For the ego (1) notices (correctly) that its own nature is functionally correlated with the body's experience, (2) observes (correctly) that it cannot survive the death of its body, and (3) concludes (incorrectly) that mind, or conscious experience, perishes with the death of the body. This error is popular among academics who, when they read passages in Spinoza such as the one to be cited below, conclude that Spinoza is a materialist like themselves. But (3) follows from (2) and (1) only under the assumption that the ego is the *only* form of consciousness possible—which assumption is an example of what we have been calling the arrogance of the ego. As soon as we understand that the imagination is a structure within the Attribute of Thought which, as such, is contained within a larger structure of consciousness, which itself is contained within a still larger mental structure, etc., and that time pertains only to the imagination, it is not difficult to see that the imagination may be transformed into something other than itself—that is, it may cease to exist—without any detriment to the larger whole in which it has its being.

Thus, when Spinoza tells us that the mind "can imagine nothing, nor can it recollect anything, except while the body exists" (*Ethics,* pt. 5, prop. 30, note), he is claiming, not that the mind perishes with the body, but rather that the mind, which in its true nature or essence is eternal, is more than its imaginative portion, which is temporal. We are far more than what we take ourselves to be.

The mind, therefore, participates in the temporal order only insofar as the body exists, but remains eternal in its essence, even while participating in the temporal order. It appears, however, that while participating in the temporal order—that is, while the body exists—it is susceptible to the "illusion" that the temporal order is the only reality there is and that it, the mind, is identical to the imagination. The imagination is unable to conceive of any mental reality other than itself, and will not easily allow itself to quiet down so that consciousness can relax into a wider awareness. The consequence of this illusion, the "human condition," is the suffering that arises from the separation of the personality from our whole self—the pain of loneliness, anxiety, and fear, from which suffering we attempt to escape, usually through dysfunctional and addictive behaviors.

A brief metaphysical review

Any demonstration must begin from principles that reason already accepts, therefore our demonstration of the mind's eternal nature begins with the principle of sufficient reason, which we discussed in chapter 1, and without which the mind cannot reason at all. The application of this principle to any specific thing or event tells us that the specific thing or event is causally linked with other things and events, and when applied to the spatio-temporal order as a whole, tells us that this order as a whole must itself have a cause. Just as physical objects do not pop in and out of existence for no reason, so also the physical universe considered as a whole—by which we mean the entire series of spatio-temporal events which is believed to have originated from the big bang—cannot pop into existence for no reason, but must itself have a cause.

We note that the principle of sufficient reason pertains only to the activity of reasoning or knowledge of the second kind; it does not pertain to the imagination. The mind can easily *imagine* objects popping in and out of existence for no reason, and it can just as easily *imagine* that the big bang could have "just happened," for no reason, or without cause. We wish to remind the reader of our discussion in Part I where we showed both (a) that the mind can *understand*, through reason, many things that cannot be imagined or pictured, e.g., infinite sets, the concept of God, quantum physics, etc.; and (b) that the mind can picture or *imagine* many things which cannot be *understood*, e.g., that a given thing could be other than what it in fact is, that something could happen without a cause, that horses could fly, etc. The eternality of our mind, like the concept of God, is an example of something that can be *understood* but not *imagined*.

Indeed, Spinoza tells us that "the human mind possesses an adequate knowledge of God's eternal and infinite essence" (*Ethics*, pt. 2 prop. 27). If it be objected that we are not conscious of having this knowledge, the reply is that our conscious awareness is engaged mostly in imaginative thinking, which generates the constant background noise we called the inner dialogue. Largely because of this background noise, the things that we know by reason alone do not stand vividly in our awareness. Mystics of all cultures have claimed that knowledge of God, the "Kingdom of Heaven," is already within us but is obscured from our awareness by layers upon layers of imaginative thinking. As Spinoza puts it, the reason "that men do not have so clear a knowledge of God as they do of the common notions comes from the fact that they cannot *imagine* God as they can bodies, and they have joined the name 'God' to the *images* of things they are used to seeing" (*Ethics*, pt. 2, prop. 47, note, italics mine). He warns his readers repeatedly to "distinguish accurately between an idea of the mind and the images of things that we imagine.... Indeed, those who think that ideas consist in images which are formed in us from encounters with external bodies, are convinced that those ideas of things which can make no trace in our brain, or of which we can form no similar image in our brain are not ideas, but only fictions" (*Ethics*, pt. 2, prop. 49, note 2). And, of course, the eternality of the mind is not the kind of knowledge which comes "from encounters with external bodies," i.e., from sense experience, and so we cannot form any image of it. We can, however, come to understand it.

Returning to our demonstration, we wish the reader to recall the chain of reasoning that began with the principle of sufficient reasoning and culminated in the idea that the physical universe is continuously emanating from its eternal source. The links along this chain are as follows: applying (1) the principle of sufficient reason to the physical universe, i.e., to the entire series of events which, according to physics, originated in the big bang, we affirm that (2) the physical universe as a whole has a cause. Then, because space and time themselves come into existence with the big bang, the concepts of space and time cannot apply to anything that is not *within* the physical universe. Since the cause of the big bang is *not* a thing or event existing within the universe, the concepts of space and time do not apply to it, and hence, as we concluded, (3) the cause of the big bang, and hence of the physical universe as a whole, is eternal. We note again that by "eternal" we do not mean something that endures forever in time—which is how the imagination commonly pictures eternity—but, on the contrary, we mean something that exists outside of time altogether. "By eternity I understand existence itself... such existence, like the essence of a thing, cannot be explained by duration or time, even if the duration is conceived to be without beginning or end" (*Ethics,* pt. 1, def. 8).

Now, because the cause of the universe is eternal, it is unaffected by spatial-temporal events occurring within the universe and, hence, is unaffected by the passage of time. Therefore, the cause must be acting "now" with the same creative power with which it generated the big bang. Consequently, (4) the physical universe is continuously emanating from its eternal source.

If the reader feels any resistance to accepting this conclusion, or regards it as anything other than straightforward and obvious, consider whether there might be some conceptual residue of an *image* of God as the Old Testament Creator who, having created the world, retires to his throne and does nothing else but contemplate and judge. This is the *image* of God that most Western people have, for most picture God as creating the world some very long time ago, and that the world, once created, is sufficient unto itself so that God does not need to keep creating it, so to speak. This *image* of an "absentee Creator" is very strong in our culture, and people generally do not see the absurdity of such a conception. But once we understand that the cause which brought this universe into existence is itself eternal and hence, that its creative power cannot be limited by the passage of time—especially when we consider that time is itself something this power created—our conclusion, that (4) the universe is continuously emanating from its eternal source, follows easily.

Now, although we used the word "God" in the above paragraph, we must take care not to identify the cause of the physical universe with God per se. For God is constituted by *all* the Attributes, whereas the cause of the physical universe must be something that exists within the Attribute of Extension. If we recall Spinoza's parallelism, according to which there can be no causation across the Attributes of Thought and Extension, it follows that the cause of the physical universe cannot be anything in the Attribute of Thought, such as an idea in God's Mind, or an act of God's will, etc. Rather, the cause of the physical universe must itself be something in Extension. That is (5) the cause of the spatial-temporal universe must be something physical.

The concept of something that is both eternal *and* physical might seem a bit unusual. But, as we discussed in Part I, contemporary physics appears to utilize just such concepts. For, in the example we discussed there, it is possible that the black hole out of which the spatial-temporal universe emerged is the same as the black hole into which it will collapse. This "black hole," which contains the space-time universe within itself, is a good model for an eternal physical object, since both "prior to" the big bang and "after" the final collapse, the black hole exists but time does not. Its existence, therefore, lies outside the temporal order, which order is internal to it, and is thus an eternal object.

We call attention to this example from physics because it helps us to see, with the mind's eye, how the temporal universe can be conceived as being contained or embedded within its eternal cause and is not really separate from it. The more common "Humean" concept of causation, according to which the cause of an event is separate from it and precedes it in time, is plausible only within the temporal order. The Humean concept of causation, therefore, pertains only to imaginative thinking and really explains nothing; it merely states the customary appearance of things to the imagination. According to Spinoza, on the other hand, "it is of the nature of reason to understand things under the form of eternity" (*Ethics,* pt. 5, prop. 29), not temporally. Scientific understanding, for example, generally endeavors to explain a thing's observed behavior and properties in terms of its internal structure. But even though the properties of a given thing, indeed, (1) the thing itself, is an effect of, or is caused by (2) the nature and arrangement of the molecules that constitute the thing, (2) neither precedes (1) in time, nor are they really separate from one another. The thing, together with all its non-relational properties, is a manifestation of the arrangement of the particular molecules that constitute it. So, when we say that (2) produces or causes (1), we do not mean that (2) is separate from (1) or precedes it in time, but only that (2) involves a more fundamental level of physical reality than (1). For the molecules can exist without being in the particular arrangement that constitutes the being of (1).

Similarly, when we say that the temporal universe is caused by an eternal object, we mean neither that the latter precedes the former in time (which would be absurd), nor that they are really separate, but rather that the eternal cause exists at a more fundamental level of physical reality than does the temporal universe, since the former can exist without the latter, but not vice versa. The timelessness of the causal relation between the temporal world and its eternal cause is perhaps better rendered when we use expressions such as "the temporal order is *embedded in* its eternal cause," or "the temporal order is a *manifestation of* its eternal cause," or "the temporal order *continuously emanates* from its eternal source," etc.

The essence of the body

We now examine the relationship between finite modes that exist within the temporal order, such as a particular human body, and the eternal order. It is clear that since each and every body within the temporal order is produced by that order, and since the temporal order as a whole is produced by, or embedded in, the eternal order, it follows that each and every body within the temporal order is embedded in, or emanates from, the eternal order. This raises the following important question: does each particular body within the temporal order, like the order itself, emanate from the eternal order taken as a whole? Or, is the eternal order, like the temporal order, richly differentiated into "parts" or "elements" or "modes," so that any given temporal body is more closely associated with a particular element of the eternal order than with other such elements, or with the order taken as a whole?

A few analogies will clarify our meaning here. According to genetic theory, each characteristic of an organism is determined by its genetic structure. But the genetic structure is richly differentiated into numerous components, so that each characteristic is determined by a specific gene within the structure taken as a whole. Although it is certainly true to say that a given characteristic is produced by the whole genetic structure, it is also true to say that there is a component of the genetic structure, a specific gene, which is more closely involved in the production of the given characteristic than are the other genes or the structure of genes taken as a whole.

Or again, consider the relationship between a movie projected onto a screen and the film or laser disc that produces the images. The series of images that appear on the screen is caused by, and contained within, the film or disc as a whole; nevertheless, the film or disc as a whole has an internal structure, just as the series of images on the screen does, such that, for any particular image, or for any part of any image, there is a specific component of the film or disc which produces that particular image and which may be considered the cause of the given image. So, for example, the image of a man and a tree appear on the screen; there must then be information encoded in the film or disc that causes the appearance of the man on the screen and different information that causes the appearance of the tree. Thus, when we seek for the cause of a specific image on the screen, we say that it is a specific element within the film or disc, rather than the film or disc as a whole.

So the picture looks something like this: the big bang, or the temporal universe, is caused by, or is emanating from, an eternal physical object, or mode. This eternal mode has a rich internal structure, so just as the temporal universe is a whole that is constituted by numerous temporal modes, or bodies, so also the cause of the temporal universe is a whole that is itself constituted by numerous eternal modes, which latter Spinoza calls *essences*. Therefore, for each temporal mode, such as a particular human body, there exists within the cause of the temporal order as a whole, a specific eternal mode or essence that is the cause of the given temporal object, or out of which the given temporal object emanates or manifests. Thus, the essence of a given temporal body or mode is an eternal mode and, as such, it bears the same relation to the given body as the eternal cause of the whole temporal order bears to that order.

To summarize:

1. My body is a temporal object that is produced by and exists within the temporal order.

2. The temporal order is itself produced by and exists within its eternal cause.

3. An eternal object is unaffected by the passage of time.

4. Therefore, the temporal order, including my body, is *now* being produced and existing within its eternal cause.

5. The eternal cause, like the temporal order, is not featureless, but has an internal structure.

6. For any given body in the temporal order, there is a specific portion of this structure with which it is intimately connected.

7. This portion of the eternal order is called the *essence* of the given temporal body.

8. The essence of my body, therefore, is an eternal mode of extension, which is *now* producing my body, or from which my body is *now* emanating.

And just as a moving image on a screen is a projection onto a two-dimensional surface of information stored on a three-dimensional object (the film or disc), so also my body is a spatial-temporal projection of a "higher-dimensional," if I might use that expression, essence. This metaphor, incidentally, is very useful in combating the imaginative error of conceiving that the essence of a body is something "in" the body. On the contrary, the body is something which is "in" its essence. The duration of the body in time is the "moving image"—as Plato puts it—of its eternal essence, and is as intimately related to its essence as the images on a movie screen are related to and dependent upon the information stored on the film or disc. It is clear that, ontologically speaking, the essence is the "real being" of which the body is a passing temporal manifestation.

The eternality of the mind
So far, everything we have discussed here involves only the Attribute of Extension. Since "the order and connection of things is the same as the order and connection of ideas," it follows that there must be, in the Attribute of Thought, an idea that correlates with, or is the mind of, each essence. Given the essence of a specific human body, there is, in the Attribute of Thought, an idea that, as Spinoza variously puts it, expresses that essence, or conceives that essence, or has that essence for its object. This idea—which we previously called the "whole mind"—is eternal, since its object, the given essence, is eternal. As the given essence manifests into the temporal order as a specific human body, the idea of that essence—the whole mind—following its object, manifests a portion of itself into the temporal order and becomes, so to speak, the imaginative portion of the whole mind.

Let us follow Spinoza's own reasoning. He begins his discussion by stating that "the mind can neither imagine anything, nor recollect past things, except while the body endures" (*Ethics,* pt. 5, prop. 21). Thus, imagination and memory perish with the body. This may be of little comfort to the reader, since the human condition is such that we identify ourselves with imagination and memory—that is, with personality or ego. Yet it is not surprising, for mystics everywhere tell us that it is precisely this personality or ego that must be, and is, transcended in the experience of union with God. The way to take comfort in Spinoza's statement is to construe it positively: the mind is something far more than its ability to form images and have memories. What is this something more?

As we have said, because each body is the projection of an eternal essence, "in God there is necessarily an idea (or mind) that expresses the essence of this or that body under a species of eternity" (*Ethics,* pt. 5, prop. 22). This idea or mind, which is itself eternal, "is necessarily something that pertains to the essence of the human mind." That is, just as our temporal physical body is related to an eternal mode in the Attribute of Extension, so also our temporal human mind is related to an eternal mode in the Attribute of Thought. There is, therefore, "something" of the latter in the former, and hence "the human mind cannot be absolutely destroyed with the body, but something of it remains which is eternal" (*Ethics,* pt. 5, prop. 23).

This is admittedly somewhat abstract. Even though we may follow Spinoza's reasoning, which leads to the conclusion that "this idea which expresses the essence of the body under the form of eternity is...a certain mode of thought which pertains to the essence of the mind, and which is necessarily eternal" (*Ethics,* pt. 5, p. 23), it is difficult, at least initially, to know how to connect with this more concretely. The relationship between time and eternity, between the temporal order and the eternal order, is the most difficult conceptual problem for any mystical philosophy to explain clearly. To the awakened mind, which experiences the eternal order directly, no explanation is needed; to the imaginative mind, which experiences only the temporal order, no explanation, perhaps, is possible—or at least, no explanation is possible that will be completely satisfying to the imagination. Yet, in Spinoza's philosophy, our *reason* is something in between the first kind of knowledge, or imaginative knowledge, and the third kind of knowledge, or mystical insight. It is, as we have said, a vehicle that can take us from the former to the latter. It is to our reason, then, that these considerations are addressed. "For the mind feels those things that it conceives in understanding [the second kind of knowledge] no less than those it has in memory. For the eyes of the mind, by which it sees and observes things, are the demonstrations themselves. Therefore, though we do not recollect that we existed before the body, we nevertheless feel that our mind, insofar as it involves the essence of the body under a species of eternity, is eternal, and that this existence it has cannot be defined by time or explained through duration" (*Ethics,* pt. 5, prop 23, note). It is to our reason, then, that these considerations are addressed.

Nevertheless, I think we can make these ideas more vivid, even to the imagination. For our reason, we are supposing, is now convinced that there is a "something" that is eternal and that is related to our mind as we *presently* experience it. That is to say, this eternal "something" is related to our mind's present, temporal experience of itself. We should be able to get at this "something." Spinoza gives us a hint: "if we attend to the common opinion of men, we shall see that they are indeed conscious of the eternity of their mind, but that they confuse it with duration, and assign it to imagination, or to memory, which they believe to continue after death" (*Ethics*, pt. 5, prop. 34). The phrase, "common opinion," indicates that Spinoza is referring, not to reason or mystical insight, but rather, to ordinary imaginative thinking. Spinoza appears to be claiming that ordinary imaginative thinking is (1) conscious of the eternity of the mind, but mistakenly believes that (2) it is itself or memory that survives forever and forever in time. Now, as we have discussed, most people who believe in an afterlife do in fact believe (2). What concerns us here, however, is (1), which is a quite extraordinary claim. For the implication is that the eternity of our mind is something that we are *now* consciously experiencing. What is this "something" that we are now consciously experiencing, which is really eternal and so "remains" after death, but which we confuse with duration and memory?

There is only one possible answer to this question: it is the feeling of "I-ness," or "selfness," or awareness per se. The feeling of I-ness is common to all modes of thinking and is necessarily constitutive of every conscious experience. We "feel and know" this I-ness, not because it is an object of which we are aware, like some external body or even our own body, but rather because it is what we essentially *are*. The reason why this I-ness, which is our true identity and which is eternal, tends to confuse its own nature with duration is that it has so deeply identified with the body's experiences that it comes to believe that it has the same temporal nature as do the modifications of the body. This identification with, or bondage to, the experiences of its body confuses the mind into thinking that its own nature is temporal, and this confusion engenders the two errors discussed earlier: (1) that the I-ness will cease to exist when the body dies and (2) that it will continue to exist forever in time. It is as if a person, while watching a movie, has so identified with the main protagonist that he comes to believe that when the movie is over, either (1) he will cease to exist or (2) he will continue to exist as the character with whom he has identified. But even while watching the movie, that portion of the person's mind which has identified with the hero of the movie is not itself "in" the movie. Similarly, even while enmeshed in imaginative experience, our mind—the feeling of I-ness—is not itself "in" the field of temporal experience.

Imagine a bright nine-year-old child who, upon hearing of the transformations brought about by puberty, asks "Will I survive my puberty?" If by "I" the child means the present content of his consciousness, the answer, it would seem, is "no." For very little of a nine-year-old child's concerns, desires, relationships, etc.—what the child thinks about from day to day—will remain after puberty. But if by "I" the child means the feeling of I-ness itself, then the answer is "yes." For, as we might explain to the child, before, during, and after the transformation called puberty, this feeling of I-ness remains; there will never be a time where you cease to experience yourself as yourself. And it is the same with the transformation called "death."

"Becoming" eternal, or the possibility of direct experience
Through reason, we know that the temporal order is an expression of, is embedded in, or continuously emanates from, an eternal order. Hence, the mind's experience of a temporal order is itself embedded in the eternal order. The eternal order must therefore be present to the mind even insofar as it follows the body's experience in time; that is to say, even insofar as it constitutes the imagination. If it is asked, why do we not now experience the eternality of our mind, Spinoza's response is that we *do* experience it—it is the feeling of I-ness, which we are experiencing *now,* even as we read these very words. But because of our bondage to the body we get confused and come to believe that this feeling of I-ness is temporal, like the body. If it be asked further, well okay, but how can we become unconfused and *experience* this feeling of I-ness as the eternal mode of thinking which it truly is, the answer will be the same as is found in mystical philosophies everywhere. The eternality of our mind can be known directly only insofar as we detach from the body and its modifications, that is, only insofar as we are able to detach from sense experience, from emotions, and from personal memory. And this, as all mystics, including Spinoza, insist, is very difficult.

Quite obviously there can be no "exercise" through which we can realize the eternality of our mind—would that it were so easy! Yet, I think there are perhaps some things we can do that may enliven, even if only a little, what our reason has convinced us must be true. We know from experience that our sense of *I-ness*, although present in every conscious experience, fluctuates in degree or intensity. Our sense of self is relatively greater during episodes of second order awareness; it is relatively less when we are caught up in obsessive, repetitive, or addictive behaviors. Therefore, the more we move into second order awareness, the more we experience, or "become," a self that is constant even as first order experiences vary in time. The following exercise may be helpful.

> **EXERCISE 30:** (a) Consider several past events that evoked emotional responses in you when they occurred, but which have no emotional residue now, so you are able to recollect them without emotion. Suppose, for concreteness, that you recollect three events during which you were respectively proud, angry, and depressed. Since, as we are supposing, these events no longer have any emotional residue, the recollection of them does not evoke the above emotions. Thus, it is the same "I," the same sense of selfness, that recollects now one event, now another.
>
> (b) Now consider several past events that still carry emotional residue. In this case, recollecting the past events is sufficient to trigger the respective emotions, so that your sense of *I-ness* changes as it identifies with, or becomes, now angry, now depressed, now proud.
>
> In (a) you have a sense of yourself as something more than the temporal experiences of pride, anger, and depression; your sense of self is of something which *has* these experiences, but does not change as you recall the different experiences. In (b) your sense of self is of something which *is* proud, angry, or depressed, and which hence fluctuates along with the various emotions. In (a) we have our emotions; in (b) our emotions have us. The more we practice second-order awareness, which is a self-remembrance, the more we gain a sense of I-ness, or selfness, which is temporally invariant. For in second order awareness, but not in first, even as the content of our awareness changes in time, it is the same "I" that is now aware of joy, now of sorrow.

This feeling of I-ness, which "pertains to the essence of our mind" (even to its imaginative portion), which is always with us, and which we feel most clearly in second order awareness, is the "something" that remains when the body dies. The more we are able to identify, not with the content of our awareness, which in imaginative experience is temporal and perishes with the body, but rather with the awareness itself, whatever the content, we identify with that in us which is eternal. For the *I-ness* that "remains" after the death of the body also "remains" during the life of the body. And because this "something which remains" is present to us *now*, it must be possible to experience it *now*, even while the body and its associated personality exist in time. In this experience the mind transcends its imaginative portion and knows itself as an eternal mode of thinking in the Mind of God.

It is thus possible for the mind, even while the body exists in time, to directly experience itself as eternal. To put this another way, it is possible for the *body* to change in such a way that the mind with which it is correlated knows and experiences itself as eternal. "Inasmuch as human bodies are fit for many things, we cannot doubt the possibility of their possessing such a nature that they may be related to minds which have a large knowledge of themselves and of God, and whose greatest or principle part is eternal, so that they scarcely fear death" (*Ethics,* pt. 5, prop. 39, note). In this experience, the mind transcends its imaginative portion and knows, or identifies with, or "becomes" the eternal mode of thinking that it already is. This experience constitutes our "continuous, supreme, and unending happiness," for in this experience the mind knows itself as an eternal idea embedded in the Mind of God. It knows itself as "an eternal mode of thinking, which is determined by another mode of thinking, and this again by another, and so on, to infinity; so that together, they all constitute God's eternal and infinite intellect" (*Ethics,* pt. 5, prop. 40, note). And this knowledge necessarily involves the greatest possible feelings of joy and love.

Spiritual love
In his discussion of the love and joy the mind feels as it awakens to its own eternal nature and to its union with God, Spinoza uses the expression "the intellectual love of God." This expression is perhaps unfortunate for us, because the term "intellectual" means something quite different to us from what it meant to Spinoza. For us, an "intellectual" is, as we have said before, someone who has read a lot of books, retained a lot of information, and has a better than average ability to manipulate symbols. This is what we have called "cleverness." Furthermore, an "intellectual" often has a great ability to dissociate what he thinks from how he feels, so much so that he often has only a very limited access to his own emotions. In other words, his consciousness has become truncated and limited to words, concepts, and other symbols, all of which, of course, pertain to the imagination. I suppose it would be not entirely unfair to say that an intellectual, according to today's usage of the term, is someone who has distanced himself from the emotional portion of his imagination and lives entirely within the non-emotional portion, which latter consists of memory, facts, symbols, etc. Thus the term "intellectual" connotes a sort of dryness, a remoteness from the fullness of human living; and the expression "intellectual love" sounds almost like a contradiction in terms, referring at best to a joyless respect with which one computer might regard another.

Nothing could be further from Spinoza's intention. What Spinoza calls "intellectual love" is the very culmination of the fullness of human living. The intellect, for Spinoza, is that part of the mind that transcends the imagination, and which remains even when the personality dissolves. For Spinoza, "intellectual love" refers to the joy that accompanies the mind's awakening to the knowledge of its own eternity, which he also calls "blessedness" and "salvation." To avoid misunderstanding, I will use the term "spiritual" instead of "intellectual," since, in today's English, the connotations of the former are much closer than that of the latter to Spinoza's intentions.

Spiritual love is a very different kind of love than that which pertains to imaginative experience. Whereas the latter pertains to the drama of the personality and its body, spiritual love pertains to the mind insofar as it is eternal, without relation to the body. In imaginative experience, it will be recalled, *joy* involves an increase in, or passage to, a relatively greater "power of acting" and *love* is the emotion we experience toward whatever we believe causes this joy. Now, the imagination's power of acting is finite and limited, and ceases altogether when the body with which it has identified perishes. But a mind that experiences itself as eternal "never ceases to be" (*Ethics,* pt. 5, prop. 42), and hence, its power of action infinitely exceeds the power of any mind that is embedded in the temporal order. The joy, therefore, of a mind that has "become" eternal infinitely surpasses the joy of a mind that is embedded in time, so much so that Spinoza calls the former joy "blessedness." "If joy, then, consists in the passage to a greater perfection, blessedness must surely consist in the fact that the mind is endowed with perfection itself" (*Ethics,* pt. 5, prop. 33).

Furthermore, a mind that experiences itself as an eternal mode of thinking embedded in the Divine Mind knows that God is the cause of its joy, and hence experiences a love of God that is eternal. "From the third kind of knowledge"—that is, from the mind's experience of its own eternality—"there necessarily arises a spiritual love of God. For from this kind of knowledge there arises joy, accompanied by the idea of God as its cause, that is, love of God not insofar as we imagine him as present, but insofar as we understand God to be eternal. And this is what I call spiritual love of God" (*Ethics,* pt. 5, prop. 32). Because this spiritual love pertains only to a mind that is eternal, it follows that spiritual love is itself eternal and is, in fact, the very *same* love that God has toward us. For if we conceive the Divine Mind as manifesting into infinitely many eternal modes of thinking—of which the awakened human mind is one such mode—which themselves collectively constitute the Divine Mind, it follows that the spiritual love that each eternal mind has for God is the very same love that God has for each mind. In Spinoza's words, "the spiritual love of the mind toward God is the very love with which He loves Himself, not insofar as He is infinite"—that is, not insofar as he constitutes *all* minds—"but insofar as He can be manifested through the human mind, considered under the form of eternity; that is to say, the spiritual love of the mind toward God is part of the infinite love with which God loves Himself" (*Ethics,* pt. 5, prop. 36).

Recall that in our discussion of sexuality we said that sex is an experience of the force that holds all individual human bodies together as a single species, and that during the experience of sex our body surrenders to, or merges with, or unites with the Life Force itself. The body, while participating in the Life Force, receives from it a strength and power and joy that far exceeds any other bodily pleasure. Sexual ecstasy results from the body's uniting, momentarily, with the very same biological force that created it. Now, it is no accident that mystics often use sexual language to attempt to describe the ecstatic joy that accompanies the mind's awakening to its eternal nature. For in that experience the mind surrenders, or transcends, its imaginative portion—its personality, so to speak—and in uniting with the Divine Mind receives from the latter a strength and power and love that is "continuous, supreme and unending." And since the power of the Divine Being infinitely surpasses that of the Life Force—indeed, the latter is created by the former—how much greater than sexual ecstasy must be the joy that accompanies the mind's conscious participation in the eternal and infinite Mind of God and in the eternal spiritual love inherent in the Divine Mind. Because "God's love of humans and the mind's spiritual love of God are one and the same," it follows that "our salvation, or blessedness, or freedom, consists in a constant eternal love of God, or in God's love for humans" (*Ethics,* pt. 5 prop. 36).

The Shakespearean metaphor, "All the world's a stage"
Because the concept of eternity is impossible for the mind to imagine or picture, and because the mind that is enmeshed in imaginative experience tends to resist what it cannot picture, many spiritual teachers (*not* including Spinoza) have resorted to myth and metaphor in order to give the imagination or personality something to hold onto, thereby weakening its resistance and gaining some acquiescence. We hope that the following metaphor, developed in some detail, will help align our imagination with what our reason knows to be true and will assist the reader to get a deeper feeling for the relation between the temporal and the eternal orders, insofar as our awareness of that relation determines our experience of who we are.

Consider the Shakespearean metaphor, "All the world's a stage, and all the people in it players." Imagine now an actor who is so deeply immersed in his role that he has completely forgotten his true identity and believes himself to *be* the character he is playing. In this metaphor, the *character* the actor is playing is analogous to the imaginative portion of the mind (ego, personality); the *actor* himself is analogous to what we have called the "whole mind" or the "higher self." The *play* itself, which includes the role the actor is playing, is analogous to the temporal order. The *"real"* off-stage world, which includes the play, is analogous to the eternal order. The *amnesia* of the actor is analogous to the human condition; for our amnesic actor, like the human persona, believes the experiences of his character to be the experiences of his self and allows his emotions to be determined by those of his character.

But the role of the character is determined by the script, over which the character has no control. Indeed, the emotions, the behavior, the very lines spoken by the character, are all determined by the script. The actor, should he desire to recover from his amnesia, must first understand that he is more than the character he finds himself playing, and then begin to detach himself from the experiences of his character. As he develops "second order awareness"—which awareness has his character's experiences as its content—he develops, or "remembers," a sense of himself as something more than the character he is playing. And with this expanded sense of self there arises a joy and happiness that are constant, even though the character's emotions may fluctuate. For when memory returns, the actor's state of mind is determined more by factors external to his role than by the joys and sorrows of his character.

> EXERCISE 31: Sit in a public place, such as a park or a cafe, where you can observe people freely. Now pretend you are at the theater watching a play. Each person who comes into the cafe is an actor or actress playing a role in the play. Tell yourself that every motion and gesture, every spoken word, which table a person sits down at, what she orders, etc., has been rehearsed many times. Even the clothes the people are wearing were chosen deliberately. Notice how well, and how consistently "in character," each person plays her part. A feeling of wonderment, perhaps of humor, may begin to envelop you.
>
> After you can do this easily in public contexts, and with a sense of fun, begin to do this in scenes where *you* play a part, e.g., at work, with friends, with your family. Does a friend's (mother's, boss's, lover's, etc.) behavior annoy you? Tell yourself that

your friend (mother, boss, lover, etc.) is really a great actor or actress who has, alas, developed amnesia while acting her part. As you do this, notice that your annoyance decreases, to be replaced perhaps with an appreciation of how well your "actress"— friend is playing her role.

Can you apply this metaphor now to scenes in which *you* have a dominant role? Remind yourself that you speak your lines in accordance with the script. Does the script call for your character to be angry? Sad? Anxious? Jealous?, etc. Notice, while delivering your lines, how well you infuse them with the feelings called for by the script. Say to yourself "how well I play the role of *victim*!" "Only a truly great actor could so completely immerse himself in this *righteous indignation*!" "It takes great acting ability to wallow in guilt the way I do!" "It took years of diligent practice to enable me to project these feelings of chronic worry and anxiety as consistently as I do it!"

Allow yourself to have these second-order thoughts both as you experience the emotions (of victimization, indignation, guilt, anxiety, etc.) *and* as you deliver your lines (to another) which express these emotions. This, admittedly, is not easy to do; it is much easier to accept the possibility that others may be acting than that we are, for we tend to take our personal dramas much too seriously. Nevertheless, if we can apply the Shakespearean metaphor to ourselves and catch ourselves in the act, so to speak, a certain lightness and humor may begin to infuse itself into our roles, and our emotions will be less determined by the roles our characters are playing.

Shakespeare's metaphor and Spinoza's metaphysics

This metaphor may be used as a vehicle to better understand several aspects of Spinoza's metaphysics.

1. The character, of course, has no "free will," and neither does our amnesic actor who thinks he *is* his character. For, we are supposing, every action, behavior, emotion, spoken word, etc., which the character performs has been written into the script; the character is not "free" to choose his lines. Freedom for the actor is not to be found within the context of the play (which context is analogous to the temporal order). Freedom from bondage to the script lies in recovering from amnesia, in recollecting that his true identity is separate from that of his character (which recollection is analogous to the experiential knowledge that our mind belongs to the eternal order).

2. Furthermore, the concept of a character in a play is analogous to Spinoza's concept of an inadequate idea; for nothing that the character says or does, thinks or feels, can be understood in terms of the character himself, but only in terms of the play as a whole. A character in a play, considered by itself without relation to the other characters, the plot, etc., is an incomplete entity, requiring for its completion the rest of the play (which is analogous to the temporal order as a whole). But the true happiness of our amnesic actor does not lie within the context of the play; it lies in his waking up to his wider reality—his larger mind—which constitutes his true identity. Analogously, the imaginative portion of our mind is an incomplete, or inadequate, idea; its completion lies in its interconnectedness with the ideas of other things within the temporal order. Ultimately, the adequate idea, of which our personality or imagination is a portion, is the idea of the temporal order as a whole. But our freedom, or salvation, does not lie within the temporal order at all. Rather, it lies in our waking up to the knowledge of our true identity as an eternal mode of thought within the Mind of God.

3. We may also use this metaphor to understand why mystics have been ambivalent toward sexuality, generally advising seekers to abstain. For in terms of our metaphor, sexuality is the glue that holds the play together. To seek for the completion of our being through sex is to seek for it in the temporal order, within the context of the play. Insofar as we are the body and its personality, we are compelled to seek in this direction; but insofar as "we know and feel we are eternal," we know that our true completion, or salvation, lies in a different direction altogether. To seek for "continuous, supreme, and unending happiness" in the temporal order is to look for it where it cannot be found.

Nevertheless, the healthy experience of sexuality is not without value. For sexuality, insofar as it is the force that connects the various elements of the play into a single whole, transcends, so to speak, the details of the play. Therefore, to the extent that we are able to experience sex with clarity of mind—that is, without emotions such as guilt and anxiety that decrease our power of acting, and without possessive attachment to the body or personality of our partner, which attachment sustains the illusions of the temporal order—and insofar as we are able to feel in our heart connected with our partner and the Earth, we gain a momentary taste of the eternal order.

The difference between a "momentary taste" and the "continuous, supreme, and unending happiness" that accompanies the knowledge of the eternity of our minds cannot be overemphasized. For our actor, insofar as he has amnesia, is constrained to suffer the emotions of his character, even if he has occasional glimpses of the play as a whole. But as he awakens to his true identity, he no longer suffers the emotions of his character and is able to maintain a constant peace of mind even as the emotions of his character fluctuate widely. The awakened actor's peace of mind and inner balance transcend the joys and sorrows of his character.

4. Moreover, we note that the mind of the awakened—or *awakening*, since Spinoza seems to be describing a *process* of awakening—actor contains all of the perceptions and emotions of the amnesic actor, but these constitute only a small part of his whole mind. Let us use our metaphor to interpret the following passage from Spinoza: "…that mind suffers the most whose largest part consists of inadequate ideas, so that it is distinguished by what it suffers rather than by what it does, while on the contrary, that mind acts the most whose largest part consists of adequate ideas, so that, although it may possess as many inadequate ideas as the first, it is nevertheless distinguished by those which belong to human virtue rather than by those which belong to human impotence" (*Ethics*, pt. 5, prop. 20, note).

Now consider three actors: A, who has total amnesia and believes without doubt that he is his character; B, who has partial amnesia and sometimes believes he *is* his character, and other times has thoughts and memories that pertain to his identity as an actor; and C, who has completely recovered his memory. What distinguishes the minds of A, B, and C from one another is their content—the thoughts and feelings that constitute their inner life. The mind of A is filled entirely with the thoughts and feelings that pertain to his character; that is to say, it is constituted entirely by inadequate ideas. The mind of A is passive, or in other words, it suffers because its inner life is determined externally by the role of its character. By contrast, although the minds of B and C also contain the thoughts and feelings (inadequate ideas) appropriate to their character, they contain in addition thoughts (adequate ideas) that pertain to their identity as actors. So the mind of B is more active, or suffers less, than the mind of A, and that of C is more active than that of B. That is, the inner life of C is not at all determined by that of his character; A on the other hand, has no power or "virtue" to think any thought other than those which are scripted for his character—his amnesia has rendered his mind impotent.

As the actor gradually recovers his memory (B), the ratio of adequate ideas to inadequate ideas increases, and at some point in this process of awakening, the ratio is large enough so that the content of his mind is distinguished more by thoughts that pertain to his identity as an actor than by thoughts that pertain to the role of his character. And should the script call for the death of his character, the mind of C will be totally unperturbed, but the mind of A will be filled with anxiety, since the latter mind experiences the death of his character as if it were the death of himself.

Unlike a play, however, the script for *every* human life calls for the death of its character (the personality). To the extent that we, like A, are ignorant of our true nature and identify solely with our personality, we are anxious and fearful. To the extent that, like C, we have awakened to the knowledge of the eternity of our mind, then the death of our personality is "of no consequence." "It is possible," says Spinoza, "for the human mind to be of such a nature that that part of it which we have shown perishes with its body (the imagination or personality), in comparison with that part of it which remains, is of no consequence" (*Ethics,* pt. 5, prop. 38). (The contemporary Near-Death Experience literature is filled with detailed personal testimony corroborating Spinoza's claim that the ego or personality is "of no consequence".)

5. Finally, we may use this metaphor to enliven Spinoza's concept of spiritual love. Insofar as the actor suffers from amnesia and believes herself to be her character, the loves that she feels within the play are determined by the experiences of her character. Suppose, to give a concrete example, it is determined by the script that another character in the play praises her, or gives her money, or does her a favor—that is to say, affects her with joy. Since, as we are supposing, her amnesia causes her to believe that her joy is caused by what the other did for her in the play, she will feel love toward the other character. This is analogous to imaginative love.

But now suppose that the actor suddenly recovers from her amnesia and recognizes that the character who affected her with joy in the play is really a person who, offstage, is a good friend of hers. Feelings of joy and friendliness, unconditioned by any constraints within the play, now permeate her character; the love she now feels for her friend is qualitatively different from the love that she-as-her-character felt for her friend's character. The latter is completely subsumed and transformed into the former.

Indeed, her affection for her friend remains constant even if, within the play, her friend's character inflicts her character with pain, suffering, or any kind of sorrow. The hatred of her character for her friend's character is experienced as real only insofar as she suffers from amnesia, but diminishes to nothing when she recovers her memory.

Moreover, to pursue the metaphor, the production of a play requires a spirit of cooperation among all involved. This "spirit of cooperation" permeates each actor's role, and is present even if the script calls for two actors to play the roles of adversaries. On the one hand, the "spirit of cooperation" is completely independent of the various roles within the play; on the other hand, it completely permeates each and every role. And it remains present even if an actor is so into his character that he has forgotten it. The amnesic actor is then constrained to suffer—to experience as real—the joys and sorrows of his character. But as soon as he recovers his memory, the spirit of cooperation becomes once again present to him, and the sufferings of his character are no longer real to him and are hence, as Spinoza says, "of no consequence."

Just as the spirit of cooperation is the force that holds the play together, so spiritual love is the force that creates the temporal order. Insofar as we are lost in the drama of our personalities, we are unconscious of this love. We become conscious of it insofar as we are able to transcend our personality and experience our mind as eternal—as part, along with all other minds, of the infinite Mind of God. If, like the amnesic actor, we are unconscious of this spiritual love, then we are constrained to experience the sufferings of our personalities as real; and conversely, the more we seek relief from our sufferings through the experiences of the personality within the temporal order, the more unconscious of this love we become. But as soon as we regain awareness of the union that exists between our mind and all other minds, the joys and sorrows of our personalities dissolve into and are transformed by the eternal spiritual love in which our essential nature has its being. The following, and final, exercise will illustrate these ideas.

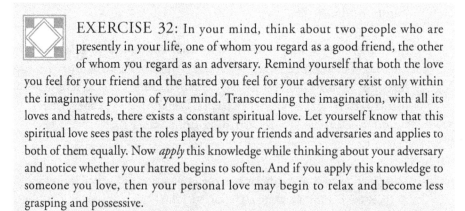

EXERCISE 32: In your mind, think about two people who are presently in your life, one of whom you regard as a good friend, the other of whom you regard as an adversary. Remind yourself that both the love you feel for your friend and the hatred you feel for your adversary exist only within the imaginative portion of your mind. Transcending the imagination, with all its loves and hatreds, there exists a constant spiritual love. Let yourself know that this spiritual love sees past the roles played by your friends and adversaries and applies to both of them equally. Now *apply* this knowledge while thinking about your adversary and notice whether your hatred begins to soften. And if you apply this knowledge to someone you love, then your personal love may begin to relax and become less grasping and possessive.

We can extend this exercise to include the entire domain of our personal lives. Make a list of all the people with whom you are connected emotionally; this list constitutes the cast of characters in the play that is your life. In constructing this list, include not only the obvious (parents, children, friends, lovers, enemies, etc.), but also anyone whom you devote time thinking about. For the true measure of your connections with others is the amount of emotional energy you expend thinking about them. If, for example, you spend more time thinking about how to please your boss than you spend thinking about how to please your spouse, then you are more strongly connected to the former than the latter. If you spend more time feeling upset with (and hence thinking about) someone you believe has wronged you than you spend thinking about your children, then you are more strongly connected with your adversary than with your children. (Hopefully there is no longer any need for self-deception here). When you complete your list, contemplate each person one at a time, noticing the thoughts and feelings you have toward each. As you do this, apply the knowledge that these thoughts and feelings pertain to the personality only—yours and theirs—and are transcended by the spiritual love that applies equally to each person in your life, and which, like the cooperation required for producing a play, holds together the entire cast of characters, including your own.

This exercise may foster a deeper sense of appreciation for *all* with whom we are connected, not just those who affect our personality with joy. And from this deeper sense of appreciation there may arise some glimmerings, however vague or faint, of spiritual love, the experience alone of which releases us from the drama of our personal lives, and which constitutes our salvation and our blessedness.

For after the play is over, the cast goes out and celebrates. How wonderful it could be to make that knowledge lively—to create a spirit of celebration and joy—even while the play unfolds. But the actor who suffers from amnesia will have as much difficulty enjoying the celebration afterward as he has enjoying his role, for he believes he *is* his character, and that the end of the play is the end of himself. How tragic, how humorous, to attempt to relate to your fellow actors, when the play is over, as if you were still your character and they were theirs!

"The ignorant man," who has totally identified with his character (imagination, personality, ego) and goes through life without faith, grasping whatever he can, "is not only agitated by external causes in many ways, and never enjoys true peace of mind, but lives also ignorant, as it were, of God and of things, and as soon as he ceases to suffer ceases also to be. On the other hand, the wise man...is scarcely ever moved in his mind, but being conscious by a certain eternal necessity of himself, of God, and of things, never ceases to be, and always enjoys true peace of mind" (*Ethics,* pt. 5, prop. 42, note). In terms of our metaphor, the amnesic actor, who has totally identified with his character, is not only agitated by other characters and events within the play and never enjoys true peace of mind, but plays his part also ignorant, as it were, of the true nature and causes of the play, and as soon as he ceases to suffer the experiences of his character, ceases also to be. On the other hand, the actor whose memory is intact is scarcely ever moved in his mind by the role he is playing, but being conscious of his true identity, and of the play and production as a whole, does not cease to be himself when the play is over and always enjoys true peace of mind, regardless of the circumstances of his character.

Rational faith and the satisfaction of longing

"We feel and know," Spinoza tells us, "that we are eternal." And yet, until we become fully conscious of our eternal nature, we also feel and know that we are incomplete. For the personality, in its state of separation from the knowledge of its union with the Mind of God, feels its incompleteness very deeply, which manifests consciously as a chronic *longing*. We generally seek to satisfy this longing through imaginative experience, where satisfaction is impossible in principle. The completion of our being, salvation, does not lie in the experiences of our body in the physical world; rather, it lies in expanding the scope of our consciousness, so that we experience our self as the eternal mode of thought that we in fact are.

This all-too-human habit of seeking for our completion where it cannot be found arises from, and sustains, the belief that our personality is all that we are. Imagine the absurdity of our amnesic actor who, feeling that something is missing, seeks for the satisfaction of his ensuing longing solely within the confines of his character and the play. But the longing, we are supposing, is caused by his amnesia, and its satisfaction lies outside the context of the play. If our actor has (1) a strong faith that his longing can be satisfied, and (2) an equally strong conviction that it cannot be satisfied within the drama of the play, then he will gradually cease identifying with the experiences of his character. That is to say, he will gradually regain some of his "power of action," which he had totally invested in his character, and this will create some space within his mind for an occasional memory of his "real" life to pop in. These memories, scattered at first, will reinforce his initial faith, causing him to further cease endeavoring to find happiness through the experiences of his character, creating more space within his mind for more memories to return, and so on until eventually, he regains the full knowledge of who he really is.

And like our amnesic actor, we humans, if we are to satisfy the longing for our completeness, must cease searching for it where it can't be found—in the temporal order, in the drama in which our character (the personality or imagination) participates. We must do everything we can to strengthen both our faith that our longing can be satisfied *and* our understanding that it cannot be satisfied within the temporal order.

The importance of nurturing within ourselves a conscious faith that our longing *can* be satisfied cannot be overemphasized. For many people come to believe, through their own experience, that longing cannot be satisfied within the temporal order, but erroneously conclude that their longing cannot be satisfied period, and hence, that "angst" and suffering are a necessary feature of their lives. This leads invariably to despair and cynicism. Indeed, cynicism is the emotional consequence of (1) longing—a strongly felt sense of one's own incompleteness; (2) the understanding that longing cannot be satisfied through imaginative experiences within the temporal order; and (3) the (false) belief that the temporal order is all there is. The reader is urged to guard against cynicism, for once it has infected and taken hold of the mind, it saps the mind of strength and vitality and is very difficult to eradicate. The actor who wholeheartedly believes without any doubt that the play is all there is will never recover her memory.

Nevertheless, the cynic might focus on her own longing and consider whether the faith that we urge is not simply an application of the principle of sufficient reason, which we discussed at the beginning of this book. Can there be such a thing, in the whole order of nature in which we exist, as a need that has no satisfaction? Certainly every felt need of the body—hunger, thirst, sex, warmth, etc.—has its satisfaction. But *longing* is a felt need that remains after, and even during, the satisfaction of all bodily needs. It remains during, and even after, the pursuit and satisfaction of all imagined needs of the personality—for status, wealth, and worldly power. For the longing of which we speak is not caused by the absence of any of these; nor can it be satisfied by the acquisition of such things, as everyone knows from experience.

Rather, *longing* pertains to the separation of the personality from its eternal source, from which it continuously emanates. *Longing* is the emotional component of the imagination's knowledge, conscious or unconscious, that it is in itself incomplete. Hence, the satisfaction of *longing* lies in the healing of this incompleteness, or separation, which healing is the knowledge of the union that exists between itself and the "larger mind" in which it is embedded. For, to consult our metaphor, the mind of the amnesic actor is still united to, or embedded in, the mind of his real self, regardless of whether or not he is conscious of that union. And the single most important requirement for becoming conscious of this union is the belief that this union exists and that it is possible to experience it directly.

This is why we stress the importance of rational faith, for no one undertakes to do anything the outcome of which is deemed impossible or remote. No one who believes that her personal drama is all she is will endeavor to regain awareness of the connection that exists between her personality and the larger mind in which her personality is embedded. And to the extent that her faith in the existence of such a connection is only partial, or fluctuates, to that extent her effort to disengage from her personal drama in order to awaken into the knowledge of union will also be only partial. Therefore, everything that supports our faith, everything that reminds us wherein lies our true happiness, is of great benefit to us.

Concluding words

It is time now to close. The philosophy of Spinoza is a cognitive map; it provides us with a sense of direction for finding our way through the drama of human life. But a map must be followed, and this philosophy must be applied in order to be effective. For no one can take from another the responsibility for living his or her own life. The way to the knowledge of the divine lies through experiential understanding of our emotions, which form the core of our personalities. It is our emotions that hold us in bondage to our own personal dramas. We must become aware of our emotions, we must be willing to feel them deeply, we must take full responsibility for them, and we must have faith in the possibility of transcending them. And admittedly, this is not easy. "If the way which, as I have shown, leads hither seem very difficult, it can nevertheless be found. It must indeed be difficult, since it is so seldom discovered, for if salvation lay ready to hand and could be discovered without great labor, how is it possible that it should be neglected by almost everybody? But all noble things are as difficult as they are rare" (*Ethics*, pt. 5, prop. 42, note).

Even though the institutions of our culture, insofar as they run on greed and ambition, are as opposed to the pursuit of wisdom today as they were in Spinoza's time, yet there is a growing "counterculture" that actively supports this pursuit. Assistance is therefore readily available, and one need not walk this path alone; as Spinoza tells us, to join with others who are also seeking their own awakening is a great advantage and a source of much joy.

And it will be good to remind ourselves, from time to time, that walking along the path, although we are certain it leads to the goal, is not the same as achieving the goal. So we will therefore be gentle with ourselves and not berate ourselves during those times when we, too, suffer from greed, ambition, or any other kind of lust. For as we have shown, until we become conscious of the union that exists between our mind and the Mind of God, we lack the power to transcend completely our emotional nature. "[B]ecause the power to restrain the emotions is in the spirit alone, no one, therefore, delights in divine love or blessedness because he has restrained his emotions, but, on the contrary, the power of restraining his lusts springs from blessedness itself" (*Ethics,* pt. 5, prop. 42).

GLOSSARY

Perhaps the most important concept in Spinoza's system of philosophy is that of **Substance**,* defined as a being that can exist independently of any other being. Several immediate consequences of this definition are that Substance is (i) unique (there is only One Substance), (ii) self-caused (otherwise its existence would depend on other things), and (iii) contains within itself all dependent beings. Spinoza also uses the terms **God** and **Nature** to refer to the same independent being.

God or Substance expresses Itself in infinitely many, qualitatively distinct ways, called **Attributes**. Of the infinitely many Attributes of God, we humans are familiar with only two, **Extension**, the physical world, and **Thought**, the mental world. Anything within the physical world is called a **body**, and anything within the mental world is called an **idea**. Spinoza sometimes uses the word **mind** as synonymous with idea. The physical world as a whole, which includes our bodies, may be conceived as the body of God; the mental world as a whole, which includes our minds, may be conceived as the Mind of God.

Anything less than the whole of a given Attribute, such as a particular body or mind, is called a **mode**. The word "mode" is short for "modification". All things are aspects of, or modifications of, the Divine Being, and using the term "mode" makes the point that all things are created by and are dependent upon God. Using Spinoza's terminology, the human body is thus a mode of Substance conceived or expressed under the Attribute of Extension, and the human mind is that same mode of Substance conceived or expressed under the Attribute of Thought.

As human beings, we are conscious of our **desires**, but ignorant of their causes. This ignorance allows us to falsely believe that we have **free will**. But for Spinoza, our "decisions" and "acts of willing" are simply our desires conceived under the Attribute of Thought, just as our bodily **appetites** are our desires conceived under the Attribute of Extension. The body and mind thus run **parallel** to one another, since they are the same mode of Substance conceived, respectively, under the Attributes of Extension and Thought. Nothing can be "free" from the forces that create it and constitute its being, and just as the body is determined by physical forces within the Attribute of Extension to act and behave in the precise way it is acting and behaving at any given time, so also is the mind determined, by mental forces within the Attribute of Thought to think and desire the precise thought(s) and desire(s) it is experiencing at any given time. Spinoza's rigorous **determinism**

---

*Words in **bold** are technical terms in Spinoza's system of Philosophy.

may be expressed by saying that nothing could be other than what it in fact is.

The human mind is capable of experiencing **three kinds of knowledge**, although the great majority of people experience only the **first kind of Knowledge**, which Spinoza calls **Imagination.** This kind of knowledge includes sense experience, memories, thoughts that pertain to the past and/or future, fantasies, most emotions; any conscious experience that involves an image belongs to the imagination. The highest kind of knowledge of which the mind is capable Spinoza calls **Blessedness**, or **knowledge of the 3RD kind.** In this mystical state of consciousness, the mind experiences directly its union with the Mind of God, and knows itself as a thought in the infinite intellect of God. This knowledge constitutes our **salvation.** The bridge that connects the egoic "I" of imaginative experience to the universal "I" of mystical experience is called **reason.** Reason, for Spinoza, is not mere calculative thinking, or cleverness, but is the ability to discern which, of the many desires that compete for our attention, are truly in our best interests. The ability or power to follow the **dictates of reason** (such as the Golden Rule) Spinoza calls **virtue.** The great majority of human beings lack this power, and are hence in **bondage** to their own desires which have been conditioned or programmed into the imaginative portion of their minds.

A finite mode of Substance, such as an individual human being, comes to exist according to the **Laws of Nature**, which are everywhere and always the same. A given individual experiences its own existence as a **striving** or **endeavor** to **persevere** and flourish in its own being and according to its own nature. Every individual is in continuous interaction with its environment. A person's **power-of-action** is measured by the individual's ability to maintain his or her form in the face of continuous interaction with the environment. Some interactions assist the individual in his or her endeavor to flourish, increasing his or her power of action; some interactions hinder the individual's endeavor to persevere, and others neither hinder nor help. The emotions of **joy** or **sorrow** accompany an increase or decrease, respectively, of our power of action.

The mind partakes of time, or **duration**, only insofar as it is associated with a body. The true nature of our mind, its **essence**, is **eternal**. But we do not experience ourselves as eternal until we awaken into the state of consciousness called **blessedness**, in which state the mind experiences itself as "an eternal mode of thinking", which together with all other eternal modes of thinking, human and otherwise, "constitute simultaneously the eternal and infinite intellect of God." This state of consciousness is constituted by extreme and continuous joy, peace of mind, and **spiritual love.** "From this we understand clearly in what our salvation, that is, our blessedness, that is, our freedom, consists: namely in a constant and eternal love for God, or [equivalently] in the love of God for human beings. This love, that is, blessedness, is called 'glory' in the scriptures, and rightly so." (*Ethics*, Part 5, proposition 36).

INDEX

acting, power of, 133–135, 138, 140, 143, 145, 146, 169, 189, 252, 256
action, *See* acting
advertising. *See* contemporary society, irrational nature of
agnosticism, world intelligibility of, 21
All There Is, 40, 41, 43, 44; concept of, 30–33; God defined as, 31–32
anthropocentrism, 70, 86, 100
anthropomorphism, 23, 29, 85
appearance, 73, 75; visual dependency of, 75, 77, 82. *See also* sense experience; sense perception
atheism, 15
atheist, 13, 19, 238
atomism, 33–34, 37, 38, 41, 118; demise of, 35–38; metaphysical aspects, 35–37
atomistic metaphysics, 37
atomistic methodology, 37
awareness, first-order, 181, 182
awareness, second-order, 180–184, 185, 186, 187; resistance to, 188, 196, 234; shifting to, 184–186, 187, 188, 196, 199

behavior: abusive, 176; causality, 176; conditional patterns of, 193, 194, 196, 200, 226; correction of, 198–199; purposeful, 127–129; repetitive patterns, 200, 206, 226
beliefs, 150–155; delineation of, 155; resisting awareness of, 150; social awareness of, 150; social conditioning of, 150–155. *See also* human mind(s), cultural conditioning of; sense experience; values
best interests: recognition of, 194, 195
Bible, 61, 96
big bang, 39, 61–65, 241–243, 245. *See also* eternity
black holes, 61, 63–66, 243
blame, 14, 31–32, 44, 48–49, 145, 157, 183–184. *See also* emotions, human, guilt

blessedness, 17, 18, 67, 103, 105, 132, 188, 231, 237, 238, 239, 252, 253, 261, 265, 267, 268
body bondage. *See* emotional bondage
Buddhism, 14, 15
Buddhists, Ch'an, 11

causation, Humean concept of, 243. *See also* parallelism, psychophysical
choice, 47, 48; metaphysics of, 118. *See also* free will
competition in irrational society. *See* contemporary society, irrational nature of conscious experience, 54
consciousness, 51; connection with higher, 156; nervous system, apart from, 55; modes of, 105
contemporary society, irrational nature of, 213–225
continuous emanation, process of, 63
cooperation, spirit of, 259
creation: continuous process of, 41
creation: Nature, whole of, 119; Divine Forces, 119
criticism. *See* emotions, human, response to criticism
cultural conditioning. *See* human mind(s), cultural conditioning of

Dalai Lama, 14. See also *Ethics for a New Millennium*
death: fear of, 237–238; as transformation, 249
Delphi, Oracle of. *See* Oracle of Delphi
denial: cause of, 195; patterns of, 196, 198, 208–209, 226
depression. *See* emotions, human
Descartes, René, 14, 23, 35, 50, 122, 125, 222; God, concept of, 23; Spinoza, compared to, 14

desire, 103; cause of, 108–109; metaphysics of, 106; motivating forces of, 109
determinism, 112
*Deus sive Natur*a (God or Nature, Spinoza), 12
Divine Being. *See* God, being of
Divine Mind. *See* God, mind of
Divine Punishment. *See* punishment, divine
Divine Reality. *See* God, conscious union with
dreaming, 92, 130–132. *See also* parallelism. psychophysical

earth, body of, 102. *See also* Gaia Hypothesis
education. *See* contemporary society, irrational nature of; human mind(s), cultural conditioning of
efficient cause, 42, 230
ego, 21, 85, 87, 92–93, 96, 116, 118, 239–240, 246–247; arrogance of, 239–240; resisting consciousness, 85, 86
Einstein, Albert: and belief in God, 13; mysterious, sense of the, 82; on spatial separation *(see* holism); sufficient reason, acceptance of principle of, 22. *See also* sufficient reason, principle of; spirituality
Eliot, George, 12
Emendation of the Understanding, On (Spinoza), 13, 21
emotional bondage, 194; cause and structure of, 200–201; Spinoza on, 14
emotions, human, 15–16, 20, 86, 103, 136, 171; depression, 137; discernment of, 192, 194; guilt, 30–31, 44, 48–49; hurt, 175–177, 184–185; irrationality, 103–104; joy and sorrow (Spinoza), 138, 141, 157, 164; longing, 262–263; love and hate, 141, 142, 145; negative, 235; passion, 138; protective barriers to, 148; residues of, 187; response to criticism, 174–175; responses to outer (external) events, as, 147, 151, 158, 164–165 *(see also* human mind(s), cultural conditioning of); self-esteem, 166, 175–176; spectator sports in, 177, 179; Spinoza's theory of, 15, 73, 133, 140, 161, 162; spiritual love, 144; understanding of, 161. *See also* beliefs

eternal, definition of (Spinoza), 63
eternal order, 244, 246–247, 249, 254, 255
eternity, 66, 97, 239, 242, 243, 247–248, 253
Ethics (Spinoza), 12, 13, 14, 93, 145, 204
Ethics for a New Millennium (Dalai Lama), 14
evil, 44, 123, 188, 189, 193, 200, 204
expanding universe. *See* big bang
experience, sense. *See* sense experience
Extension, Attribute of, 58, 65, 70, 71, 83, 88, 93, 94, 98, 107, 108, 112, 117, 124, 125, 128, 129, 132, 140, 149, 160, 161, 163, 171, 190, 193, 201, 201, 218, 234, 243, 246, 247, 266. *See also* God

feelings. *See* emotions, human
"fight or flight response," 107
free will, 44, 46, 112–114, 115, 116, 118–119, 122, 153, 154, 169, 176, 255, 266; argument against, 116; deliberation, 48; illusion of, 46, 112. *See also* choice
freedom: from bondage, 167–227; path to, 158
Freud, Sigmund, 21, 72, 85, 212; and the superego, 148

Gaia Hypothesis, 102
Gestalt psychology, 10, 11
gnosis, 11
Gnostic, 11
God: aloneness of, 12; anthropomorphic projections of, 23, 29; Aristotle on, 26; attributes of, 109; being of, 27, 29, 50, 58, 60, 108, 119; body of, 25, 58, 59, 99, 107, 266; causal proof of, 26; causality of, 41; concept of, 23–24, 25, 29, 42, 97, 156, 241; connection with, 20, 25, 29, 144, 148, 196, 216; conscious union with, 93, 192; as creator, 25, 66, 119, 242; definition of, 23, 28; divine necessity, 44, 48, 107; Einstein, Albert, belief in, 13; erroneous concept of, 97; existence of, 23–27 ; human unification with, 14, 20, 121, 188,

193, 247, 251; independence of, 24–27; infinite attributes of, 106; intellectual love of, 132, 251–252 (see also emotions: spiritual love); Judeo-Christian concepts of, 23–27, 108; manifestations of, 125; mind of, 20, 25, 58, 59, 60, 67, 91, 92, 95, 96, 99, 103, 105, 107, 108, 110, 112, 119, 120, 121, 122, 136, 143, 180, 206, 250, 251, 253, 256, 260, 262, 264, 266, 267; nature of, 29, 31, 47, 107, 141, 160, 188; or nature, 12, 193, 213 (see also *Deus sive Natura*); substance or, 58, 98, 161; spiritual love of, 251–253; totality, of, 30, 44; union with, 14, 15, 93, 121, 187, 193, 247, 251, 262, 267. See also All There Is; Extension, Attribute of; nature, order of; Thought, Attribute of; universe, and integration with God

Goethe, Johann Wolfgang von, on *Ethics* (Spinoza), 12

good and bad: harmful consequences of belief in, 190–192; metaphysical impossibility of, 188

guilt. See emotions, guilt

hallucination. See imagination; sense perception, veridical

happiness, 13, 188; continuous, 20, 22; obstacles and limitations, 29; personality, 20; Plato and Spinoza, comparison of, 67; transitory, 20; true, 13, 20, 204, 231, 256, 264

Harlow, Harry. See nurturing

hate. See emotions, human

History of Western Philosophy (Bertrand Russell), 9

holism, 33–34, 38, 40–41, 46, 61, 99, 118, 151, 180, 206, 229; metaphysics of, 46, 229; modern science, continuity with, 40–41; physics, in harmony with, 61; quantum physics, 38; spatial contiguity, 38; spatial separation, 38, 39

homunculus, 68, 70, 73, 114, 115, 119; myth of, 68; theory of, 77, 80, 83, 113

human body, 128; atomical conception of, 33, 41; dependence upon God, 41; Dynamic Equilibrium, 133; essence of, 244 (see also efficient cause); extension of mind as, 246; harmony and construction, 128; in time (Plato), 246; optical properties of, 75–77; part of God, 129; perseverance of, 193; physical interaction with external bodies, 85; striving of, 202–205; substance of God, as a, 129. See also God

human condition, 20, 44, 88, 96, 99, 100, 103, 118, 188, 196, 240, 246, 254

human mind(s), 134, 135, 136; awakening of, 253; cultural conditioning of, 150, 152, 193; group, 100; imaginative (see ego); imagine, ability to, 240–241, 246; immortality of, 93, 237–238; infections of, 209, 212, 216 (see also behavior, conditional patterns of); mode of God, 72; perception by, 70; philosophical theory of, 106; programming of, 147, 152, 153, 155, 157, 165, 178, 216; psychic organization within, 160

hypnosis, 153

idea, 70

"idea of an idea" (Spinoza), 180

illusion, 92

imagine, ability to, 26

imagination, 85–87, 91, 93, 94, 96, 98, 99, 103, 105, 116, 136, 160, 235–236; confusion with understanding, 101; definition of, 45; limits of, 61 (see also big bang); Spinoza's use of, 168

imagination, Spinoza on, 85, 94

imaginative experience, 91–92, 96, 97, 99, 103, 116, 149

Improvement of the Understanding, On the (Spinoza), 10

"I-ness," 116, 248–250

inner dialogue, 168–180, 183, 235–236, 241

inquiry, rational, 22

intellectual identification. See "knowledge of the second kind"

intellectual love of God. See God, intellectual love of

intuition, 105; Spinoza on, 85

James, William: "On Human Immortality," 54

Kantians, 9
"kingdom within a kingdom" (Spinoza), 86, 110
knowledge, intuitive, 91, 105, 116, 132, 224
"knowledge of the second kind," (Spinoza), 86, 121, 231, 238, 241
"knowledge of the third kind," 121, 231, 238. *See also* Near Death Experience
knowledge, self, 105, 112, 113, 118, 148, 154, 188, 190, 199, 225. *See also* human mind(s), programming of

larger mind, concept of, 86, 91–93, 94, 99, 121–122, 124, 136. *See* also God, mind of; soul
Leibniz, Gottfried Wilhelm, 14
Life Force. *See* sexuality
love. *See* emotions, human; sex, love

Maslow, Abraham: peak experiences, 128
materialism, 51, 54, 55
Maya, 11
mentally healthy culture: Freud on, 212; principles for, 212–213
metaphysics: definition, of, 20; etymological sense, 11; first principles of, 20, 21–23; review of, 240–244; symbols, 11
mind and body: coexistence of, 57; perturbations of, 84; relationship of, 56–57; relationship of (Spinoza's account of), 58–60
mind(s). *See* human mind(s)
mind, whole, 91, 93–94, 96, 99–100, 136, 236, 246, 254; constitution of, 91. *See also* soul
mode, definition of, 69
modification, definition of, 69
Moses: Mount Sinai, vision of, 8

motion and rest: Spinoza on (pre-Newtonian), 43

naive realism, 68
natural order, 47, 48, 103, 104, 189, 200, 213
nature: laws of, 52, 107, 193, 200, 267; Spinoza on, 267. *See also* creation
NDE. *See* Near Death Experience
Near Death Experience, 16, 52, 238. *See also* "knowledge of the third kind"
nervous system, consciousness apart from, 54–55
neurophysiology, 55, 68
New Age: philosophy, 172; spirituality, 228
nurturing, 263. *See also* contemporary society, irrational nature of

Oracle of Delphi, 148

parallelism: metaphysical (Spinoza), 83; objections to, 126; psychophysical, 130, 149, 243
passion. *See* emotions, human
past lives. *See* reincarnation
peace of mind. *See* happiness
perception, mental, 126
perception, sense. *See* sense perception
perseverance. *See* human body, perseverance of
philosophers, mystical, 20, 67, 91, 92
philosophers, rationalist, 14
Plato: compared to Spinoza, 11; dialogues of *(Allegory of the Cave)*, 8, 66, 182; on sense experience, 67; on sexuality, 229; on World-Soul, 144. *See also* human body, in time (Plato)
Platonists, 9
Plotinus, 70
praise, 157, 205
psychedelic drug, 82
psychology: happiness, 21. *See also* spiritual psychotherapy

psychophysical parallelism. *See* parallelism, psychophysical
punishment, divine, 188, 204

rational culture. *See* mentally healthy culture
rational faith, 162–163
rationalism, western, 10
reality, intelligibility of, 22
reason, 193–194; discernment of, 194
"reason, dictates of" (Spinoza), 194, 218, 267
"reason, man of" (Spinoza), 203, 234
reincarnation, 97–99, 152
religion, organized. *See* human mind(s), cultural conditioning of; human mind(s), programming of
Russell, Bertrand (*History of Western Philosophy*), 9

schizophrenia, social, 158–159
Schopenhauer, Arthur, 229
self-deception, 143, 144, 155, 165. *See also* human mind(s), programming of
self-esteem. *See* emotions, human, self-esteem
"self-ness." *See* "I-ness"
sensation. *See* sense experience
sense experience, 84–85, 87, 90–91, 93; general nature of, 67–68, 73; homunculus, myth of, 68; illusion of, 73, 163; mind-body interaction, 68; sensations, 68; veridical, 167
sense perception, 69, 70, 74, 77, 84, 90–91, 130; light, 76; mechanics of, 75–77, stages of, 75–76; touch, 80
sex: enablement of the species, 229–231; love, 236; natural appetite for, 232; nourishment of body and mind, 236; surrender to the experience of, 231, 235–236, 253. *See also* sexuality; sexual patterns
sexuality: of child, 233; as human experience, 249; holism and, 229; impact of religion on, 238; Life Force as, 231, 233, 235, 253; masturbation, 234; Plato on, 229; societal manipulation of desires, 217, 228; transcendence of the body, 235–236. *See also* sexuality; sexual patterns
sexual patterns: programming of, 233. *See also* sexuality; sex
Shakespeare, William, 253, 255; metaphor compared with metaphysics (Spinoza), 255–259
sin, concept of, 11, 119, 204. *See also* free will
singularity, 64
social awareness. *See* beliefs
social conditioning. *See* beliefs
soul, 194–102, 120; spiritual love of, 144 *(see also* emotions, human)
space and time. *See* big bang
spatial-temporal connections, 63–64
Spinoza, Benedict de: excommunication of, 10; as a Jewish theologian, 13; Moses Maimonides, compared to, 13; name, Hebrew origin of, 9; as a student, 13
Spinozists, 9, 11
spiritual love. *See* emotions. *See also* God, intellectual love of
spiritual psychotherapy, 14
spirituality, Einstein on, 52. *See also* "knowledge of the third kind"
striving. *See* human body, striving of
suffering: freedom from, 123
sufficient reason, principle of, 22–23, 28, 30, 34, 35, 62, 240, 241, 242, 263; violation of 35, 41*(see* atomism)
Sufis, 11. *See also* gnosis
suicide, 53, 192, 212, 213

Tantric Yoga, 229
temporal order, illusion of, 240, 243
Thomists, 9
Thought, Attribute of, 58–60, 67, 69–73, 83–84, 88, 93, 94, 95–96, 98–100, 107, 112, 117–118, 120–122, 124–125, 127, 128–131, 135, 136, 140, 144, 149, 160–161, 170, 174, 180, 181, 190, 201, 219, 239–240, 243, 246, 247, 266. *See also* God

transcendence of the mind, 237–244. *See also* blessedness
Treatise on God, Man and His Well-Being (Spinoza), 239

ultimate parts. *See* atomism
ultimate whole. *See* All There Is
unconscious idea, concept of, 73
understand, ability to, 20, 23, 26, 29, 162, 190
understanding, 105. *See also* "knowledge of the second kind"; "knowledge of the third kind"
universe: and integration with God, 133; as a whole, 43
universe, laws of, 52

values: western civilization, of, 148. *See also* human mind(s), programming of
Vedantists, 11

Wittgensteinians, 9
World: concept of, 25; intelligibility of, 21

Yoga, Tantric. *See* Tantric Yoga

www.ingramcontent.com/pod-product-compliance
Lightning Source LLC
Chambersburg PA
CBHW031145110525
26505CB00001B/36